1903
TO
1988

THE
HISTORY
of the
BRADFORD CRICKET
LEAGUE
by
PETER PICKUP

Cover design by R. Peel

Chapters

1	In the Beginning 1903	5
2	The Golden Age 1904 – 1914	7
3	Heroes of World War One 1915 – 1918	12
4	Between the Wars 1919 – 1939	21
5	Big Guns of World War Two 1940 – 1945	35
6	County Connections	47
7	Magic of the Priestley Cup	51
8	Star Comments	70
9	A Dose of Salts 1946 – 1959	76
10	Nothing Idle at Cavendish Road 1960 – 1977	90
11	Marquis of Queensbury Rules 1978 – 1988	110
12	The Future	127

Introduction

Should you be looking for a book full of controversy, disputes and back stabbing, this is not the book for you. But neither am I a Prasanna, for Erapally Prasanna, the Indian spin bowler, wrote his autobiography in 6 days. There's certainly many months and thousands of hours work gone into this publication.

The fame of the Bradford Cricket League has been made mainly because of the World Class Stars who have played in it.

If the worlds greatest bowler is Syd Barnes, then he has had 10 seasons in the League, 9 with Saltaire and 1 with Keighley. Is the finest batsman this country has ever seen, Len Hutton, well he too has graced the League along with his 3 brothers. Was Learie Constantine the finest all rounder prior to Sobers the West Indies has produced, well he also is part of the League history. In recent years Martin Crowe, Abdul Qadir, Dilip Vengsarkar, Mark Greatbatch and Mansoor Akhtar have brought their undoubted class to the League.

When I have finished telling you about the Stars there will be the little incidents, the player who was dropped 5 times in scoring 7, the batsman who could gain an extra point for his side by losing his wicket next ball, the story of the batter who nearly had his life ruined when a ball struck his pocket and set light to a box of matches. Many and varied are the stories.

After this we have the records, all ten feats, quick scoring, even a hat-trick all stumped from the bowling of a Test cricketer by the grandfather of a former England skipper.

There are clubs whom you have never heard of but who have names to enjoy, such as Bradford City Lamplighters.

Then we have the games themselves, great fightbacks, collapses, large and small totals, big wins, ties, in short 85 seasons of Cricket, glorious Cricket.

What history there is in this finest of all cricket leagues. Its a book about people, places, events and will be laid down in a style of factual reporting, not tabloid sensationalism.

A fair and true record of all that is good is my wholehearted intention. I hope you all find interest and enjoyment from its forthcoming pages.

Peter Pickup

A table tennis presentation it might have been but Bradford League cricket was well featured. Extreme left is the delightful Kathy Phillips, daughter of Gordon Phillips who played for Idle from 1940 to 1956 and skippered East Bierley thereafter. Wearing the suit and tie is the author, who was 'persuaded' to include his photo. On his left with badge on shirt is Dave Thomas who played for Baildon and Saltaire while on the extreme right is Malcolm Hartley who covered Bradford League cricket with distinction for many years but was actually banned from the Eccleshill club for his comments.

Chapter One
In the Beginning (1903)

"From Land's End to John O'Groats, from Pudsey to Brisbane you will not find a better league than the Bradford League. It has worthily upheld the finest traditions of our glorious National Game."

These are the words of the great Yorkshire and England batsman Herbert Sutcliffe, who on his far flung travels witnessed cricket at all levels and is well qualified to comment and compare a league in which he played. That league was born on a Wednesday, 17th September 1902 to be exact, at a meeting of seven clubs from the West Bradford League. The clubs concerned were Allerton, Clayton, Great Horton, Lidget Green, Manningham Mills, Queensbury and Thornton. The reason for the meeting, at the Queens Hotel, was apparently to express some dissatisfaction at:
(a) the poor gates they were getting   and
(b) at the unfair allocation of derby matches.

This seems a bit strange for if all the clubs were from West Bradford every game could surely have been classed a derby. However it was decided to form a new league and call it 'The Bradford Cricket League'. As a direct result of this meeting the league was formed to commence fixtures in 1903 and added to the original seven teams were applicants Bankfoot, Dudley Hill, Eccleshill, Shelf and Undercliffe.

Remarkable strides were to be made from these humble beginnings for in less than a decade the Bradford League had become the strongest in the World, with a vast number of County and Test stars playing in it.

Six of the original clubs, Bankfoot, Eccleshill, Great Horton, Lidget Green, Queensbury and Undercliffe have enjoyed an unbroken membership since. To say that the opening day was successful would be a gross understatement and one club, Eccleshill, stole a march on all the rest.

Their opening game against Manningham Mills was to be followed by a garden party and dance, with a brass band booked for good measure. With such festivities to be enjoyed it was decided on an early start, and this was made half an hour before the other fixtures commenced. In the second over of this game Eccleshill took a wicket, thus the first in the Leagues history. They also had the League's first centurion later that season when Joe Rogers scored a ton v Great Horton. For good measure Eccleshill had the leading wicket taker in A. Crawford who took 69 league wickets at an average of 8.33. Yet it was Shelf who were Champions for the first and only time in their history. A highly creditable performance too as they had a nine point margin, substantial as there were only two points for a win. Clayton, for whom G. Patefield claimed the League's first hat-trick (v Undercliffe), were joint second in the League with Great Horton. Horton were not only on the wrong end of that first Rogers century but also the seasons highest score came against them from the willow of C. Harris of Lidget Green who totalled 120 not out.

Manningham Mills star player was Schofield Swithenbank who was successfully making runs for the Yorkshire 2nd XI. Once while with Shelf (1904), twice after moving to Saltaire (1906 & 1909) and again while playing for Windhill (1912) Swithenbank was to make the highest score in a season. 1903 simply served notice of what was to follow. The season was undoubtedly a triumph for Shelf with only one defeat in 22 league games. The Cup Competition did not commence till 1904. Though Manningham Mills left after 1903, not to return to the League till 1974, for all other clubs it had been a highly successful beginning with excellent gates. One year later there would be a new cup competition, new champions to hail but 1903 was its birth following which it has grown into the finest of beings.

BRADFORD CRICKET LEAGUE 1903

	P	W	D	L	Pts
Shelf	22	14	7	1	35
Clayton	22	10	6	6	26
Great Horton	22	9	8	5	26
Manningham Mills	22	7	10	5	24
Lidget Green	22	8	7	7	23
Bankfoot	22	6	10	6	22
Eccleshill	22	6	10	6	22
Queensbury	22	6	10	6	22
Undercliffe	22	8	6	8	22
Allerton	22	6	6	10	18
Thornton	22	4	6	12	14
Dudley Hill	22	2	6	14	10

2 pts for a win   1 pt for a draw

Chapter Two
The Golden Age (1904 – 1914)

The period up to World War One is often called 'The Golden Age' of cricket, with W.G. Grace, Victor Trumper, Jack Hobbs, Charles Fry, etc. Personally I feel it was a Golden Age for batsmen, for it is they who feature most in the history books.

In the Bradford League however, wickets were more favourable to bowlers, providing a sporting wicket where batsmen could not dominate. Many people have remarked that spectators will only pay good money to see sparkling batting and no one pays to see bowling. Yet in 1904 the Bradford League crowds were high, and bowling rather than batting was in the ascendency.

T. Metcalfe performed the Leagues first 'All Ten' bowling feat in 1906, with 10 wickets for 15 runs in 11.4 overs, for Saltaire against Lidget Green. Four years later Lidget Green skittled Queensbury for just 12 runs. In 1913, Windhill dismissed Farsley for just 16 and the following season bowled out Baildon Green for only 10 runs. This still remains in the record books, as the Leagues lowest total.

Scorecard for the Leagues record low total
1914 – The Baildon Green innings v Windhill

H. Whitham b Elton	1
H. Claughton c Dawson b Keighley	1
W. Horsman c Dawson b Elton	0
E. Taylor c Dawson b Keighley	2
F. Greenwood c Hyde b Keighley	1
J.R. Paley c Illingworth b Elton	1
R. Graham c Hardcastle b Elton	0
J. Slack b Elton	0
H. Rhodes b Elton	0
H. Robinson not out	0
A.J. Boddy b Elton	0
Extras	4
Total	10

Windhill Bowling

C.J. Elton 7 wkts for 4 runs
E.C. Keighley 3 wkts for 2 runs

The most successful team of this period were Great Horton, one of the founder members of the League with an unbroken membership to this day. In 1903, Great Horton had dismissed Dudley Hill for just 30 runs and the first of their Championships arrived twelve months later. This was followed by a Priestley Cup win in 1906 against Clayton who were all out for 79. In 1907 Great Horton, by now a very fine all round side, finished second in the League and were beaten by one run in the semi-final of the Priestley Cup. On the way to the semi-final they had whipped out Greengates for a mere 14 runs. Another Cup triumph came in 1911 when after scoring 262, Great Horton had their opponents all out for under 100. This was the third time they had achieved this in three Finals. (Clayton 79, Lidget Green 86 and Windhill 96). In eight seasons, commencing 1904, the Club had won the Championship four times and were Cup Winners three times.

Who were the players who made Great Horton such a great side? First and foremost they had a fine respected captain in Joe Haley. He had topped the League bowling averages in 1903 with 52 wickets at 7.25 and was to appear for the club in three Priestley Cup Finals, taking a match winning 7 for 25 against Clayton in the 1906 final. Then there was the club's first Bradford League centurion, A. Bailey who had many fine knocks apart from his maiden 123 v Windhill. That came in 1906, the same year Percy Yewdall joined the club. Yewdall was to become one of the Leagues longest serving and much respected players. Prior to his signing for Great Horton, he had two years with Lidget Green, but from 1906 to 1927 he was a stalwart of both Club and League. A batsman of high quality who could, and often did, rise to the occasion. The cup brought out the best in him, a competition in which he made three centuries — 106 not out v Laisterdyke in 1908, 119 not out v Dudley Hill in 1909 and 115 v Baildon in 1920 (highest score in the Cup that year).

Great Horton were on the receiving end of an 'All Ten' in 1908 when J.K. Booth of Eccleshill took 10 for 30 against them, but still Great Horton won the match by eight runs.

For the 1910 season the League decided to have two divisions. This coincided with the decline of Great Horton even though their 2nd XI were Champions in 1911. The two divisions idea was not deemed a success and after a couple of seasons it was shelved until 1937 when it returned with resounding success. Under the two divisions, Idle (1910) and Windhill (1911) were to win their first Championships, with Mountain Mills (1910) and Laisterdyke (1911) winning the Division Two titles. In fact it was a Championship play off between Idle and Windhill in 1911, that resulted in Windhill's title by just one wicket, on neutral territory at Eccleshill. Ironically Idle lost the 1912 Championship to Bingley, again in the same way. The 2nd XI bowling averages in 1912 were won by E. Slingsby of Saltaire, his 26 league wickets costing just 3.8 each, needless to say a second team record which still stands.

The 1913 League Handbook tells us that Lidget Green and Tong Park had good stabling for anyone wishing to travel to a match on four legs. Not many people had four wheels in those days.

The highest score made in a league match during the 'Golden Age' belongs to Tong.Park. They thrashed 322 off the Saltaire attack in 1913 and their opening batsman Cecil Tyson had the highest league aggregate with 696 league runs. Tyson formed an opening partnership with Sam Cadman which was formidable to say the least.

Cadman played 375 times for Derbyshire in first class games between 1900 and 1926, scoring over 14,000 runs. Tyson on the other hand played only 5 first class games but this had nothing to do with the lack of ability but dissatisfaction with terms. Making his debut for Yorkshire he made a debut 100 not out, but after only three games left the County after a disagreement over money. Although he played a couple of games for Glamorgan at a later date it was in league cricket that he proved such a success. Tyson had not commenced playing County cricket when he first played with Tong Park. That was 1913 when he joined from Whitwood Colliery making an immediate impact by topping the League averages in his first season and included among many match winning performances, 120 not out v East Bierley and 110 v Saltaire. On occasions he would turn his arm over and 5 for 46 v Bingley in 1913 and 5 for 43 v Pudsey one year later showed that his bowling was not altogether in vain. When described to me by someone who saw Tyson play, I learned, 'he was an excellent left hand opening bat'.

Two other players of this era who should not be forgotten are R.H. 'Dickie' Moulton and Luther Sowden who made the first opening stand of over 200 runs in the League. This was for Bradford against Saltaire in 1911, when Sowden scored 100 and Moulton went on to 137 not out, after the stand had been broken at 201.

With patrons such as Lord Hawke and F.C. Toone it was a period when the League seemed to want for nothing. There was no doubt it was now well established with the standard of the cricket played rising all the time. The match of the season was one against the Yorkshire 2nd XI by a League Representative side. Very soon the Bradford League was to become so strong that it was the Yorkshire 1st XI who were to be the opposition.

BRADFORD CRICKET LEAGUE

FINAL LEAGUE POSITIONS

1904

	P	W	D (1 pt)	L	Pts
Great Horton	20	17	1	2	35
Clayton	20	14	1	5	29
Lidget Green	20	11	4	5	26
Shelf	20	8	6	6	22
Allerton	20	6	8	6	20
Thornton	20	8	4	8	20
Queensbury	20	8	3	9	19
Bankfoot	20	6	5	9	17
Undercliffe	20	5	6	9	16
Eccleshill	20	3	4	13	10
Dudley Hill	20	2	2	16	6

1905

	P	W	D (1 pt)	L	Pts
Clayton	22	12	6	4	30
Saltaire	22	10	8	4	28
Lidget Green	22	9	9	4	27
Bankfoot	22	9	9	4	27
Undercliffe	22	9	8	5	26
Shelf	22	10	6	6	26
Great Horton	22	10	5	7	25
Windhill	22	9	5	8	23
Eccleshill	22	6	4	12	16
Allerton	22	4	8	10	16
Queensbury	22	5	5	12	15
Dudley Hill	22	1	3	18	5

Batting Averages
1. F. Scott (Bankfoot) — 41.07
2. A. Wellburn (Bankfoot) — 35.15
3. W. Priestley (Bankfoot) — 34.66
4. P. Yewdall (Lidget Green) — 33.08

Bowling Averages
1. F. Ward (Clayton) — 55 wkts @ 6.96
2. T. Bland (Eccleshill) — 11 wkts @ 8.45
3. C. Duffield (Great Horton) — 52 wkts @ 9.03
4. J. Holden (Bankfoot) — 37 wkts @ 10.00

1906

	P	W	D (1 pt)	L	Pts
Great Horton	22	11	8	3	30
Bankfoot	22	9	11	2	29
Saltaire	22	10	9	3	29
Undercliffe	22	9	11	2	29
Windhill	22	9	10	3	28
Clayton	22	5	13	4	23
Idle	22	2	14	6	18
Allerton	22	5	7	10	17
Lidget Green	22	4	9	9	17
Shelf	22	4	8	10	16
Queensbury	22	2	11	9	15
Eccleshill	22	2	9	11	13

Batting Averages
1. G. Swithenbank (Saltaire) — 43.69
2. H. Spencer (Clayton) — 39.90
3. N. Firth (Saltaire) — 37.64
4. A. Bailey (Great Horton) — 36.66

Bowling Averages
1. J. Rigg (Shelf) — 26 wkts @ 6.33
2. E. Jowett (Clayton) — 39 wkts @ 6.77
3. F. Smith (Saltaire) — 18 wkts @ 7.12
4. G. Patefield (Saltaire) — 71 wkts @ 7.40

1907

	P	W	D (1 pt)	L	Pts
Undercliffe	22	12	8	2	32
Great Horton	22	12	7	3	31
Clayton	22	10	9	3	29
Windhill	22	11	6	5	28
Queensbury	22	7	11	4	25
Saltaire	22	7	10	5	24
Bankfoot	22	5	12	5	22
Lidget Green	22	5	9	8	19
Idle	22	4	10	8	18
Allerton	22	3	8	11	14
Eccleshill	22	4	5	13	13
Shelf	22	1	7	14	9

Batting Averages
1. S. Swithenbank (Saltaire) — 42.85
2. F. Hollings (Idle) — 37.66
3. F. Shackleton (Queensbury) — 37.06
4. A. Wellburn (Bankfoot) — 37.05

Bowling Averages
1. C. Duffield (Great Horton) — 70 wkts @ 6.97
2. W. Kemp (Undercliffe) — 49 wkts @ 7.04
3. W. Lumb (Great Horton) — 39 wkts @ 7.12
4. F. Halliday (Windhill) — 46 wkts @ 7.86

1908

	P	W	D (1 pt)	L	Pts
Great Horton	22	12	8	2	32
Undercliffe	22	9	10	3	28
Saltaire	22	10	7	5	27
Windhill	22	11	5	6	27
Idle	22	8	9	5	25
Queensbury	22	7	8	7	22
*Clayton	22	9	5	8	21
Bankfoot	22	5	11	6	21
Eccleshill	22	4	10	8	18
Lidget Green	22	4	9	9	17
Shelf	22	4	7	11	15
Allerton	22	1	7	14	9

* 2 pts deducted for breach of Rule.

Batting Averages
1. A. Robinson (Undercliffe) — 41.16
2. P. Yewdall (Great Horton) — 35.69
3. T.A. Brook (Idle) — 00.00
4. A. Hyde (Windhill) — 32.92

Bowling Averages
1. T. Parrington (Undercliffe) — 46 wkts @ 8.41
2. J. Haley (Great Horton) — 45 wkts @ 8.48
3. E.C. Keighley (Windhill) — 63 wkts @ 9.46
4. W. Lumb (Great Horton) — 48 wkts @ 9.56

9

1909
Division One
	P	W	D	L	Pts
Great Horton	18	12	5	1	29
Queensbury	18	8	7	3	23
Idle	18	8	6	4	22
Undercliffe	18	7	8	3	22
Lidget Green	18	6	6	6	18
Windhill	18	7	4	7	18
Saltaire	18	4	6	8	14
Bankfoot	18	3	8	7	14
Eccleshill	18	2	6	10	10
Shelf	18	1	8	9	10

Division Two
	P	W	D	L	Pts
Sticker Lane	18	11	7	0	29
Laisterdyke	18	8	9	1	25
Thornbury	18	9	6	3	24
Tong Park	18	8	6	4	22
Birkenshaw	18	7	4	7	18
Dudley Hill	18	5	6	7	16
Esholt	18	5	5	8	15
Thackley	18	4	6	8	14
Sandy Lane	18	4	5	9	13
Bradford City LL'	18	1	4	13	6

Batting Averages
1 T.A. Booth (Idle) 54.00
2 F. Shackleton (Queensbury) 38.62
3 E. Barker (Bankfoot) 31.75
4 J. Holden (Bankfoot) 30.63
5 M. Drake (Queensbury) 30.50

Bowling Averages
1 F. Dibb (Great Horton) 50 wkts @ 5.56
2 J. Haley (Great Horton) 30 wkts @ 6.83
3 W. Lumb (Idle) 51 wkts @ 8.60
4 B. Parrish (Great Horton) 40 wkts @ 8.80
5 I. Knight (Lidget Green) 49 wkts @ 10.18

In Second XI cricket only one batsman scored above 83 and that was J.W Parrington (Undercliffe). His top score being 145 not out, and he topped the 2nd XI batting averages with an average of 55.00.

1910
Division One
	P	W	D	L	Pts
Idle	22	11	8	3	30
Undercliffe	22	8	11	3	27
Great Horton**	22	8	11	3	25
Saltaire	22	6	10	6	22
Shelf	22	7	8	7	22
Lidget Green	22	6	10	6	22
Windhill	22	6	8	8	20
Bingley	22	5	10	7	20
Bradford	22	6	7	9	19
Eccleshill	22	6	7	9	19
Queensbury	22	7	5	10	19
Bankfoot	22	6	5	11	17

** Great Horton had 2 pts deducted for breach of a Rule.

Division Two
	P	W	D	L	Pts
Mountain Mills	20	15	2	3	32
Laisterdyke	20	12	6	2	30
Thackley	20	11	6	3	28
Sandy Lane	20	9	5	6	23
Tong Park	20	9	3	8	21
Birkenshaw	20	6	7	7	19
Woodlands	20	7	5	8	19
Shipley St Pauls	20	6	5	9	17
Esholt	20	5	2	13	12
Bradford City LL'	20	4	2	14	10
Crossley Hall	20	3	3	14	9

Batting Averages
1 C.W. Binns (Undercliffe) 37.43
2 T. Wilcock (Bingley) 35.13
3 J. Nelson (Eccleshill) 31.88
4 T.A. Booth (Idle) 31.83

Bowling Averages
1 E. Mann (Sandy Lane) 63 wkts @ 4.65
2 A. Chadwick (Sandy Lane) 13 wkts @ 5.61
3 J. Illingworth (Laisterdyke) 68 wkts @ 6.05

Qualification for Bowling Averages was only ten wickets thus Chadwick from Sandy Lane with only 13 wickets was able to qualify in second spot.

1911 (1 pt)
	P	W	D	L	Pts
Idle	22	14	4	4	32
Windhill	22	14	4	4	32
Great Horton	22	11	7	4	29
Undercliffe	22	11	5	6	27
Bradford	22	9	8	5	26
Bingley	22	8	4	10	20
Eccleshill	22	7	6	9	20
Shelf	22	8	4	10	20
Lidget Green	22	7	3	12	17
Saltaire	22	5	6	11	16
Bankfoot	22	4	5	13	13
Queensbury	22	2	6	14	10

NB – Idle and Windhill played off for the Championship at Eccleshill on the 23rd September – Windhill the winners.

Batting Averages
1 W. Spencer (Great Horton) 51.63
2 R.H. Moulton (Bradford) 39.00
3 T.A. Booth (Idle) 37.42
4 S. Swithenbank (Undercliffe) 37.00

Bowling Averages
1 C.J. Elton (Windhill) 68 wkts @ 8.04
2 W. Rhodes (Bankfoot) 49 wkts @ 8.24
3 H. Riley (Windhill) 92 wkts @ 8.44
4 F. Wood (Shelf) 46 wkts @ 8.90

1912
	P	W	D	L	Pts
Bingley	20	15	3	2	33
Idle	20	10	8	2	28
Windhill	20	12	4	4	28
Great Horton	20	12	3	5	27
Lidget Green	20	11	4	5	26
Undercliffe	20	10	5	5	25
Bradford	20	9	5	6	23
Saltaire	20	10	3	7	23
Low Moor	20	10	2	8	22
Laisterdyke	20	7	6	7	20
Pudsey Britannia	20	6	8	6	20
Farsley	20	7	4	9	18
Pudsey St. Lawrence	20	6	6	8	18
East Bierley	20	5	6	9	16
Stanningley & Farsley	20	5	6	9	16
Eccleshill	20	4	6	10	14
Baildon Green	20	4	4	12	12
Queensbury	20	2	8	10	12
Bankfoot	20	2	6	12	10
Tong Park	20	3	3	14	9

Batting Averages
1 E.P. Hardy (Bingley) 39.4
2 E. Walker (Pudsey Britannia) 37.3
3 S. Swithenbank (Windhill) 34.7
4 H.I. Pratt (Low Moor) 33.7
5 E. Illingworth (Undercliffe) 33.2
6 C.W. Binns (Undercliffe) 33.1

Bowling Averages
1 F. Luckhurst (Bradford) 79 wkts @ 5.40
2 C. Duffield (Bingley) 74 wkts @ 7.90
3 E. Jowett (Lidget Green) 80 wkts @ 8.02
4 B. Parrish (Great Horton) 80 wkts @ 8.05
5 A. MacKenzie (Saltaire) 60 wkts @ 8.10
6 G. Patefield (Undercliffe) 56 wkts @ 8.46

In 2nd XI cricket E. Slingsby (Saltaire) won the league bowling averages with 26 wickets at just 3.8 runs each. An amazingly low return.

1913

	P	W	D	L	Pts
Windhill	20	12	6	2	30
Laisterdyke	20	11	5	4	27
Bradford	20	11	4	5	26
Eccleshill	20	9	7	4	25
Great Horton	20	8	8	4	24
Tong Park	20	7	9	4	23
Bingley	20	7	8	5	22
Idle	20	6	8	6	20
Saltaire	20	7	6	7	20
Undercliffe	20	6	8	6	20
Pudsey St. Lawrence	20	7	5	8	19
Lidget Green	20	6	6	8	18
Bankfoot	20	6	6	8	18
Low Moor	20	5	8	7	18
East Bierley	20	5	7	8	17
Farsley	20	6	5	9	17
Stanningley & Farsley	20	5	6	9	16
Baildon Green	20	4	7	9	15
Pudsey Britannia	20	4	6	10	14
Queensbury	20	3	5	12	11

Despite finishing 2nd, three points behind Windhill, Laisterdyke exercised their right to challenge Windhill to a play-off. Laisterdyke won and so became Champions.

Batting Averages
1 C. Tyson (Tong Park)   49.70
2 A. Welburn (Great Horton)   42.60
3 S. Wilcock (Pudsey Britannia)   41.00

Bowling Averages
1 C.J. Elton (Windhill)   72 wkts @ 8.26
2 E.C. Keighley (Windhill)   76 wkts @ 9.60
3 B. Parrish (Great Horton)   54 wkts @ 10.09

Highest Innings
H.I. Pratt (Low Moor) v East Bierley   142
H. Bennett (Lidget Green) v Great Horton   141
F. Luckhurst (Bradford) v Undercliffe   141

Best Bowling
W. Kemp (Bankfoot) v Low Moor   9 for 17
T. Sheard (Eccleshill) v Baildon Green   8 for 26
J. Rider (Pudsey St. Law.) v East Bierley   8 for 28

1914

	P	W	D (1 pt)	L	Pts
Bradford	20	16	3	1	35
Windhill	20	15	1	4	31
Pudsey St. Lawrence	20	11	3	6	25
Eccleshill	20	10	4	6	24
Tong Park	20	11	2	7	24
Great Horton	20	8	7	5	23
Idle	20	10	3	7	23
Undercliffe	20	8	7	5	23
Baildon Green	20	10	2	8	22
East Bierley	20	9	3	8	21
Bingley	20	8	3	9	19
Lidget Green	20	7	3	8	19
Pudsey Britannia	20	7	4	9	18
Laisterdyke	20	6	4	10	16
Stanningley & Farsley	20	7	2	11	16
Farsley	20	6	3	11	15
Queensbury	20	5	4	11	14
Saltaire	20	5	3	12	13
Bankfoot	20	3	4	13	10
Low Moor	20	3	3	14	9

Batting Averages
1 A. Holmes (Bradford)   50.8
2 H. Sutcliffe (Pudsey Britannia)   47.6
3 S. Peck (Laisterdyke)   45.0
4 H. Whitwam (Baildon Green)   39.0

Bowling Averages
1 C.J. Elton (Windhill)   81 wkts @ 8.00
2 S. Claughton (Idle)   81 wkts @ 8.40
3 H. Claughton (Baildon Green)   56 wkts @ 9.08
4 F. Luckhurst (Bradford)   86 wkts @ 9.20

Chapter Three
Heroes of World War One (1915 – 1918)

War is futile, nothing worthy has ever emanated from it and nothing ever will. When it caused the abandonment of County Cricket, the Bradford League Secretary, W. Cockroft issued a statement in which he said, "We had serious misgivings whether or not we were justified in continuing our competitions". The players wished to play, the public thought likewise and the League's decision to continue resulted in 'the Stars' coming to Bradford, and how!

When the League was re-organised in 1912, Farsley, East Bierley, Pudsey Britannia, Low Moor, Tong Park, Stanningley & Farsley Britannia, Laisterdyke, Pudsey St. Lawrence and Baildon Green were all admitted, but none of them made an impact to equal that of Bowling Old Lane who successfully applied for admittance in 1915. So remarkable was Bowling Old Lane's first season that a whole book could be written about it. It was success all the way, for the club did the 'double'.

In the Priestley Cup, Undercliffe were beaten by 3 wickets in Round One. There was a sensation in Round Two as Great Horton were beaten by 351 runs. Batting first Old Lane totalled 455 with Charles Grimshaw making a record breaking 230. This individual record still stands. Saltaire in the Semi-final and Windhill (by 10 wkts) in the Final were beaten with consummate ease. The Championship went the way of Old Lane by virtue of just two defeats in 20 league games. Grimshaw who played 54 first class matches for Yorkshire commencing in 1904 was the 'Star' all-rounder who scored 618 league runs at an average of 47.5 and took 68 wickets at 8.4 runs apiece.

Bowling Old Lane had taken over from Bradford Cricket Club, who had resigned, as their County Ground at Park Avenue was no longer available. Bradford won the Championship in 1914 so perhaps it was fitting that the club who replaced them proved to be a winning one. One of Old Lane's two defeats that season came at the hands of Saltaire who dismissed them for just 31 runs. An advertisement which appeared in *Athletic News,* placed by Saltaire, stated 'Wanted, a Left Arm Bowler'. The club received a reply which simply said, 'Will I do' signed S.F. Barnes. Now Barnes was not a left arm bowler but such was his reputation and experience (he had played in 27 Test Matches) that a reply was sent straight away saying, "Come to Bowling Old Lane Saturday. Terms will be arranged!"

Barnes did go to Old Lane and on his debut took 8 wickets for 8 runs. It was obviously a sparkling debut, yet in the following match Syd Barnes took all ten wickets against Baildon Green. It included five wickets in successive balls and his 10 for 14 meant that in two games he had taken an incredible 18 wickets for 22 runs. The most sensational bowling figures, for two consecutive games I have ever found. At the seasons end Barnes had taken 92 league wickets at just 4.42 runs each. He added another 15 wickets in three Priestley Cup Ties.

Another forward looking club, Idle, made an approach, somewhat tentatively, to Jack Hobbs but they really thought he would ask too much. Hobbs however replied that he wanted just £5 per week plus travelling expenses and that he would be pleased to sign. So the Idle officials acted with the speed of light. At the seasons end he had batted in ten league games and averaged over 40 runs per innings. Despite his presence Idle finished 6 points behind Old Lane, while Saltaire, with Barnes making short work of most teams, finished 5 points behind the leaders. That illustrates perfectly just how 'special' the Old Lane side of 1915 was.

Crowds grew, there were record takings when in 1916 Idle were at home to Lidget Green. The cricket was obviously 'crowd pleasing' and when Old Lane met Great Horton there was a

Idle Cricket Club
Bpfy

May 24/15

Mr. J. Hobbs
Dear Sir

Please say if you are open to take a weekly on Saturday afternoon engagement for the above club in the Bradford Cricket League for remainder of season, and if so what would your terms be? An early reply will oblige.

Yours &c.

SURREY COUNTY CRICKET CLUB,
KENNINGTON OVAL,
S.E.

May 25th 1915

Dear Sir

I am in receipt of yours of yesterday's date for which I thank you. Subject to the approval of the Surrey County C.C. I would accept an engagement to play on Saturday providing of course that your terms were satisfactory.

Will you please let me know what terms you are prepared to offer.

Yours Faithfully
J.B. Hobbs

A. Fletcher Esq.
Hon. Sec. Idle C.C.
Bradford

IDLE OFFERED £5 per match plus £2 expenses & Jack Hobbs duly accepted and joined the club May 29th 1915.

century on each side for the first time in a Bradford League game. E. Cummins scored 117 not out for Bowling, but the innings of George Leach for Great Horton was a League record, though his 173 not out lasted only three seasons before being topped.

If the Barnes debut was startling in one way, so was that of George Leach in an all-round sense, for Leach had a debut 'all ten' feat for just 16 runs against Pudsey Britannia and scored 65 runs. He had the best Batting and Bowling performance in the League on the same day, an unparalleled feat.

Inspired by Hobbs, Idle became Champions in 1916 with 'The Master' making 784 league runs at an average of 56.00 and also taking 59 league wickets at just 6.58 runs each. Now this was an unexpected bonus for Idle for Hobbs the Master Batsman had never been considered for regular bowling stints. Yet here he was in the best league cricket of the day, dismissing batsmen regularly on wickets Hobbs himself found ideal for run making. In his 30 year County and Test career Hobbs took only 109 wickets, yet here with his right arm medium pace he took 59 at a very low cost in 18 matches. His best statistical performance was ironically against the might of Barnes and Saltaire. In two matches in 1916 Hobbs took 9 for 39 and 7 for 24 while scoring 87 runs in one of them. It was the nerve and experience of Hobbs which was largely responsible for the Title going to the Cavendish Road club. A play-off was needed with Lidget Green to decide the Championship and it was largely a steadying 72 from Jack which led to victory. Idle lost their 'top spot' in 1917 and slumped alarmingly. Even so the club reached the semi-final of the Priestley Cup, and the victory over Saltaire which got them that far included 132 by Hobbs, the highest individual score in the competition that year.

1917 was the first season in which a side went through the season without a win. The bad luck fell the way of Queensbury who had four draws and sixteen defeats from their twenty league games.

The signing of 'top' players was by now commonplace and Undercliffe had acquired the services of Charlie Llewelyn, the South African Test player, who had already played in 15 Test Matches and 196 games for Hampshire. Playing against Bankfoot in 1917 Llewelyn performed the hat-trick, all stumped, and the wicketkeeper was William Close, grandfather of that much respected man of positive thinking, tremendous courage and oustanding cricket ability, Brian.

The season also had another first with the double defeat, by 10 wickets, of Farsley by Lidget Green, the first instance of a side winning both games in such a manner. Four years later it happened again with Baildon Green beating Tong Park by 10 wickets in each meeting.

After 'all ten' feats in 1915 and 1916 it was surprising to find another in 1917. This time it was performed by Cecil Parkin, who had played for both Yorkshire and Lancashire and would later play in 10 Test Matches. He took 10 wickets for 15 runs against Baildon Green, the side which just two years before had been victims of a similar feat by Syd Barnes. In fact in 1927 Baildon were on the receiving end of a third 'all ten' feat. The attendance at the Keighley v Saltaire match in 1917 was 4,897 which created a record soon to be broken. Barnes and Saltaire were always an attraction but Keighley too had 'stars' and a fine side. Their 1917 fixture v Bingley brought them a record league partnership when Thomas Arthur Booth and Willie Huddlestone put on 167 for the 4th wicket. Keighley had among their ranks that year Jack Hearne, Schofield Haigh and Frank Woolley. Woolley joined Keighley for their first Bradford League season of 1916. That year he took centuries from Idle, Bingley and East Bierley, while in the Priestley Cup he took 7 for 16 v Lidget Green and 5 for 44 v Low Moor to help his new side reach the semi-final. Jack Hearne, Schofield Haigh and George Crawford joined him for 1917. Crawford is the lesser known of the quartet but it was he who took four wickets with the first four balls of the game when Keighley met Pudsey Britannia in 1918. Keighley added Emmott Robinson to their side for 1918 and positions of 9th, 6th and 5th commencing 1916 clearly illustrated the Club's rising status.

Yet it was that man Barnes who was having most to say about where the trophies went. He led Saltaire to the Championship of both 1917 and 1918. The first of those was a season in which Barnes took 116 league wickets at 5.52 runs each. He topped the League bowling averages, a feat he performed in all the nine seasons he was with the club. His 1918 performance was quite out of the pages of fiction. He took 10 for 36 v Keighley which was one better than his 9 for 41 against them the previous year. He performed the hat-trick against Bankfoot and his six wickets in seven balls, which of course included another hat-trick, was part of an eight wickets for just four runs feat against the unfortunate Windhill who were all out for just 16 runs. Bingley 20 all out, Bankfoot 34 all out, (and 43 in the return game), Tong Park 46 all out were testimony to his magical powers. The Priestley Cup exploits, which included the seasons highest score from the bat of Barnes, is described elsewhere. Only two defeats in 1917 and one in 1918 made Saltaire the toughest of nuts to crack but no side had yet gone through a season unbeaten.

In 1918 Barnes was the only Saltaire player to take five wickets in an innings, not surprisingly I suppose but you had to feel sorry for his opening partner Herbert Sedgwick. It was as a Staffordshire player that Sedgwick had his most prominent cricket days, though three times Yorkshire had called on his services, as a 23 year old, when he took 16 First Class wickets at 20.43. Not bad in only three games, but places in the Yorkshire side have always been difficult to secure, so the right arm fast bowling he was so good at found its audience in Minor County and League cricket. Despite Barnes he did manage 42 league wickets in 1917, at an economic 12.11 runs each. Saltaire had become the first team for eleven years to retain their title, which they did in the 1918 season. So strong were all the sides in the Bradford League that commencing in 1909 the next ten years produced eight different clubs at the top.

Many were the 'stars' who performed during the War years and great was their entertainment value, as well as their stature. One who was perhaps under-rated was John Thomas Newstead. Between 1903 and 1913 Newstead played 96 times for his native County, Yorkshire. His best performance was 7 for 10 at County level and when he brought his medium pace off breaks to the Bradford League he could at times be quite unplayable. His first Bradford League Club was Lidget Green for whom he played in 1916 and 1917. With Lidget he made three half centuries but his bowling was pure mean-ness. Poor old Queensbury suffered more than most. Playing against them in 1916 he took 8 for 25 and 6 for 15. The following year he took 5 for 18 and scored 64 not out. After that he left Lidget and joined East Bierley for the 1918 season. Then in his first match for Bierley against Queensbury had the amazing analysis of nine wickets for five runs. There would be many relieved batsmen at Queensbury when Newstead left the League after the 1918 season.

The war took from cricket many lives needlessly wasted. I abhor violence in any form, though I hasten to add that the smiting of a cricket ball in a full blooded drive to the boundary I do not consider to be violence, this being against an inanimate object. To Bradford League fans the most famous of all those tragically lost in the First World War was Major William Booth. Major was his Christian name, not a rank, and Booth who was born in Pudsey had already played 144 matches for Yorkshire, been on tour to South Africa and played in TWO Test Matches. Booth had made a double hundred against Worcestershire and was a tremendous prospect for the future. He played some cricket with Pudsey St. Lawrence when County commitments allowed and was the first from the Yorkshire town to learn his trade in the area and then go off and show the world. Alas on July 1st 1916, Booth lost his life, killed in action, in France.

Another of the men from Pudsey was Herbert Sutcliffe. Not actually born in Pudsey, but in Harrogate. Herbert played for the Pudsey Britannia team and also St. Lawrence. It is not known if he played when the two sides had their extraordinary match of 1916. It remains the shortest match in League history. Batting first Pudsey St. Lawrence made only 22 runs. It took Britannia just 22 balls to knock off the required runs. Sutcliffe was a Corporal with the Sherwood Foresters and each Saturday he cycled away the 20 miles from York, where he was stationed, to Killingbeck from where he caught a tram and to avoid detection played under an assumed name. Only in later years was Herbert safely able to reveal this. What was not revealed was the name he played under. He did once recall though that on three consecutive Saturdays he was out for a 'duck' and L.B.W. on all three occasions. A lot of cycling for now't.

At Yorkshire the name of Percy Holmes was very often coupled with Herbert Sutcliffe. Holmes too played in the Bradford League with Great Horton whom he joined in 1917. Percy had just two seasons at Horton before going back to his County career which did not end until

1933 and which included two tours to South Africa and one to the West Indies. Here was yet another stylish opener to honour the Bradford League with his presence. His 36 league innings brought him 1091 runs averaging over thirty. Among them was a century (100 not out v Eccleshill) and a dozen half centuries. Although the likes of Percy Holmes went back to sample the two-day matches of County cricket in 1919, the League was by now well established.

The quality of wickets had attracted some of the countries top cricketers and the rewards from collections and high standards of play meant, 'The Word was Out'. You couldn't do better than join a Bradford League Club. Injured one wintry morning in France, in 1916, Fred Root was in St. Lukes War Hospital in Bradford when he awoke. Finding he was in Bradford, Root although told by a specialist he should never play cricket again, started making arrangements to play Bradford League cricket. A healthy 26 year old at the time he had to wait until 1918 before his wish was granted, when he assisted Bowling Old Lane. Born in Derbyshire, Root had played County Cricket with his native County before moving on to Worcestershire. He was to play in three Test Matches after his Bradford League days so was far from being a has been when he made his debut.

There was a shock in store for Root when he travelled up to Bradford for that debut in 1918. On arrival at the station he saw placards which said, 'Idle Hobbs not playing'—rather disrespectful thought Root for poor old Hobbs, for at that time Root was not aware of a Club called Idle and thought it a comment on Hobbs's apparent laziness. The Club Root was on his way to play for was Bowling Old Lane against Lidget Green. The reason for his choice was because while at St. Lukes Hospital two years earlier he met Mrs Ernest Holdsworth, the wife of Yorkshire's 2nd XI Captain. Holdsworth was captain of Bowling Old Lane for over 20 years and in their double year of 1915 he took 5 for 13 in the Semi-Final of the Priestley Cup against Saltaire (Barnes and All). Root was regaled with tales by Mrs Holdsworth of T'Owd Loin. In his first season Fred's best analysis was 5 for 32 against Keighley, while in 1918 Lidget Green (8 for 46), Great Horton (7 for 41) and Farsley (6 for 17) felt the penetration of his Leg Theory more than most. There is little difference between Bodyline and Leg Theory and often the two get confused but Root was probably the first in County and Bradford League cricket to regularly bowl at the leg stump with a packed legside field. Root was amazed that there was only one division and too many sides to be able to play each other twice during a season. The fixture arrangement baffled more than he, and for those interested in how fixtures were arranged in those days I will do my best to explain.

When the League had twenty clubs, e.g. 1918, they were, for fixture purposes split into divisions of five clubs by virtue of their positions in the previous seasons championship. When fixtures were arranged the clubs in the top five spots would play against each other and make up their lists from the lower groups in proportion. Thus these groups of five govern the quality and drawing power of future fixtures. The method ensured that many of the matches were thus contested by teams of near equal strength. If at the seasons end the side in 2nd place had not met the top team they were allowed to challenge them for the title. An indication of the power of the League when drawing crowds is that in 1918 there was a higher attendance at the Priestley Cup Final than a football match at Bradford City's Valley Parade ground, which took place simultaneously.

Various representative matches took place at Park Avenue during the War so that while the likes of Barnes, Woolley and Hobbs were regularly playing in the City, other notables such as P.F. 'Plum' Warner, Percy Fender, Nigel Haig, etc. were able to visit the city and get some competitive cricket. It is sad to think that it took another World War before so many great cricketers were regularly in one city for so long again.

When 1918 ended, Saltaire were the Champions and would be seeking to complete a hat-trick in 1919, but a new Champion was on the horizon, a club who would win their first title in 1919 and then wait 27 years before they could repeat the feat.

BRADFORD LEAGUE CRICKET CLUB V YORKSHIRE C.C.C. CLUB

PLAYED AT PARK AVENUE ON 14th AUG. 19 16

INNINGS OF YORKS. C.C.C.

	BATSMEN	HOW OUT	BOWLER	TOTAL
1	G. HIRST	LLEWELYN	WOOLLEY	20
2	A.J.C. HIRST	c LLEWELYN	PARKIN	9
3	RHODES	b	COOK	19
4	CAPT. D.C.F. BURTON	st. TOULSON	LLEWELYN	14
5	LANCE CORP. SUTCLIFFE	c & b	WOOLLEY	11
6	FLT. COM. J.P. WILSON	b	COOK	22
7	CAPT. J. TASKER	c WOOLLEY	LEACH	14
8	DRAKE	c HOLDSWORTH	LEACH.	21
9	SIR. A. WHITE (CAPT)	b	PARKIN	21
10	HAIGH	NOT	OUT	8
11	WATSON	c WOOLLEY	PARKIN	0
12	WHITEHEAD	b	PARKIN	0

EXTRAS 13
TOTAL 172 FOR 11 WKTS.

FALL OF EACH WICKET

MATCH DRAWN

BOWLERS

		OVERS	MDNS	RUNS	WKTS	AVGE
1	F.E. WOOLLEY	23	5	51	2	25.5
2	W. COOK	15	3	28	2	14.0
3	C.H. PARKIN	13	0	40	4	10.0
4	CB LLEWELLYN	9	1	22	1	22.0
5	G. LEACH	5	1	18	2	9.0

12 A-SIDE MATCH

INNINGS OF BRADFORD LEAGUE.

	BATSMEN	HOW OUT	BOWLER	TOTAL
1	J.B. HOBBS	c DRAKE	HIRST	43
2	F.E. WOOLLEY	c BURTON	DRAKE	21
3	G. LEACH	b	DRAKE	6
4	C.B. LLEWELYN	b	DRAKE	7
5	E. ROBINSON	b	DRAKE	9
6	E.F. (CAPT) HOLDSWORTH	b	RHODES	11
7	C.F. TYSON	NOT	OUT	12
8	W. COOK	b	RHODES	0
9	A. HYDE			
10	C.H. PARKIN	D.N.B.		
11	A.L. RICHARDSON			
12	T. TOULSON			

EXTRAS 1
TOTAL 110 FOR 7 WKTS.

FALL OF EACH WICKET

MATCH DRAWN.

BOWLERS

		OVERS	MDNS	RUNS	WKTS	AVGE
1	WHITEHEAD	5	0	37	0	-
2	DRAKE	12	2	37	4	9.25
3	G. HIRST	8	0	33	1	33.0
4	RHODES	.4	1	2	2	1.0

12 A-SIDE MATCH

BRADFORD LEAGUE XI. v YORKSHIRE COUNTY XI

PLAYED AT PARK AVENUE   DATE 13TH & 14TH. AUG. 1917

BFD. LGE XI.

1st INNINGS

	BATSMEN	HOW OUT	BOWLER	TOTAL
1	C.F. TYSON	c CRAWFORD	HAIGH	10
2	E. ROBINSON	b	DRAKE	3
3	J.W. HEARNE	b	HAIGH	0
4	F. JEBSON	b	DRAKE	3
5	C.B. LLEWELYN	b	HAIGH	0
6	C.P. CHARLESWORTH	b	HAIGH	3
7	S.F. BARNES	b	HAIGH	2
8	A.W. SPRING	b	DRAKE	5
9	C.L. PARKER	NOT	OUT	5
10	A.L. BAIRSTOW	lbw	HAIGH	2
11	C.H. PARKIN	ST. PLOWRIGHT	HAIGH	0
12	E.F. HOLDSWORTH (CAPT)	b	HAIGH	0
			EXTRAS	3
			TOTAL FOR 11 WKTS	36

2nd INNINGS

HOW OUT	BOWLER	TOTAL
HT/WKT.	DRAKE	2
c PLOWRIGHT	SMITH	9
c DENTON	RHODES	24
b	HAIGH	0
c DRAKE	HAIGH	4
c PLOWRIGHT	HAIGH	13
RUN	OUT	3
c HOLMES	DRAKE	3
ST. PLOWRIGHT	HAIGH	0
NOT	OUT	0
c RHODES	DRAKE	0
b	HAIGH	0
EXTRAS		13
TOTAL FOR 11 WKTS		71

BOWLERS (1st)

	BOWLERS	OVERS	M'D'NS	RUNS	WKTS	AV'GE
1	A. DRAKE	18	8	15	3	5·0
2	S. HAIGH	17.4	9	18	8	2·25

BOWLERS (2nd)

	BOWLERS	OVERS	M'D'NS	RUNS	WKTS	AV'GE
1	A. DRAKE	18·1	7	32	3	10·6
2	S. HAIGH	21	7	24	5	4·8
3	W. RHODES	6	5	1	1	1·0
4	E. SMITH	3	2	1	1	1·0

YORKS. COUNTY XI.

1st INNINGS

	BATSMEN	HOW OUT	BOWLER	TOTAL
1	F.W. ELAM	c & b	BARNES	0
2	P. HOLMES	c SPRING	PARKER	2
3	D. DENTON	c SPRING	BARNES	18
4	R. KILNER	b	PARKER	1
5	W. RHODES	b	PARKER	2
6	LT. SALE-PENNINGTON	c PARKIN	PARKER	0
7	A. DRAKE	c BARNES	PARKER	16
8	G. HIRST (CAPT)	lbw	PARKER	16
9	S. HAIGH	b	PARKER	7
10	E. SMITH	b	PARKER	0
11	H.P. PLOWRIGHT	c LLEWELYN	BARNES	6
12	G.H. CRAWFORD	NOT	OUT	0
			EXTRAS	0
			TOTAL FOR 11 WKTS	68

2nd INNINGS

HOW OUT	BOWLER	TOTAL
NOT	OUT	15
NOT	OUT	24
	D.N.B.	
EXTRAS		1
TOTAL FOR 0 WKTS		40

BOWLERS (1st)

	BOWLERS	OVERS	M'D'NS	RUNS	WKTS	AV'GE
1	S.F. BARNES	15	4	33	3	11·0
2	C.L. PARKER	15	5	35	8	4·4

BOWLERS (2nd)

	BOWLERS	OVERS	M'D'NS	RUNS	WKTS	AV'GE
1	S.F. BARNES	4	1	4	0	—
2	C.L. PARKER	7	3	6	0	—
3	C.H. PARKIN	6	1	16	0	—
4	C.B. LLEWELYN	2·2	0	13	0	—

MATCH — 12 a-side.

RESULT YORKS XI. WON BY 10 WKTS.

Bradford Cricket League v P.F. Warner's International XI

Played at Park Avenue Date 21st & 22nd Aug. 1918

P.F. Warner's XI

1st Innings

#	Batsmen	How Out	Bowler	Total
1	Air Mec. J.B. Hobbs	c Robinson	Parkin	70
2	Sgt. Major H.W.T. Hardinge	b	Barnes	19
3	Major. Hon. L.H. Tennyson	b	Barnes	4
4	Coxswain F.E. Woolley	b	Field	31
5	Capt. N. Haig	st. Gaukroger	Llewelyn	11
6	Lieut. P.G.H. Fender	b	Parkin	1
7	Rev. F.H. Gillingham	b	Parkin	35
8	Midsh. Man. G.T.S. Stevens	b	Parkin	11
9	Capt. (Capt) P.F. Warner	b	Robinson	12
10	Lieut. E.J. Long	not	out	0
11	A.B. A.E. Pollard	b	Robinson	0
			Extras	24
			Total	220
			For 10 wkts.	

2nd Innings

How Out	Bowler	Total
run	out	22
c Parkin	Robinson	2
lbw	Parkin	14
c & b	Barnes	8
c Barnes	Parkin	4
c Barnes	Parkin	10
c & b	Robinson	16
not	out	9
c Haigh	Barnes	0
b	Barnes	5
c Ingham	Robinson	4
Extras		4
Total		98
For 10 wkts.		

Bowlers (1st Innings)

#	Bowler	Overs	Mdns	Runs	Wkts	Avge
1	C.H. Parkin	21	2	76	4	19.8
2	F.E. Field	10	3	44	1	44.0
3	C.B. Llewelyn	11	1	47	1	47.0
4	S.F. Barnes	7	1	18	2	9.0
5	E. Robinson	1.1	0	9	2	4.5

Bowlers (2nd Innings)

#	Bowler	Overs	Mdns	Runs	Wkts
1	E. Robinson	12.5	2	30	3
2	C.H. Parkin	12	0	39	2
3	F.E. Field	1	0	1	0
4	S.F. Barnes	12	3	24	4

Bradford League

1st Innings

#	Batsmen	How Out	Bowler	Total
1	G. Gunn	b	Pollard	1
2	H. Haigh	c Fender	Pollard	23
3	J.W. Hearne	c Fender	Woolley	19
4	E. Robinson	run	out	18
5	S. Cadman	c Warner	Woolley	0
6	C.B. Llewelyn	c Haig	Pollard	16
7	S.F. Barnes	c Gillingham	Fender	4
8	Gaukroger	st. Long	Pollard	42
9	C.H. Parkin	c Warner	Woolley	1
10	Gun. R. Ingham (Capt)	not	out	2
11	F.E. Field	c Warner	Woolley	0
			Extras	11
			Total	137
			For 10 wkts.	

2nd Innings

How Out	Bowler	Total
c Fender	Stevens	5
c Fender	Woolley	5
lbw	Pollard	33
c & b	Woolley	7
st. Tennyson	Woolley	7
c Warner	Fender	31
lbw	Fender	6
b	Woolley	11
c & b	Fender	1
c Woolley	Fender	8
not	out	2
Extras		12
Total		128
For 10 wkts.		

Bowlers (1st Innings)

#	Bowler	Overs	Mdns	Runs	Wkts	Avge
1	N. Haig	3	1	10	0	—
2	A.E. Pollard	16	4	41	4	10.25
3	P.G.H. Fender	9	0	48	1	48.0
4	H.W.T. Hardinge	1	1	0	0	—
5	F.E. Woolley	12.3	3	27	4	6.75

Bowlers (2nd Innings)

#	Bowler	Overs	Mdns	Runs	Wkts	Av
1	A.E. Pollard	8	1	19	1	19
2	F.E. Woolley	23	6	51	4	12
3	G.T.S. Stevens	10	2	31	1	31
4	P.G.H. Fender	6	1	15	4	3

Umpires G.P. Harrison & H. Noble

Result P.F. Warner's XI won by 53

FINAL LEAGUE POSITIONS

(1 pt)

1915	P	W	D	L	Pts
Bowling Old Lane	20	11	7	2	29
Bingley	20	10	8	2	28
Lidget Green	20	9	8	3	26
Pudsey St. Lawrence	20	9	7	4	25
Windhill	20	10	5	5	25
Saltaire	20	10	4	6	24
Idle	20	9	5	6	23
Bankfoot	20	8	6	6	22
Laisterdyke	20	9	4	7	22
Great Horton	20	7	7	6	21
Undercliffe	20	5	8	7	18
Baildon Green	20	5	7	8	17
Eccleshill	20	6	5	9	17
Queensbury	20	4	9	7	17
Tong Park	20	5	7	8	17
East Bierley	20	6	4	10	16
Farsley	20	5	6	9	16
Low Moor	20	5	6	9	16
Pudsey Britannia	20	3	5	12	11
Stanningley & Farsley	20	3	4	13	10

Batting Averages
1 H. Booth (Undercliffe) 55.4
2 C.H. Grimshaw (Bowling Old Lane) 47.5
3 J.B. Hobbs (Idle) 40.5
4 G. Sargent (Idle) 38.0

Bowling Averages
1 S.F. Barnes (Saltaire) 92 wkts @ 4.42
2 E.C. Keighley (Windhill) 82 wkts @ 8.30
3 C.H. Grimshaw (Bowling O L) 68 wkts @ 8.40
4 R.C. Sargent (Idle) 51 wkts @ 8.50

Bradford left the League and their place was taken by Bowling Old Lane.

1916	P	W	D	L	Pts
Idle	20	13	4	3	30
Lidget Green	20	13	4	3	30
Undercliffe	20	12	3	5	27
Pudsey Britannia	20	11	3	6	25
Bowling Old Lane	20	9	6	5	24
Tong Park	20	10	3	7	23
Bankfoot	20	9	4	7	22
Farsley	20	9	4	7	22
Keighley	20	8	6	6	22
Saltaire	20	8	6	6	22
Windhill	20	9	3	8	21
Laisterdyke	20	7	5	8	19
Baildon Green	20	7	4	9	18
Bingley	20	5	7	8	17
Queensbury	20	7	2	11	16
East Bierley	20	5	5	10	15
Great Horton	20	5	5	10	15
Pudsey St. Lawrence	20	4	6	10	14
Low Moor	20	4	5	11	13
Eccleshill	20	1	3	16	5

Idle beat Lidget Green in deciding match by 158 runs. (Idle 254 – Lidget Green 96)

Batting Averages
1 A. Hepworth (East Bierley) 62.20
2 J.B. Hobbs (Idle) 56.00
3 F.E. Woolley (Keighley) 49.70

Bowling Averages
1 S.F. Barnes (Saltaire) 93 wkts @ 6.48
2 J.B. Hobbs (Idle) 59 wkts @ 6.57
3 C.H. Parkin (Undercliffe) 95 wkts @ 6.65

Best batting of the season came from George Leach (Great Horton) 173 not out v Bowling Old Lane. Leach also had the best bowling of the season 10 for 16 v Pudsey Britannia.
Other top bowling performances were by:
C.H. Parkin (Undercliffe) 9 for 25 v Baildon Green and 9 for 26 v Tong Park.
Jack Hobbs also had nine wickets in an innings, 9 for 39 v Saltaire.

1917	P	W	D	L	Pts
Saltaire	20	13	5	2	31
Windhill	20	12	5	3	29
Bowling Old Lane	20	11	6	3	28
Lidget Green	20	10	7	3	27
Bankfoot	20	11	4	5	26
Keighley	20	9	8	3	26
Bingley	20	10	5	5	25
Great Horton	20	10	5	5	25
Pudsey Britannia	20	10	4	6	24
Laisterdyke	20	9	4	7	22
Tong Park	20	8	4	8	20
Eccleshill	20	8	4	8	20
East Bierley	20	8	3	9	19
Undercliffe	20	8	2	10	18
Farsley	20	5	4	11	14
Baildon Green	20	4	5	11	13
Idle	20	3	6	11	12
Low Moor	20	4	2	14	10
Pudsey St. Lawrence	20	2	2	16	6
Queensbury	20	0	4	16	4

Batting Averages
1 J.W. Hearne (Keighley) 50.50
2 P. Holmes (Great Horton) 42.07
3 H. Sutcliffe (Pudsey Britannia) 30.27
4 F. Jebson (Windhill) 30.06

Bowling Averages
1 S.F. Barnes (Saltaire) 107 wkts @ 4.92
2 C.J. Elton (Pudsey Britannia) 74 wkts @ 7.33
3 H. Spencer (Windhill) 36 wkts @ 7.86
4 E. Robinson (Bankfoot) 77 wkts @ 8.02

Highest Innings
A. Hodgson (East Bierley) v Idle 156

Best Bowling
C.H. Parkin (U'cliffe) v Baildon Green 10 for 15
S.F. Barnes (Saltaire) v Tong Park 9 for 19
E. Robinson (Bankfoot) v Keighley 9 for 29
J.T. Newstead (Lidget Green) v Und'cliffe 9 for 35
S.F. Barnes (Saltaire) v Keighley 9 for 41

1918	P	W	D	L	Pts
Saltaire	20	14	5	1	33
Keighley	20	12	6	2	30
Pudsey St. Lawrence	20	10	7	3	27
Undercliffe	20	8	10	2	26
Bowling Old Lane	20	8	9	3	25
East Bierley	20	6	9	5	21
Windhill	20	8	5	7	21
Baildon Green	20	7	6	7	20
Bingley	20	7	6	7	20
Low Moor	20	7	6	7	20
Laisterdyke	20	4	11	5	19
Pudsey Britannia	20	6	7	7	19
Great Horton	20	4	10	6	18
Lidget Green	20	4	9	7	17
Tong Park	20	6	5	9	17
Eccleshill	20	4	8	8	16
Farsley	20	5	6	9	16
Bankfoot	20	4	6	10	14
Queensbury	20	2	8	10	12
Idle	20	3	3	14	9

Batting Averages
1 C. Tyson (Tong Park) 48.81
2 S. Haigh (Keighley) 39.11
3 P. Yewdall (Great Horton) 36.77
4 W. Payton (Bankfoot) 36.85

Bowling Averages
1 S.F. Barnes (Saltaire) 112 wkts @ 5.20
2 F. Horner (Keighley) 48 wkts @ 9.10
3 H. Atkinson (Pudsey St. Law.) 35 wkts @ 10.05
4 E. Robinson (Keighley) 39 wkts @ 10.28
5 W. Rhodes (Baildon Green) 68 wkts @ 10.83

Highest Innings
W. Payton (Bankfoot) v East Bierley 135 no

Best Bowling
S.F. Barnes (Saltaire) v Keighley 10 for 36
J.T. Newstead (East Bierley) v Queensbury 9 for 5

J. Cupitt (Windhill) had an average of more than his highest score, as follows:
Inns 13   no 10   H.S. 30   Runs 91   Av. 30.33

Chapter Four
Between the Wars
(1919 – 1939)

Keighley were the Champions in 1919, just one league defeat in twenty matches and probably they would have been the bookies favourites at the start of the season with a team which consisted of Frank Woolley, Schofield Haigh, Jack Hearne, George Crawford, Willis Walker and Herbert Haigh. It was certainly strong on paper and that strength was transferred to performances, none better than the 6 wickets for 2 runs taken by Frank Woolley when Pudsey St. Lawrence were humbled for only 13 runs. More was to follow, Queensbury dismissed for 21, Baildon Green for 28 and Lidget Green for 44. Hearne and Woolley played only 5 and 11 times respectively but both averaged over forty five while Herbert Haigh with two centuries and ten half centuries scored over 800 league runs at 50.31. Chief rivals to Keighley were Bowling Old Lane, Farsley and Undercliffe. Yet it was against Bowling Old Lane that Keighley made their highest score of the season (289 for 5). When they played Undercliffe both Herbert Haigh (53) and Jack Hearne (76) made half centuries. There was a new first wicket league record too when Herbert Haigh (112 not out) and W. Morley scored 261 without being parted against Bingley.

While Keighley were worthy Champions there were other events of note. George Gunn and W.H. Hickton broke the 5th wicket partnership record when 177 was gathered from the Pudsey St. Lawrence attack. Wilf Payton who had made 135 not out, for Bankfoot v East Bierley in 1918, the highest individual score of the season, broke George Leach's record of 173 by scoring 187 not out against Great Horton. Payton was in the middle of a career with Nottinghamshire for whom he played almost 500 times and scored over 1,000 runs in nine different seasons. Payton helped Bankfoot into 5th spot in the League, thirteen places higher than the previous season.

The resumption of the County Championship was to result in Yorkshire being able to send only their 2nd XI to Park Avenue in August for the Annual game against a representative side from the League. The League made the County bowlers toil, when, after trailing by 87 on the first innings the Bradford League scored 288 for 3 in their second innings. Tyson (Tong Park) 84, H. Haigh (Keighley) 35, Dibb (Undercliffe) 44, Read (Farsley) 37 not out and Cole (B.O.L.) 64 not out making it a real team effort.

Opener Cecil Tyson created a new aggregate record in 1919 with his 867 runs in league games, and he and Sam Cadman were most unlucky not to hold the first wicket partnership record when their match against Lidget Green brought them 258 runs without being parted. Cadman 100 not out and Tyson 143 not out. It was just three runs less than the partnership between Haigh and Morley of Keighley in the same season. The match after that 258 v Lidget, Cadman and Tyson put on 136 v Laisterdyke, again without being parted. Tong Park were on the receiving end of a partnership record however in 1919 when E.J. Parkin (59) and B.B. Wilson (134 not out) playing for Pudsey Britannia had a second wicket stand of 203.

Despite having Kent batsman James Seymour in their side Keighley slipped to 4th spot with Saltaire taking over at the top. This was the first time a side had gone through a league season unbeaten. It was impressive too as fifteen outright wins came from the twenty matches. Sedgwick topped 500 runs at 35.13 and was ably assisted by N. Robinson who averaged 53.40 from his ten innings with S. Smith and T. Craven both of whom topped 400 runs for the club averaged over 25 runs per innings. The 94 league wickets that Barnes took was obviously the major contribution. There was a big shock in store however for despite the 6 wickets taken by Barnes, Bingley beat Saltaire in the 1st round of the Priestley Cup. Twenty one years later Saltaire did go through a cup and league season without defeat.

21

One of the League's most remarkable matches took place in 1921. Eccleshill against Saltaire. Batting first Saltaire were all out for a mere 35 runs. Along came Barnes with not many runs to play with, took 7 for 17 and Eccleshill were all out for 34, so failing by one run. Eccleshill however were used to low scores, usually their own, for in 1919 they set a record which still stands today and is probably the most unwanted record in the League. Meeting Queensbury they were dismissed for 28. One week later Windhill dismissed them for 26 and after Farsley had also bowled them out for 26 seven days later, it meant that in three consecutive completed innings Eccleshill had totalled 80 runs whilst losing 30 wickets. It wasn't as if Eccleshill were a bad side that year for they lost only three more of their seventeen remaining fixtures that season. That three weeks of humiliation is better not mentioned to Eccleshill members—that's if you value our hide.

Bingley removed the Saltaire dominance in 1921 if only for one year. Their win revolved mainly around four men. Arthur Hyde and John Hardcastle for runs, Oyston and Judson for wickets. With a century and six half centuries Hyde led the way but Hardcastle too (102 not out v Windhill) had a 'ton' and four fifties and wasn't far behind. The taking of 143 league wickets between them by Oyston and Judson often resulted in the other bowlers not being able to turn their arm. When Pudsey Britannia were all out for 47, the two bowlers had 5 wickets each, a not unusual occurence for eleven times between them five wickets were earned in an innings.

On the opening day of the 1921 season G.W. Brooke, a Yorkshireman born at Mirfield (he went on to play 150 games for Worcestershire) playing for Keighley, took nine wickets for just four runs. What a way to start a season!! Tong Park were dismissed for 14 as a result and while Keighley had a successful season (cup winners and 2nd in the League) Tong Park went through the season without a win and were replaced for the 1922 season by the Bradford Club. Opening the bowling at Keighley in 1921 was Alex Skelding, a man who hated dogs. He played 177 times for Leicestershire his native county and later became a much respected umpire known for his eccentricities. Skelding bowled more overs in 1921 than anyone else in the League and at the seasons end was rewarded with 64 wickets at 14.76 runs apiece and also a cup winners medal.

Sydney Barnes was 49 years of age in 1922 which makes all the more astounding his record breaking season. Barnes took 122 league wickets at an unbelievably low average of 4.10 runs each. Both wickets and average are a record never likely to be beaten. His 100th wicket that season came as early as the 29th July and, as if he hadn't already proved his worth in shattering fashion he was the top Saltaire batsman also, averaging 32.00 which was 8.13 more than his nearest club challenger. Now it was Barnes the all-rounder. Despite all this and the clinching of their 4th title in six years, they failed to make it a resounding double by a 23 run defeat in the Priestley Cup Final.

The side who beat them in that Final was Bowling Old Lane and it was they who took the title from Saltaire in 1923 and then retained it in 1924. The first of these was made a little bit easier when Barnes, after taking 62 league wickets at 4.17 runs each, which was enough to win him the 'top spot' in the League averages for the ninth successive season, left the League. He wrote to Saltaire from Wales saying that he had taken over the Royal Hotel in Colwyn Bay and asked to be released from his contract. The club reluctantly agreed. So ended the Barnes era when he literally re-wrote the record books. His nine years at Saltaire equalled his longest period with any one club (he had nine years also with Porthill commencing in 1906).

The season after Barnes left, Saltaire actually went through the season unbeaten in their twenty league games. There were however contributory factors like rain and fifteen draws in a miserable summer. It brought them 3rd spot in the League with Bowling Old Lane worthy winners having managed nine victories. In runners-up spot for the second season in succession were Bradford. They were quickly into their stride after their enforced absence during the First World War. T.W. Patefield was the main run maker at this time while Frank Luckhurst and Stanley Douglas were destroyers in chief and did so with wickets always costing less than twelve runs each.

The 1924 season contained an extra ingredient in the form of Bert Vogler. Having played in fifteen Test Matches for South Africa, taking 64 Test wickets, the right arm leg break and googly bowler was signed by Windhill. His unusual repertoire of deliveries dismissed 61 batsmen in the League at 12.90 while his batting which brought 212 runs in 10 completed innings was quite useful and the club reached the semi-final of the Priestley Cup where he took 5 for 41 but could not inspire his colleagues to a Final place. One man almost dominated the scene in 1924. Charles Grimshaw who won both the batting and bowling averages in the same season. He had comfortable margins in both too.

Grimshaw was an inspiration to all those around him. Born in 1880 Charlie was a First Class cricketer with Yorkshire between 1904 and 1908. He was a left hander when batting but right arm medium when bowling. He played in Old Lane's first Bradford League season of 1915 and had such loyalty that he was turning out match winning performances for them for the next twenty two seasons. Apart from his 230 record in the Priestley Cup in 1915 he became the first to bat through a completed innings for Old Lane with his 72 not out against Saltaire the same season. When he topped both the League averages in 1924 he did not only a hat-trick playing against Low Moor but 4 in 4 v Keighley. When he ended his playing days at the age of 56 years he had taken 1273 league wickets for Bowling Old Lane. Only once since then has a player taken so many in the League. Seven times he represented the club in a Priestley Cup Final yet was a winner only twice. He took 6 wickets in two of those Finals, 5 wickets in another and scored 55 and 56 in yet two more. Three Championships won by the club while he was with them were due in no small way to the great all-round ability of 'Charlie' Grimshaw.

Bowling Old Lane came extremely near a 'hat-trick' of Championship wins in 1925 when Undercliffe stole their thunder and pipped them by just one point. It was perhaps a surprising win, for in the year previously Undercliffe were in sixth position. You wouldn't find an Undercliffe player in the top three of the League averages either in 1924 or their winning year 1925. The indication is clearly that this was a team effort with everyone pulling their weight. No one made more than three fifties in the season, Parrington, Robinson and Dibb reaching the half century three times each with Ainley, Cooke and Holden once each. The bowling was really a two man affair, Arthur Bastow and Percy Coates had 60 and 41 wickets respectively, while it was unusual in a Championship winning side to find no bowler taking more than six wickets in any innings. Bastow's 6 for 22 v Laisterdyke and Coates's 6 for 39 v Keighley being the best. Dibb and Robinson were an opening pair to rival that of Cadman and Tyson in days gone by. On the 6th June 1925 Robinson and Dibb put on 113 runs for the first wicket v Lightcliffe. One week later they had an opening stand of 100 v Low Moor and in the two following matches against Laisterdyke and Idle made 145 and 100 before being parted. Four consecutive century opening stands. Sixty three years on and that record still stands.

There was a new aggregate record in 1925 when George Lund of Brighouse scored 954 league runs. Runs were plentiful that season. When Bingley met Laisterdyke it was the first time there had been three centuries in the same Bradford League game. H. Firth and H. Briggs started the ball rolling (frequently to the boundary no doubt) making 270 for a new 2nd wicket partnership record. Not to be outdone Laisterdyke's J.W. Williamson then scored 117 in his sides spirited reply. Bingley had declared at 308 for 1 and when the Laisterdyke reply ended, after a really great fight, at 294 for 8, it was the highest number of runs scored in the League on one day.

Eric Petts became the eigth bowler to take 'all ten' in a league game when he produced figures of 10 for 59 for Great Horton v Farsley. Saltaire after finishing with only four teams beneath them in 1925 stormed back to win the most exciting title race so far, in 1926. Only one point separated the top four teams and play-offs were needed.

The first play-off was between Windhill and Queensbury. Windhill scraped home by one wicket when Alf Morris took 9 for 33, then went on to play Saltaire to decide the title. Helped by 5 for 39 from T. Mawson, Saltaire dismissed Windhill for 127 and took the title, winning by four wickets. Top of the Saltaire batting and with 38 wickets at 12.57 was another one of the fine all-rounders who made a large contribution to the League's history. Amos Spring was a bit of a wanderer though not as bad as some who have played in the League. He started his Bradford League career with Bankfoot in 1917 moving to Baildon Green for 1924 and 1925 before joining Saltaire. He then moved on to Windhill playing for them for three years starting in 1927. Spring was born in Dulwich and played 68 matches for Surrey before coming to the League. He left his mark with his 143 not out against Baildon Green, it being the League's highest score in 1926 and he had topped the League bowling averages in 1925 proving he was a top class all-rounder. Spring almost scored centuries for four different clubs, making a 'ton' for Bankfoot, Windhill and Saltaire, while reaching 98 for Baildon v Eccleshill in 1924.

Many performances of players like Spring are lost alas in the passage of time. Not much cricket history is left without statistics and a player who may have saved his side with thirty odd runs on a sticky wicket against the odds will not find it recorded to do his memory justice.

Bradford had only managed an average season in 1926 but did total the highest losing score so far in a Bradford League match when they made 327 against Laisterdyke and lost by four wickets. Bradford were to become the most outstanding side in the League when they lost only three games in three years. That was sixty league matches of which 34 were won, 23 drawn and only the three reverses. It brought the Park Avenue based club three Championships and made household names of Stanley Douglas, William Alfred Hutton, Frank Luckhurst and Jack Crossley. Hutton played with the Bradford club from 1922 to 1935 and came back for a season in 1940. He was not one of the famous Hutton brothers, but he was good enough to win the League batting with an average of 61.27 in 1929. Frank Luckhurst was another Kentish son to find his way North and he joined Bradford in 1912, played for three seasons and returned to the club in 1923 staying for twelve more years. Luckhurst was a bowler pure and simple, and not a bowler who could bat as his run making was almost non-existent. However with the ball he could be deadly. His first Bradford League season saw figures of 9 for 53 v Great Horton, 8 for 28 v Pudsey Britannia, 8 for 42 v Windhill and 8 for 46 v Queensbury. No wonder Bradford were pleased to have him in their ranks. He proved a lucky mascot in Priestley Cup games too, for Luckhurst played in four Priestley Cup Finals for Bradford in 1913, 1914, 1929 and 1934 all of which were won.

The story of J.M. Crossley is rather strange. His first league season was 1928 when he joined Bradford, 'Champs' of the previous season, and took part in their 2nd and 3rd consecutive Championship seasons. In 1931 he left to join Brighouse who had won the title in 1930 and he stayed with them for two years helping them also to their 2nd and 3rd consecutive Championship wins. Thus he had four championship medals and also shared in the League's first two Championship hat-tricks. His 167 not out v Baildon Green in 1932 was not only the third highest score in the League's history but was also part of a record partnership for the fourth wicket when he and Jackie Hill (Snr) put on 248, Hill making 81 not out.

Stanley J. Douglas first played Bradford League cricket in 1924 for Bradford. His left arm spin making him the second league bowler to complete 1000 wickets. He was 21 years old when he made his debut and 40 years when he played his last game in 1943 but the years between did nothing but illustrate his tremendous skills. His worst season was 1928 when he took 31 League wickets at 17.96. In 1932 he took his highest number of wickets in a season, 80 at an average of 11.47 and although taking fewer in 1927 (50), 1936 (55) and 1937 (69), his average on all three occasions was below eleven. Douglas was one of the League's long servants and perhaps a man for the big occasion. Of his three fifties two were responsible for bringing a trophy to his club, Bradford. The Championship play-off with Brighouse in 1929 brought him 59 runs and he repeated that score, this time unbeaten in the following years Priestley Cup Final. His ability was such that Yorkshire called on him for 23 matches at the height of their power in the left arm bowling department. Yet another man of high class left his mark.

Another record maker with Bradford was Fred Popplewell who, in 1926 became the first man to score three successive centuries in the League. This was later equalled by J. 'Vic' Wilson, former Yorkshire captain, in 1944 and eventually beaten.

Brighouse won the first of their three successive championships in 1930 with East Bierley and Bowling Old Lane just one point behind. The Club had only been in the League since 1925 and had surprised many, in 1928, when only a 47 run defeat in a play-off with Bradford stopped them taking the title sooner. Their 1930 triumph was a real team effort. Runs flowed from the bats of Hill, Outram, Barker, Robinson, and Hirst while Render, Hirst, Metcalfe and Harrison captured the wickets. Although Brighouse lost one of the great cup games that year (by one wicket after scoring 231) and that in round one, their first trophy made them hungry.

In 1931 Crossley arrived after assisting Bradford to two of their titles. Jackie Hill took a liking to the Bowling Old Lane attack and made 89 and 74 not out in the two games against them, while Crossley himself favoured Idle against whom he scored 92 and 72 not out. Once more, despite being Champions with only two defeats, Brighouse failed in the cup 1st round. No great encounter this time as Undercliffe romped home by 48 runs. Their highest score in 1930 had been only 228 for 8 in a league match and was only improved by five runs in 1931 but in 1932 Saltaire were taken for 258 for 4 wkts and Baildon Green hit for 278 for 2 wkts when Hill and Crossley had their record breaking knock. Jack Hill (Snr) topped the League averages with a record average of 99.11. His 18 innings may have contained 9 not outs but his steady play had brought him 892 runs, one century and nine half centuries.

Windhill's N. Walton went to town in 1932 taking 48 runs from two consecutive overs from Freddie Wharton, playing with Spen Victoria. Miles Coope playing for Bingley in 1946 beat this with 50 runs from two consecutive overs, but it must have been quite a surprise around the city in 1932 that one of the League's finest and steadiest bowlers such as Wharton should have suffered so badly. It was with Spen Victoria that Freddie Wharton began his Bradford League career as a bowler who was quite useful with the 'willow' also, without perhaps being a genuine all-rounder. The season before the Walton onslaught his 35 wickets had cost just over 12 each and he was making a name for himself as 'Mr Economy'. Fortunately there was no lasting damage and Freddie went on to Undercliffe, Farsley, Yeadon, Idle and Windhill with equal success. It is perhaps odd that in his last season, 1953, for Windhill he should enter the Batting records, for against Bankfoot, he and Tony Wain put on 117 for the 8th wicket. It was Freddie who did most of the scoring too with 77 but perhaps he was most proud of his century in 1937 against East Bierley.

The 30's were no different to any other decade in the Bradford League, it contained as always great players the highest of league standards and many memorable matches. Of the players one who was to be known world-wide later, as an umpire, was Syd Buller. He entered 'league life' with the Bradford club in 1932. Playing against Great Horton, Syd saw two Horton batsmen rattle up speedy centuries—Halstead 107 not out and W. Smith 104. He then made Horton pay dearly for all the 'leather chasing' he had to do and thrashed 137 not out, the third century of the game. This was only the second time such a happening had occured in the League. Born in Bramley, just down the road from Pudsey, for those who didn't know, Buller did indeed play for his native county once. That was 1930 and then off to play 110 games for Worcestershire. When time allowed he turned out for Bradford and won himself a cup winners medal in the 1934 Priestley Cup Final. In 1939 he was involved in a car accident in which his team mate Charles Bull was killed. Syd was awarded the MBE in 1965 and died five years later when he collapsed during an interval for rain at a county match in which he was an umpire. During the Second World War, Syd came to play in the Bradford League renewing old acquaintances, making new friends and making 90 runs in the cup for Windhill against Undercliffe. The highest cup score of that year.

Perhaps this is an ideal spot in the book to give a few details of the Hutton brothers. Elsewhere you will read some comments from Sir Leonard Hutton himself, given to me in 1987. The first of the four brothers to play Bradford League cricket was Edmund who turned out when 20 years of age. His first notable contribution being 52 not out against Tong Park in 1921. Maybe it isn't so strange that all four brothers were batsmen. Edmund didn't play regularly in the League again till the 1933 and 1934 seasons. George was next and he like Edmund and later Leonard played only for Pudsey St. Lawrence. It was in 1924 that George made the first of his twenty six half centuries for the club. He also had a hundred to his credit in 1940 against Bankfoot. Described in his day as a very dependable batsman George Hutton batted through for Pudsey St. Lawrence no less than four times. The first was in 1926 when he made 63 not out v Low Moor. His second such feat came in 1935 with 31 not out against Brighouse but the third instance of him carrying his bat was against Windhill in 1936 and while losing his ten partners George scored just 11 not

25

out. Three years later his 66 not out gave him an unrivalled Bradford League record of batting through four times for the same club.

In 1932 Len Hutton made his first '50' for the St. Lawrence 1st XI, in fact it was an 82 not out v Queensbury with his maiden Bradford League century 108 not out in the Priestley Cup in 1933 against Bradford. His County and Test career from 1934 obviously restricted his league appearances but that did not stop him making four centuries and thirty two half centuries when he did play. The match v Undercliffe in 1940 brought his highest score for St. Lawrence, that of 133. We must not forget the bowling of Len Hutton which is certainly not as well documented as his batting but which nevertheless was more than useful. Take 1943 for example, when despite bowling only 104.4 overs he took 43 Bradford League wickets. What a strike rate and at only 8.97 runs each too. This gave him 5th spot in the League bowling averages. Two cup medals were earned while playing for Pudsey, one a victors medal and one a runners-up medal. His winners medal came in the 1943 Priestley Cup Final when his 64 was only one run short of the entire Brighouse total. In Len Hutton's last Bradford League season, 1945, his twelve innings brought an average of 50.55. The fourth Hutton brother Reg. played at Pudsey in 1937 and although scoring 50 v Baildon Green he did not make his mark again in the League until he returned to it, with Eccleshill in 1950. That year he managed 71 v Queensbury and his top score for Eccleshill came in 1952, his last season, when he cracked 75 not out from the Windhill attack.

All the Hutton brothers were fine, honest upstanding citizens, well respected where ever they went. Of all the Hutton stories, and there are plenty, I love best the one Sir Leonard tells against himself concerning his son Richard. When Richard started to play a bit of Bradford League cricket Dad would go along to watch when other commitments allowed. One Saturday when Dad was not present Richard made 50 runs. He was an opener at the time. He came home and boasted to Dad of his innings, showering his collection in the form of dozens of small coins all over the table. There were a few words with Dad not wanting son to get too bigheaded about it all. The following week the two had an argument resulting in Sir Len refusing to take Richard to the away game, at East Bierley, by car. Concerned about the progress of his son, Sir Leonard went to Bierley, arriving to see the home side in the field and the scoreboard showing one wicket down for no runs. Richard not at the wicket had obviously got a 'duck'. His father went home and on Richards arrival that evening feeling the need to bring the lad down a peg or two, said glibly, 'Where's your collection money this week then'. 'Here', said Richard, once more spilling his well earned gains all over the room. But I came and you were 0 for 1 and not at the crease exclaimed Dad. 'Yes', said Richard because I had to go by bus I arrived half an hour late and went in No. 6, but still got another fifty and a collection, so there. Not many men would let it be known that they argued with a son and were made to look a little foolish, but then there have not been many men like Len Hutton.

After finishing tenth in 1933, Keighley created an absolute sensation by signing a 61 year old for the following season. His name—Sydney Barnes. Yes Barnes was back in the League where his records remain still from his earlier days with Saltaire. What could a 61 year old do in any class of cricket, not a lot, unless he was unique. Sydney Barnes certainly was that, and in 1934 while helping Keighley to third position in the League, just two points behind first place, he helped himself to 76 league wickets at 10.32 each. During this 1934 season Barnes passed 1000 wickets in the League and Cup, and when the seasons end arrived had reached 909 league wickets. Now for those who add up his nine seasons at Saltaire and the 76 he got for Keighley you'll find that the total is 908 wickets. I shall now reveal where the odd wicket comes from. In 1928 Brighouse asked Barnes if it were possible to help them out. 'Alas', he said, that he was able to manage only the Whit Monday holiday fixture which was at home to Windhill. He made just one run and took one wicket for twenty six runs. This helps with the trick question, 'Which three Bradford League clubs did Sydney Barnes play for? Everyone knows Saltaire, a few know Keighley but Brighouse. Well as Michael Caine may say, 'not a lot of people know that'.

Bradford were 1934 Champions but what must they have thought after playing a Barnes inspired Keighley? Bradford were humbled when the old-timer took eight wickets for nine runs. I never saw Barnes play, much before my time, but on statistics alone he surely was the greatest ever.

The Championship win of Undercliffe in 1935 would I am certain have been well received. No one likes monopoly of trophies and since 1927 only Bradford five times, and Brighouse three times had won the title. Undercliffe had a comfortable margin of five points too and winning at least three games more than any other club had obviously been positive in their outlook. No team drew fewer matches and in Thomas Alec 'Sandy' Jacques they had a match winner to almost rival the great Barnes himself. Sandy Jacques was a fine bowler. He played County Cricket with Yorkshire on 28 occasions and in all First Class cricket made over 30 appearances never once being on the losing side. He had taken an unprecedented 'all ten' in 1933, taking 10 for 25 against Bankfoot—all his victims being bowled. I am aware that John Wisden was the first cricketer to perform such a feat but Jacques did it in the Bradford League!! He topped the League bowling with Saltaire in 1933 and again in 1935 with Undercliffe, taking 93 wickets at 8.24 runs each which was quite exceptional.

After breaking the dominance of Saltaire and Bradford, the Undercliffe side slid unexpectedly to eleventh position in 1936 and Bradford were back as Champions. Prior to the commencement of the season it was felt three points for a win would have beneficial effects and although the top three in 1936 would have been the same under the old system the change did help to cut down the number of draws. Season 1935 produced 75 drawn games which was reduced to 52 under the new system, as teams more than ever before went all out to win.

The seasons highest individual score came from Willie Sutcliffe of Farsley. Often wrongly confused with Herbert Sutcliffe or Billy Sutcliffe. Willie was no relation to either but was a fine batsman. His 158 v Windhill may have been his highest score in his Bradford League days but he thrashed many an attack. Other centuries came against Saltaire (148) and Eccleshill (134) both in 1933, while he had 124 v Brighouse in 1936 and 119 not out against local rivals Pudsey St. Lawrence in 1940. Willie Sutcliffe was by all accounts a hitter, a crowd pleaser who cared now't for averages. He would average between 25 and 35 each season but would rarely if ever let the paying public down. His playing days were all with Farsley, his first team period stretching from 1927 to 1940.

While Bradford were winning the title, Jack Swift was scoring a lot of runs for Windhill. Jack Swift was one of those people when given a ball game to play was always likely to excel. Mainly as a batsman he will be remembered in Bradford League history but he could keep wicket to a high standard and was second in the League wicketkeeping averages in 1948. He could bowl a bit too and just as his top batting performance was against Windhill so was his only five wicket feat with 5 for 30 against them in 1932. As a 19 year old, Jack Swift played a few games for Idle in 1923 but it was not till 1931 that he again played and having joined Eccleshill became a man of some considerable reputation. He went back to Idle in 1933 for two seasons before joining Windhill. I'm sure they were pleased to play with him rather than have damage inflicted against them. By 1942 Jack was playing for Yeadon whom he left in 1947 for Bingley. By now the wandering run machine was getting near the record for the most fifties made by a player in the League, but it took further moves to Eccleshill in 1948 and to Bowling Old Lane in 1951 before he recorded his record breaking half century while with Old Lane. When his league career ended in 1953 Jack Swift had scored ten centuries and ninety half centuries. Both his records lasted for over thirty years. Of his ninety half centuries only seven were scored in cup ties, but he did appear in four Priestley Cup Finals winning with Idle (1923) and Yeadon (1945) and losing with Windhill (1938) and Yeadon (1944).

Jack's son, Malcolm, followed his father's footsteps into the League, first joining Yeadon in 1959. Although more of an all-rounder than Dad constant comparisons were being made and maybe it weighed heavily on Malcolm's shoulders. Even so between 1959 and 1973 he turned in some fine performances. Though his chequered career did not bring a century, (his highest was 90 runs for Salts v Great Horton in 1969), it brought him a championship medal with Idle in Division Two in 1962. Malcolm's most penetrative bowling came early, 7 for 39 against Eccleshill in 1960 and 7 for 59 v Great Horton in 1962. So with 22 half centuries, four clubs in Yeadon, Idle, Salts and Bingley he carved out his own little niche of Bradford League History.

In the late 1930's the West Indians arrived. It was something of a novelty seeing coloured players in the League but not unique. A quartet of great West Indian cricketers were to grace the League with their considerable talents. The first of these being Edwin St. Hill. Known as 'Enoch' he was often confused with Wilton St. Hill, who though born eleven years earlier also played in Tests against England in the 29/30 series. Wilton could bat high in any order, Enoch could not. Whatever limitations Enoch had with his batting he sure made up for it with a ball in his hands. He was right arm, medium rather than fast and he set tongues wagging in 1935 when he made his debut for East Bierley and ended his first season with 63 league wickets at 14.57. In his second year this had risen to 87 league wickets at only 10.60. Players and spectators became fully aware that 'ere we had a good un'. Before naming the second of this amazing quartet let me immediately add that in 1937, 1938 and 1939 Windhill had a hat-trick of Championship wins without him. The 'him' to whom I refer, you will read about in the next chapter, Learie Constantine. Martindale and Achong arrived too. Manny joined Bingley (1940) and Achong joined Windhill in 1944.

The fact that Windhill did so well before he joined may have influenced his decision, but in 1937 Windhill obviously had a fine side. Obvious from the standard of opposition whom they swept aside, obvious too from the fact that eight different batsmen made half centuries, six of them at least twice. Then there was the bowling of Johnnie Lawrence and Squire Render.

Johnnie Lawrence was born in the Leeds area of Carlton and by 1937 he was 23 years old and just finding his way in the game. His leg breaks and googlies were eventually to earn him 281 First Class games with Somerset, after which he became one of the most highly respected coaches this country has seen. Geoffrey Boycott was just one 'Star' to benefit from the Lawrence experience. In 1936 he had made his debut for Windhill and his bowling contribution to their 1937 title was 40 wickets. His last Bradford League matches came in 1969 when he was in his mid-fifties but even then his high degree of skill brought dividends on a regular basis. One or two highlights Johnnie no doubt relished are his 8 for 27 against Undercliffe in 1939, his hat-trick v East Bierley in 1945, his 8 for 18 v Yeadon in 1957 and 9 for 43 v Bowling Old Lane eleven years later. The passing years had little effect on J.H. Lawrence and it must be recalled that his batting was rather more than average, witnessed by his 141 for Bingley v Keighley in 1943. Two sons, Miles and Steve have also played Bradford League cricket. Miles with Idle, Farsley and East Bierley and Steve with Lightcliffe, Cleckheaton and East Bierley. Although good players in their own right they will make a rod for their own backs if trying to emulate an outstanding Dad.

Partnering Johnnie Lawrence in opening the Windhill attack in 1937 was Squire Render. One of the League's loyal servants, Render started at Low Moor in 1925 and concluded his Bradford League days at Idle in 1946. A vast amount could be written about the happenings between these dates, for Render went on year after year taking wickets, with great regularity if a supporter, great monotony if an opponent. It seems that Render was a real tailender in the old tradition. In 1928 for example his batting average was 3.2 which leads to wonder, even amazement, when you realise in 1925 he made 55 not out for Low Moor against Baildon Green. To relate that Render once scored fifty in a Bradford League innings would lead to ridicule from those who saw some of his performances.

Render was however good enough to 'top' the League averages with his main love, bowling, this he did in 1928 and again in 1929 while other proud moments would no doubt be his hat-trick in 1928 for Brighouse v Bingley, his 9 for 35 against Bankfoot in 1926. Six times he had eight wickets in an innings for 35 runs or less. In 1938 Render played in a losing Cup Final and was deprived of a winners medal in 1943 only through injury but that, as they say, is another story. After a break lasting twenty six years the League went back to the two division format in 1937. Playing all the top sides did not bother Windhill who in 1938 won their second consecutive Championship despite the fact that only three half centuries came during the season. Swift, Hipkin and Spencer had one each, so it was perhaps surprising in view of that statistic to find the club at the top of the League with only one league defeat.

Completing a hat-trick by again finishing top in 1939 they did have improved batting performances but were indebted to Lawrence and Davison who took 107 league wickets between them. After becoming yet another club to chalk up a Championship hat-trick, people thought, so I am reliably informed, that the bubble would burst. It did not and any chance of a fall following immense pride was scuppered by a significant signing, that of Learie Nicholas Constantine.

The best was yet to come.

BRADFORD CRICKET LEAGUE

FINAL LEAGUE POSITIONS

1919	P	W	D	L	Pts
Keighley	20	13	6	1	32
Bowling Old Lane	20	9	8	3	26
Farsley	20	9	8	3	26
Undercliffe	20	9	8	3	26
Bankfoot	20	9	6	5	24
Low Moor	20	10	4	6	24
Tong Park	20	8	7	5	23
Eccleshill	20	8	6	6	22
Pudsey St. Lawrence	20	7	8	5	22
Saltaire	20	8	6	6	22
Queensbury	20	9	3	8	21
Lidget Green	20	8	4	8	20
East Bierley	20	7	5	8	19
Pudsey Britannia	20	6	7	7	19
Windhill	20	6	5	9	17
Laisterdyke	20	4	5	11	13
Baildon Green	20	4	4	12	12
Bingley	20	4	4	12	12
Great Horton	20	2	8	10	12
Idle	20	1	6	13	8

Batting Averages
1 George Gunn (Undercliffe)   60.88
2 Cecil Tyson (Tong Park)   57.80
3 Herbert Haigh (Keighley)   50.31

Bowling Averages
1 S.F. Barnes (Saltaire)   62 wkts @ 8.43
2 Frank Woolley (Keighley)   47 wkts @ 8.97
3 Irvine Boocock (Eccleshill)   30 wkts @ 9.23

Frank Woolley scored 134 v Saltaire and 109 v Bankfoot but did not bat the 12 times needed to qualify for the batting averages.

1920	P	W	D	L	Pts
Saltaire	20	15	5	0	35
Bowling Old Lane	20	14	5	1	33
Great Horton	20	10	5	5	25
Keighley	20	8	7	5	23
Tong Park	20	9	4	7	22
Bingley	20	8	5	7	21
Pudsey Britannia	20	6	8	6	20
Pudsey St. Lawrence	20	7	6	7	20
Undercliffe	20	8	4	8	20
Laisterdyke	20	7	5	8	19
Bankfoot	20	6	6	8	18
Farsley	20	6	6	8	18
Idle	20	4	9	7	17
Baildon Green	20	6	5	9	17
East Bierley	20	4	9	7	17
Low Moor	20	7	3	10	17
Queensbury	20	5	6	9	16
Lidget Green	20	4	7	9	15
Eccleshill	20	4	6	10	14
Windhill	20	2	9	9	13

Batting Averages
1 T.G. Dobson (East Bierley)   48.41
2 Ben Wilson (Pudsey Britannia)   48.28
3 Charles Lee (Undercliffe)   44.80

Bowling Averages
1 S.F. Barnes (Saltaire)   94 wkts @ 5.30
2 C.H. Grimshaw (Bowling O L)   74 wkts @ 8.05
2 R. Whitehead (Great Horton)   71 wkts @ 8.05

Best Batting
Ben Wilson (Pudsey Britannia) v Undercliffe   151 not out

Best Bowling
L. Richmond (Pudsey St. Lawrence) v Low Moor   10 for 39

1921	P	W	D	L	Pts
Bingley	20	11	7	2	29
Keighley	20	10	8	2	28
Saltaire	20	9	9	2	27
Baildon Green	20	10	6	4	26
Great Horton	20	9	7	4	25
Bankfoot	20	7	8	5	22
Laisterdyke	20	6	10	4	22
Queensbury	20	7	8	5	22
Undercliffe	20	6	9	5	21
Bowling Old Lane	20	6	8	6	20
Eccleshill	20	5	10	5	20
Lidget Green	20	6	6	8	18
Windhill	20	6	6	8	18
Farsley	20	4	9	7	17
Low Moor	20	6	5	9	17
Pudsey Britannia	20	3	10	7	16
Pudsey St. Lawrence	20	4	8	8	16
East Bierley	20	4	7	9	15
Idle	20	2	11	7	15
Tong Park	20	0	6	14	6

Batting Averages
1 Arthur Hyde (Bingley)   52.07
2 George Beet (Baildon Green)   50.75
3 Richard Moulton (Baildon Green)   40.18

Bowling Averages
1 S.F. Barnes (Saltaire)   88 wkts @ 5.62
2 G.W. Brooke (Keighley)   85 wkts @ 8.49
3 E. Clark (Bankfoot)   50 wkts @ 8.92

Best Batting
Richard Moulton (Baildon Green) v Idle   135

Best Bowling
G.W. Brooke (Keighley)   9 for 4 v Tong Park

29

1922

	P	W	D	L	Pts
Saltaire	20	14	4	2	32
Keighley	20	11	7	2	29
Baildon Green	20	10	7	2	27
Bowling Old Lane	20	7	10	3	24
Bradford	20	8	8	4	24
Bankfoot	20	6	9	5	21
Bingley	20	6	9	5	21
Farsley	20	6	9	5	21
Idle	20	6	9	5	21
Undercliffe	20	4	12	4	20
East Bierley	20	6	8	6	20
Lidget Green	20	7	6	7	20
Great Horton	20	6	6	8	18
Laisterdyke	20	3	11	6	17
Pudsey St. Lawrence	20	4	7	9	15
Eccleshill	20	1	13	6	15
Low Moor	20	3	9	8	15
Pudsey Britannia	20	3	9	8	15
Queensbury	20	4	7	9	15
Windhill	20	2	6	12	10

Batting Averages
1 J.T. Bell (Undercliffe)   65.63
2 A. Turner (Farsley)   58.50
3 Festus Mawson (Idle)   45.55

Bowling Averages
1 S.F. Barnes (Saltaire)   122 wkts @ 4.10
    (League Record)
2 G.W. Brooke (Keighley)   75 wkts @ 7.62
3 A. Morris (Bradford)   79 wkts @ 8.53

Best Batting
Festus Mawson (Idle) v Pudsey Britannia   138 no

Best Bowling
S.F. Barnes (Saltaire)   9 for 19 v Laisterdyke
C.J. Elton (Windhill)   9 for 20 v Eccleshill

1924

	P	W	D	L	Pts
Bowling Old Lane	20	9	11	0	29
Bradford	20	6	13	1	25
Saltaire	20	5	15	0	25
Lidget Green	20	5	14	1	24
Windhill	20	6	12	2	24
Undercliffe	20	7	10	3	24
Keighley	20	6	11	3	23
Idle	20	5	12	3	22
Lightcliffe	20	6	10	4	22
Pudsey St Lawrence	20	4	14	2	22
Bankfoot	20	6	9	5	21
Great Horton	20	5	11	4	21
Farsley	20	5	10	5	20
Bingley	20	1	14	5	16
Laisterdyke	20	2	12	6	16
Baildon Green	20	3	9	8	15
Eccleshill	20	2	11	7	15
Low Moor	20	1	12	7	14
Queensbury	20	0	13	7	13
East Bierley	20	0	9	11	9

An amazing season, Pudsey St. Lawrence with only two defeats in twenty games were as low as 10th, while Bingley with only one win in twenty games had 6 teams beneath them.

Batting Averages
1 Charles Grimshaw (Bowling Old Lane)   47.80
2 Elijah Haigh (Queensbury)   44.83
3 J.R. Hardcastle (Bingley)   37.71

Bowling Averages
1 Charles Grimshaw (Bowling O L)   60 wkts @ 6.38
2 F. Pratt (Lightcliffe)   31 wkts @ 8.35
3 A. Judson (Keighley)   53 wkts @ 9.15

Best Batting
E.M. Smeeth (Bradford) v Bingley   160 not out

Best Bowling
C.H. Grimshaw (Bowling O L)   9 for 28 v Low Moor
R. Blackburn (Bankfoot)   9 for 30 v Great Horton

This was a double for C.H. Grimshaw

1923

	P	W	D	L	Pts
Bowling Old Lane	20	14	5	1	33
Bradford	20	9	8	3	26
Idle	20	9	8	3	26
Saltaire	20	8	10	2	26
Bingley	20	8	9	3	25
Farsley	20	10	4	6	24
Windhill	20	8	8	4	24
Keighley	20	7	9	4	23
Queensbury	20	7	9	4	23
Pudsey St. Lawrence	20	7	8	5	22
Laisterdyke	20	8	4	12	4	20
Great Horton	20	5	8	7	18
East Bierley	20	4	9	7	17
Lidget Green	20	5	4	11	14
Undercliffe	20	3	7	10	13
Baildon Green	20	3	7	10	13
Low Moor	20	1	9	10	11
Bankfoot	20	3	5	12	11
Eccleshill	20	2	6	12	10
Pudsey Britannia	20	2	6	12	10

Four groups of five clubs – each club must play every club in its own group plus two clubs from each of the other groups.

Batting Averages
1 E. Kearney (Bowling Old Lane)   43.90
2 H. Haigh (Keighley)   41.38
3 H. Turland (Windhill)   41.25
4 A. Turner (Farsley)   41.06

Bowling Averages
1 S.F. Barnes (Saltaire)   62 wkts @ 4.17
2 A. Morris (Bradford)   70 wkts @ 8.12
3 C.H. Grimshaw (Bowling O L)   82 wkts @ 8.15
4 W. Browne (Farsley)   70 wkts @ 8.61

1925

	P	W	D	L	Pts
Undercliffe	20	10	8	2	28
Bowling Old Lane	20	9	9	2	27
Bradford	20	7	9	4	23
Great Horton	20	6	11	3	23
Lightcliffe	20	5	13	2	23
Keighley	20	7	8	5	22
Lidget Green	20	5	12	3	22
Baildon Green	20	8	5	7	21
Bingley	20	5	11	4	21
Pudsey St. Lawrence	20	4	13	3	21
Brighouse	20	4	13	3	21
Windhill	20	4	13	3	21
Queensbury	20	4	12	4	20
Bankfoot	20	5	8	7	18
Farsley	20	5	8	7	18
Saltaire	20	5	8	7	18
Low Moor	20	4	8	8	16
Laisterdyke	20	3	8	9	14
Eccleshill	20	4	5	11	13
Idle	20	0	10	10	10

Batting Averages
1 A. Mitchell (Saltaire)   81.12
2 G.A. Lund (Brighouse)   56.11
3 H. Taylor (Bowling Old Lane)   49.90

Bowling Averages
1 A.W. Spring (Baildon Green)   67 wkts @ 9.50
2 E.C. Keighley (Lidget Green)   54 wkts @ 9.68
3 D.V. Norbury (Keighley)   64 wkts @ 9.87

Best Batting
H. Firth (Bingley) v Laisterdyke   142 not out
C. Harrison (Lidget Green) v Bradford   142 not out

Best Bowling
E. Petts (Great Horton)   10 for 59 v Farsley

30

1926

	P	W	D	L	Pts
Saltaire	20	10	8	2	28
Queensbury	20	11	6	3	28
Windhill	20	11	6	3	28
Undercliffe	20	9	9	2	27
Lidget Green	20	8	8	4	24
Bingley	20	7	9	4	23
Bowling Old Lane	20	8	6	6	22
Bradford	20	7	8	5	22
Farsley	20	7	7	6	21
Lightcliffe	20	7	7	6	21
Brighouse	20	5	10	5	20
Keighley	20	6	7	7	19
Idle	20	4	10	6	18
Bankfoot	20	6	5	9	17
Pudsey St. Lawrence	20	6	5	9	17
Low Moor	20	3	10	7	16
Laisterdyke	20	2	10	8	14
Eccleshill	20	3	7	10	13
Great Horton	20	1	10	9	12
Baildon Green	20	3	4	13	10

Saltaire won Championship after play offs.

Batting Averages
1 E. Whitaker (Idle) — 37.50
2 G.A. Lund (Brighouse) — 37.13
3 H. Petts (Bankfoot) — 35.58

Bowling Averages
1 A. Morris (Windhill) — 83 wkts @ 8.63
2 L. Powell (Pudsey St. Lawrence) — 52 wkts @ 9.07
3 W. Hirst (Lightcliffe) — 32 wkts @ 9.84

Best Batting
A.W. Spring (Saltaire) v Baildon Green — 143 not out

Best Bowling
H. Brown (Bankfoot) — 9 for 22 v Baildon Green

1928

	P	W	D	L	Pts
Bradford	20	9	10	1	28
Brighouse	20	11	6	3	28
Bingley	20	10	6	4	26
Bowling Old Lane	20	6	12	2	24
Saltaire	20	6	12	2	24
Keighley	20	7	8	5	22
Queensbury	20	6	10	4	22
Baildon Green	20	8	5	7	21
Idle	20	3	14	3	20
Windhill	20	5	9	6	19
East Bierley	20	5	9	6	19
Bankfoot	20	5	8	7	18
Farsley	20	5	8	7	18
Lidget Green	20	3	12	5	18
Low Moor	20	5	7	8	17
Lightcliffe	20	2	13	5	17
Undercliffe	20	5	7	8	17
Eccleshill	20	3	10	7	16
Pudsey St. Lawrence	20	3	8	9	14
Great Horton	20	3	6	11	12

* Bradford were Champions after a play off.

Batting Averages
1 H. Taylor (Lightcliffe) — 60.70
2 K.R. Davidson (Bingley) — 47.33
3 A. Lister (Eccleshill) — 43.92

Bowling Averages
1 S. Render (Brighouse) — 68 wkts @ 9.63
2 A. Schofield (Queensbury) — 65 wkts @ 10.89
3 C.H. Grimshaw (Bowling Old Lane) — 54 wkts @ 11.25

Best Batting
J.C. Lee (Saltaire) v Farsley — 124
J.M. Crossley (Bradford) v Eccleshill — 123

Best Bowling
J. Sunderland (Gt. Horton) — 8 for 12 v Low Moor

1927

	P	W	D	L	Pts
Bradford	20	10	9	1	29
Bowling Old Lane	20	10	6	4	26
Idle	20	9	8	3	26
Windhill	20	9	8	3	26
Saltaire	20	8	8	4	24
Keighley	20	8	6	6	22
Lidget Green	20	6	10	4	22
Lightcliffe	20	6	10	4	22
Queensbury	20	6	10	4	22
Undercliffe	20	8	5	7	21
Farsley	20	8	4	8	20
Bankfoot	20	6	7	7	19
Low Moor	20	7	5	8	19
Brighouse	20	5	7	8	17
Great Horton	20	6	5	9	17
Bingley	20	4	8	8	16
Baildon Green	20	3	8	9	14
Laisterdyke	20	6	2	12	14
Eccleshill	20	5	2	13	12
Pudsey St. Lawrence	20	3	6	11	12

Batting Averages
1 Wilf Barber (Brighouse) — 53.15
2 J. Hill (Low Moor) — 40.25
3 A. Widdop (Lidget Green) — 37.40

Bowling Averages
1 Charles Grimshaw (Bowling Old Lane) — 63 wkts @ 9.04
2 Norman Sugden (Eccleshill) — 46 wkts @ 10.17
3 Stanley Douglas (Bradford) — 50 wkts @ 10.28

Best Batting
Wilf Barber (Brighouse) v Bankfoot — 121 not out

Best Bowling
Sutcliffe Culpan (Great Horton) — 10 for 44 v Baildon Green

1929

	P	W	D	L	Pts
Bradford	20	15	4	1	34
Bowling Old Lane	20	12	5	3	29
Lightcliffe	20	11	7	2	29
Undercliffe	20	11	3	6	25
Windhill	20	9	6	5	24
Keighley	20	7	9	4	23
Saltaire	20	8	7	5	23
Idle	20	10	2	8	22
Lidget Green	20	7	7	6	21
Queensbury	20	8	5	7	21
Bingley	20	6	9	5	21
Brighouse	20	5	9	6	19
Farsley	20	9	1	10	19
Bankfoot	20	4	10	6	18
East Bierley	20	4	7	9	15
Baildon Green	20	6	2	12	14
Eccleshill	20	5	4	11	14
Low Moor	20	3	7	10	13
Great Horton	20	3	3	14	9
Pudsey St. Lawrence	20	2	3	15	7

Batting Averages
1 W.A. Hutton (Bradford) — 61.27
2 J.C. Lee (Saltaire) — 51.46
3 T.W. Patefield (Lightcliffe) — 50.86

Bowling Averages
1 S. Render (Idle) — 93 wkts @ 10.34
2 P. Sharples (Queensbury) — 71 wkts @ 10.74
3 C.H. Grimshaw (Bowling Old Lane) — 63 wkts @ 11.34

Best Batting
T.W. Patefield (Lightcliffe) v Eccleshill — 118
H. Smith (East Bierley) v Bankfoot — 117 not out

Best Bowling
S. Douglas (Bradford) — 8 for 18 v Eccleshill
F.W. Luckhurst (Bradford) — 8 for 28 v Low Moor
S. Render (Idle) — 8 for 30 v Undercliffe
S. Render (Idle) — 8 for 31 v Baildon Green

31

1930

	P	W	D	L	Pts
Brighouse	20	10	8	2	28
East Bierley	20	10	7	3	27
Bowling Old Lane	20	10	7	3	27
Lidget Green	20	10	6	4	26
Undercliffe	20	9	7	4	25
Bradford	20	9	7	4	25
Keighley	20	8	8	4	24
Queensbury	20	7	8	5	22
Windhill	20	6	10	4	22
Lightcliffe	20	5	10	5	20
Bankfoot	20	6	7	7	19
Farsley	20	7	5	8	19
Baildon Green	20	7	4	9	18
Saltaire	20	5	8	7	18
Pudsey St. Lawrence	20	5	6	9	16
Eccleshill	20	3	10	7	16
Bingley	20	4	5	11	13
Idle	20	3	7	10	13
Bradford A	20	1	9	10	11
Great Horton	20	2	7	11	11

Batting Averages
1 J. Hill (Brighouse) 52.28
2 H. Taylor (Lightcliffe) 49.00
3 J.C. Lee (Saltaire) 44.30
4 R.D. Somers (Lightcliffe) 43.50

Bowling Averages
1 A.L. Claughton (Undercliffe) 78 wkts @ 8.80
2 J. Ludlam (Queensbury) 66 wkts @ 11.30
3 G.F. Terry (Baildon Green) 31 wkts @ 11.30
4 P. Coates (Bankfoot) 57 wkts @ 12.28

Best Batting
C.H. Grimshaw (Bowling Old Lane) v East Bierley 127 no
R.D. Somers (Lightcliffe) v Keighley 124 no
A. Hartley (Lightcliffe) v Farsley 119 no

Best Bowling
P. Coates (Bankfoot) 9 for 37 v Great Horton
J.W. Lamb (Keighley) 8 for 27 v Queensbury
A.L. Claughton (Undercliffe) 8 for 32 v Great Horton and 8 for 33 in the return

1932

	P	W	D	L	Pts
Brighouse	20	15	2	3	32
Windhill	20	13	4	3	30
Undercliffe	20	10	7	3	27
Bradford	20	10	4	6	24
Bowling Old Lane	20	7	7	6	21
Farsley	20	6	9	5	21
Keighley	20	7	6	7	20
Pudsey St. Lawrence	20	8	4	8	20
Baildon Green	20	5	9	6	19
East Bierley	20	5	9	6	19
Lightcliffe	20	6	7	7	19
Queensbury	20	6	7	7	19
Idle	20	4	10	6	18
Eccleshill	20	7	4	9	18
Great Horton	20	4	9	7	17
Lidget Green	20	4	8	8	16
Spen Victoria	20	5	6	9	16
Bingley	20	4	7	9	15
Saltaire	20	5	5	10	15
Bankfoot	20	4	6	10	14

Batting Averages
1 J. Hill (Brighouse) (18 inns, 9 no) 99.11
2 G. Senior (Baildon) 52.75
3 T. Patefield (Lightcliffe) 40.33

Bowling Averages
1 H.V. Douglas (Bowling Old Lane) 35 wkts @ 9.84
2 N. Jackson (Pudsey St. Lawrence) 43 wkts @ 10.55
3 F. Berry (Windhill) 37 wkts @ 10.86

Best Batting
J.M. Crossley (Brighouse) v Lidget Green 167 no

Best Bowling
C.H. Grimshaw (Bowling Old Lane) 9 for 25 v Bradford

1931

	P	W	D	L	Pts
Brighouse	20	11	7	2	29
Spen Victoria	20	9	8	3	26
Bankfoot	20	9	7	4	25
Bradford	20	9	7	4	25
Keighley	20	9	7	4	25
Lidget Green	20	6	11	3	23
Bowling Old Lane	20	7	7	6	21
East Bierley	20	7	7	6	21
Lightcliffe	20	7	6	7	20
Eccleshill	20	7	6	7	20
Undercliffe	20	7	6	7	20
Saltaire	20	6	7	7	19
Idle	20	4	9	7	17
Windhill	20	4	9	7	17
Bingley	20	3	10	7	16
Great Horton	20	3	9	8	15
Queensbury	20	3	9	8	15
Farsley	20	4	6	10	14
Pudsey St Lawrence	20	2	7	11	11

Batting Averages
1 A.C. Rhodes (Spen Victoria) 46.88
2 J. Hill (Brighouse) 43.07
3 R. Whatmough (Idle) 36.92

Bowling Averages
1 S. Brown (Keighley) 41 wkts @ 9.53
2 B. Hargreaves (East Bierley) 44 wkts @ 10.20
3 F.W. Luckhurst (Bradford) 62 wkts @ 10.45

Best Batting
J. Drake (Windhill) v Lidget Green 138 no
J. Drake (Windhill) v Queensbury 134

Best Bowling
N. Sugden (Eccleshill) 8 for 20 v Pudsey St. Lawrence
P. Sharp (Saltaire) 8 for 25 v East Bierley

In 1931 only 4 centuries were scored in first team league games. Drake (Windhill) scored two, Williams (East Bierley) and Butterfield (Keighley) the others.

1933

	P	W	D	L	Pts
Bradford	20	10	9	1	29
Spen Victoria	20	10	9	1	29
Brighouse	20	7	11	2	25
Idle	20	5	15	0	25
Saltaire	20	8	8	4	24
Bowling Old Lane	20	6	12	2	24
Queensbury	20	7	8	5	22
Great Horton	20	5	11	4	21
Windhill	20	5	11	4	21
Keighley*	20	7	8	5	20
Pudsey St Lawrence +	20	5	11	4	19
Lightcliffe	20	3	13	4	19
East Bierley	20	3	12	5	18
Lidget Green	20	2	13	5	17
Undercliffe	20	3	10	7	16
Farsley	20	2	10	8	14
Eccleshill	20	1	11	8	13
Bankfoot	20	2	9	9	13
Baildon Green	20	1	9	10	11
Bingley	20	1	9	10	11

*Keighley 2 pts deducted, + Pudsey 1 pt deducted

Bradford were 1933 Champions after a play-off with Spen Victoria, winning by 16 runs.

Batting Averages
1 E. Oldroyd (Pudsey St. Lawrence) 86.16
2 W. Halstead (Spen Victoria) 66.66
3 M.T. Wade (Brighouse) 51.00

Bowling Averages
1 T.A. Jacques (Saltaire) 63 wkts @ 10.90
2 C. Harrison (Spen Victoria) 40 wkts @ 11.90
3 W. Hirst (Brighouse) 57 wkts @ 12.24

Best Batting
W. Sutcliffe (Farsley) v Saltaire 148

Best Bowling
T.A. Jacques (Saltaire) 10 for 25 v Bankfoot (all bowled)

1934

	P	W	D	L	Pts
Bradford	20	14	2	4	30
Bingley	20	13	3	4	29
Keighley	20	11	6	3	28
Lightcliffe	20	12	3	5	27
Undercliffe	20	11	4	5	26
Idle	20	11	3	6	25
Bowling Old Lane	20	10	3	7	23
Farsley	20	9	5	6	23
Windhill	20	10	2	8	22
Spen Victoria	20	6	8	6	20
Brighouse	20	7	5	8	19
Queensbury	20	8	3	9	19
Great Horton	20	6	5	9	17
Pudsey St. Lawrence	20	6	5	9	17
Bankfoot	20	5	4	11	14
East Bierley	20	3	8	9	14
Saltaire	20	6	2	12	14
Baildon Green	20	3	6	11	12
Eccleshill	20	4	3	13	11
Lidget Green	20	3	2	15	8

Batting Averages
1 W.A. Shackleton (Bowling Old Lane)   51.09
2 J. Swift (Idle)   50.93
3 A. Davison (Idle)   50.58

Bowling Averages
1 N. Sugden (Idle)   43 wkts @ 9.88
2 H. Wilkinson (Bingley)   50 wkts @ 10.10
3 S.F. Barnes (Keighley) (Aged 61)   76 wkts @ 10.32

Best Batting
J. Swift (Idle) v Great Horton   154 not out

Best Bowling
G.H. Crimshaw (Bowling Old Lane)   9 for 37 v Baildon
D. Waterhouse (Pudsey St. Lawrence)   9 for 56 v Idle
E.L. Cooper (Windhill)   9 for 60 v Pudsey St. Lawrence
S.F. Barnes (Keighley)   8 for 9 v Bradford

1936 (Points increased to 3 for a win)

	P	W	D	L	Pts
Bradford	20	13	5	2	44
Lightcliffe	20	13	4	3	43
Windhill	20	13	4	3	43
Brighouse	20	9	9	2	36
East Bierley	20	9	5	6	32
Great Horton	20	8	7	5	31
Keighley	20	9	4	7	31
Queensbury	20	9	4	7	31
Lidget Green	20	8	5	7	29
Bingley	20	8	3	9	27
Undercliffe	20	7	6	7	27
Idle	20	7	4	9	25
Spen Victoria	20	6	7	7	25
Farsley	20	6	6	8	24
Saltaire	20	5	6	9	21
Bowling Old Lane	20	5	5	10	20
Eccleshill	20	4	8	8	20
Baildon Green	20	4	6	10	18
Bankfoot	20	3	4	13	13
Pudsey St. Lawrence	20	2	2	16	8

Batting Averages
1 H. Taylor (Lightcliffe)   49.76
2 J. Swift (Windhill)   46.11
3 W. Horner (Queensbury)   44.84

Bowling Averages
1 H. Jefferson (Keighley)   58 wkts @ 6.77
2 J.S. Douglas (Bradford)   55 wkts @ 10.14
3 H. Blowes (Bingley)   40 wkts @ 10.42

Best Batting
W. Sutcliffe (Farsley) v Windhill   158
G. Senior (Baildon Green) v Great Horton   142

Best Bowling
J.W. Lamb (Eccleshill)   9 for 14 v Farsley
T. Tetley (Great Horton)   9 for 72 v Bowling Old Lane
L. Powell (Queensbury)   8 for 29 v Pudsey St. Lawrence
E. Pawson (Bowling Old Lane)   8 for 32 v East Bierley
T.A. Jacques (Undercliffe)   8 for 43 v Baildon Green
E. St. Hill (East Bierley)   8 for 50 v Pudsey St. Lawrence

1935

	P	W	D	L	Pts
Undercliffe	20	12	6	2	30
Brighouse	20	7	11	2	25
East Bierley	20	9	6	5	24
Keighley	20	9	6	5	24
Lightcliffe	20	8	8	4	24
Saltaire	20	7	9	4	23
Bankfoot	20	7	8	5	22
Bowling Old Lane	20	8	6	6	22
Idle	20	7	8	5	22
Lidget Green	20	5	10	5	20
Windhill	20	7	6	7	20
Spen Victoria	20	5	9	6	19
Baildon Green	20	4	10	6	18
Bingley	20	6	6	8	18
Bradford	20	5	7	8	17
Eccleshill	20	4	8	8	16
Queensbury	20	5	6	9	16
Farsley	20	4	7	9	15
Great Horton	20	3	7	10	13
Pudsey St. Lawrence	20	3	6	11	12

Batting Averages
1 H. Hutchinson (Brighouse)   53.60
2 H. Taylor (Lightcliffe)   51.66
3 J.C. Lee (Saltaire)   43.11

Bowling Averages
1 T.A. Jacques (Undercliffe)   93 wkts @ 8.24
2 C.H. Hall (Brighouse)   48 wkts @ 10.64
3 W.P. Fryer (Bingley)   35 wkts @ 11.82

Best Batting
M.T. Wade (Bingley) v Baildon Green   136

Best Bowling
T.A. Jacques (Undercliffe)   9 for 25 v Bradford
G. Mellor (Spen Victoria)   9 for 40 v Farsley
T.A. Jacques (Undercliffe)   8 for 14 v Keighley
T.A. Jacques (Undercliffe)   8 for 25 v Bankfoot

1937

Division A

	P	W	D	L	Pts
Windhill	18	12	4	2	40
Brighouse	18	9	7	2	34
Spen Victoria	18	7	8	5	29
Lightcliffe	18	7	6	5	27
Farsley	18	8	2	8	26
Bradford	18	7	4	7	25
East Bierley	18	6	5	7	23
Lidget Green	18	6	2	10	20
Saltaire	18	2	6	10	12
Queensbury	18	2	4	12	10

Division B

	P	W	D	L	Pts
Idle	18	11	6	1	39
Bingley	18	9	7	2	34
Bowling Old Lane	18	8	5	5	30*
Great Horton	18	7	8	3	29
Undercliffe	18	8	4	6	28
Eccleshill	18	5	5	8	22*
Keighley	18	4	8	6	20
Baildon Green	18	3	6	9	15
Pudsey St. Lawrence	18	3	5	10	14
Bankfoot	18	3	4	11	14*

* 3 clubs awarded extra points for tied matches

Batting Averages
1 M.T. Wade (Brighouse)   46.40
2 H. Mortimer (Spen Victoria)   45.44
3 J.A. Swift (Windhill)   39.35

Bowling Averages
L. Powell (Bowling Old Lane)   67 wkts @ 8.65
L. Bullock (Bingley)   60 wkts @ 8.71
H. Jefferson (Keighley)   31 wkts @ 8.83

33

1938

Division A	P	W	D	L	Pts
Windhill	18	9	8	1	35
East Bierley	18	8	4	6	28
Brighouse	18	6	9	3	27
Bowling Old Lane	18	7	5	6	26
Bingley	18	5	10	3	25
Spen Victoria	18	5	9	4	24
Bradford	18	6	5	7	23
Idle	18	5	4	9	19
Lightcliffe	18	3	9	6	18
Farsley	18	2	5	11	11

Division B	P	W	D	L	Pts
Pudsey St. Lawrence	18	10	5	3	35
Keighley	18	8	6	4	30
Undercliffe	18	8	6	4	30
Eccleshill	18	6	7	5	25
Baildon Green	18	6	6	6	24
Queensbury	18	6	5	7	23
Great Horton	18	5	6	7	21
Bankfoot	18	5	5	8	20
Lidget Green	18	4	7	7	19
Saltaire	18	2	7	9	13

Batting Averages
1 W. Horner (Queensbury)   49.65
2 C.S. Hainsworth (Pudsey St. Lawrence)   47.92
3 R.E. Ednie (Baildon Green)   47.10

Bowling Averages
T.A. Jacques (Undercliffe)   77 wkts @ 8.19
H. Jefferson (Keighley)   43 wkts @ 8.51
P. Coates (Bankfoot)   50 wkts @ 10.50

1939

Division A	P	W	D	L	Pts
Windhill	18	11	4	3	37
Bingley	18	8	7	3	31
Spen Victoria	18	8	5	3	29
Brighouse	18	6	8	4	26
Bradford	18	5	9	4	24
Keighley	18	5	9	4	24
Bowling Old Lane	18	5	7	6	22
Undercliffe	18	3	6	9	15
Pudsey St. Lawrence	18	2	8	8	14
East Bierley	18	2	7	9	13

Division B	P	W	D	L	Pts
Lightcliffe	18	11	7	0	40
Baildon Green	18	8	8	2	32
Great Horton	18	8	7	3	31
Bankfoot	18	6	6	6	24
Queensbury	18	6	6	6	24
Idle	18	7	3	8	24
Eccleshill	18	4	7	7	19
Farsley	18	4	6	8	18
Saltaire	18	3	7	8	16
Lidget Green	18	1	7	10	10

Batting Averages
1 A. Hartley (Lightcliffe)   54.60
2 F. Woodhouse (Brighouse)   54.20
3 H. Taylor (Lightcliffe)   53.50

Bowling Averages
1 W. Johnson (Great Horton)   53 wkts @ 7.86
2 O. Glover (Queensbury)   34 wkts @ 8.29
3 A. Mason (Keighley)   31 wkts @ 9.35
4 J. Lawrence (Windhill)   63 wkts @ 9.87

Chapter Five
Big Guns of World War Two (1940 – 1945)

Learie Constantine was born in Trinidad in 1902. His father played for the local Victoria XI and was the first mentor young Constantine had.

By the time he joined Windhill for the 1940 season Learie had become a caring young man, a fine upstanding human being, a man of fun about whom there was nothing dull and above all a gentleman.

It has always been difficult to find accurate ways of rewarding fielding, yet from all quarters I understand Learie Constantine was undoubtedly the best of all. He himself said that the fielding in the Bradford League during his time in the League was, and I quote, 'very poor'. I can understand that remark for anything judged by his standards, would be of a lower class. One must also remember that the League in the 1940's contained quite a number of players who were past the height of their physical powers—many had seen better days.

When Windhill won the 1940 Championship for the 4th consecutive season, Constantine took 70 league wickets at 11.80 runs each and averaged 30.50 with the bat, which included 105 not out against Brighouse. There was a hat-trick for him too in 1940, Spen Victoria being on the receiving end. His 8 for 39 against them in the League and 6 for 34 in the Cup must have made them utterly relieved that they did not face him every week. Lightcliffe would however be even more pleased to see the back of him. Two league games against them gave Learie figures of 6 for 54 and 5 for 40, they, like Spen met him also in the Priestley Cup and lost six of their batsmen to him for only 35 runs. Yet I have it on the best authority that it was not in figures that Learie Constantine could be measured but in attitude, fitness and enthusiasm. Yes, he bowled 'Bodyline' too, at England on the West Indies Tour here in 1939, but in his words, 'that sort of attack can be meat and drink to a right thinking batsman who should take many legside boundaries'.

I had the pleasure of meeting the then Sir Learie Constantine at Park Avenue while he was on one of his last journalistic assignments, a year or two before his death. It was a short chat but a pleasant one and I shall always remember his obvious love for all things. Whatever he spoke about he did so with relish. Sir Learie, a barrister, then went on to join the Diplomatic Service. An excellent 'after dinner' speaker, he displayed his talents in this direction at an official Bradford League Dinner in the late sixties.

Bradford League followers had much to enjoy at their grounds, during their wartime viewing but I seriously doubt if any other human being had the same ability and willingness, almost an obsession to please. In 1939 Arthur Wood was dismissed in three consecutive Test innings by Constantine, once caught and bowled, twice bowled, which seemed to add extra rivalry later to their Bradford League days.

The wide margin of ten points shows that the 1940 championship was virtually a one horse race. Despite 89 wickets from Arthur Booth, Bowling Old Lane could get no nearer. Keighley in 3rd position were a further five points away, but certainly pulled in the crowds. Not too surprisingly with Eddie Paynter and Winston Place delighting the Lawkholme Lane faithful with their stroke play.

Winston Place may have been small in stature but he had a big heart and was a very courageous player. He played First Class cricket from 1937 to 1955 and his three Test Matches came after many fine Bradford League performances. His average of 57.30 in 1940 earned third spot in the League averages, while his 172 not out for Keighley against Brighouse would have been good enough most seasons as top Individual score but Edgar Robinson of Great Horton stole that honour scoring just one run more against Lightcliffe.

Eddie Paynter was born on Guy Fawkes day in 1901 so it was not too surprising that his left handed batting should contain an explosive quality. He first played for Keighley in 1940 and topped the League averages in each of his first three seasons. Scores of 150 not out v Lightcliffe, 114 v Baildon Green, 101 v Windhill and 100 not out v Spen Victoria equalled the highest number of centuries in a season and came within just a 'six hit' of the record with 94 in the first meeting with Windhill.

His consistency was second to none. Commencing on 4th May 1940, when he made 60 on his debut at Spen Victoria followed by 56 against Bingley, the Bradford League had found another player to bring money through the turnstiles. Although the four centuries did not break the League record he did smash one other. Previously only Edgar Oldroyd (1934) had topped 1,000 league runs in a season. At Windhill the home side batted first making a total of 161 and when Paynter and Place went out to open in reply, Paynter was on 939 runs. He needed 61 for the thousand and 96 for a new record aggregate. It was the last day of the season too and only 162 runs were required to win. Constantine soon dismissed Place but Paynter stood firm, gradually he passed the first target of 61 runs and although losing two more partners, Keighley won by seven wickets and Eddie Paynter carried his bat for 101—a new record by just six runs.

Two centuries and seven half centuries came in 1941 but 1942 saw him break another League record. Commencing 27th June his next seven innings were, 60 not out v Farsley, 121 v Baildon Green, 94 not out v Pudsey St Lawrence, 65 v Queensbury, 51 not out v Bankfoot, 57 not out v East Bierley and 52 v Eccleshill. Seven consecutive half centuries. A total of fifteen league innings brought three centuries and nine half centuries, thus in only three innings did he fail to reach fifty. In addition he had 51 and 84 in the Priestley Cup-ties and his seasons average of 138.55 was the sort one only reads about in fiction, normally that is, but was Eddie Paynter normal?

Explosive batting was also seen that year in the East Bierley v Queensbury fixture. When Queensbury scored 130 for 1, it took only 47 minutes. George Senior, opening, scored 110. Senior had recorded the League's fastest century (45 mins) which was equalled in 1945 by Les Ames for Windhill against Spen Victoria. In 1951, Norman Kitson made 100 not out for Idle against Yeadon, also in under 50 minutes but in the Cup. Now Norman (if he'll forgive me for saying so) was a bowler. His Bradford League career ran from 1944 to 1965 and although he did have another century and six half-centuries, he will be remembered most for his accurate bowling. Kitson's finest season was in 1957 with 81 league wickets at 11.02 runs each, yet it is that 100 in 48 minutes which keeps him in the Priestley Cup record books. Idle, Bingley, East Bierley, Keighley and Baildon have all been the better for signing him.

If Paynter's seven consecutive fifties in 1942 took most of the 'Headlines', there was one record created in the bowling department which can never be beaten. No one took a league wicket for Lidget Green during the whole season but the opening bowlers, Tommy Mitchell and Arthur Bastow. As far back as 1925 Bastow had entered the League by way of Undercliffe. His first season had brought 60 wickets at 10.23 each but in 1926 he fell away somewhat, his 6 for 24 v Keighley was the only 5 wicket return. His 1942 returns took him to the top of the League averages with 63 wickets at 6.96, and when you consider he had the likes of Horace Fisher, Bill Copson, George Pope, Alf Pope, Manny Martindale, Jim Smith, Ellis Robinson, Alex Coxon, Sandy Jacques and 'Enoch' St. Hill beneath him, it illustrates what a stupendous feat it was.

Tommy Mitchell took more wickets (78) but at a higher cost (8.94). All 141 wickets Lidget captured that season went to Bastow and Mitchell. No one else got a look in. Mitchell was of course very experienced. Born 1902, a leg break and googly bowler who was on the 'Bodyline' tour of Australia in 1932/33. Known as the 'Merry Hearted Cricketer' he had taken 'all ten' in a county match. It was 10 for 64 for Derbyshire (with whom he had over 300 games) against Leicestershire, at Leicester in 1935. 1942 was Mitchell's first Bradford League season and although 9 for 43, against Great Horton was his best performance, perhaps it was the Brighouse batsmen who had most trouble with his leg breaks. In two league and one cup game against them, Mitchell took 7 for 40, 5 for 55 and 8 for 37.

R.E.S. Wyatt, when England skipper, once prolonged a selection meeting by seven hours until the selectors agreed to include Tommy Mitchell in a particular Test. Three seasons with Lidget Green brought him 204 league wickets at 11.40.

If Mitchell had the measure of Brighouse it was Keighley whom Bastow favoured. In 1943 he had just one five wicket plus feat (7 for 39 v Keighley). In 1944 only twice did he take 5 wickets in an innings, home and away to Keighley, and in 1945 his best performance was 5 for 21 also against Keighley. How Keighley must have dreaded their fixture with Lidget Green.

The year 1942 was not all success, for Bankfoot went through the season without a win, but at Queensbury they could not have been closer to a success. Bankfoot made only 85 and after Butler struck two early blows, Dobson and Bartle took the score past 60 without further loss. In obvious desperation Bankfoot put Arthur Longthorne on to bowl with just 24 runs needed to win and 8 wickets still to fall. Longthorne immediately dismissed Dobson for thirty and Bartle for twenty seven. Aided by two wickets from Smith, Longthorne then took three more to reach 5 for 12. At 81 for 9 Queensbury had lost 7 wickets for 19 runs when Smith bowling to Oliver Glover committed the cardinal sin. He bowled a no-ball and very gratefully Glover lashed out and sent the ball screeching to the boundary. Perhaps it travelled, in the words of John Arlott, the greatest of all cricket writers and BBC commentators, 'like a marble across a skating rink'. The scores were now level. Up came Smith to atone for his error magnificently by spreadeagling Glover's wicket and ending the game in a tie. Needing 24 with 8 wickets left Queensbury had failed, but so had Bankfoot who never got so near victory again that year.

This unwanted record by Bankfoot was in marked contrast to Saltaire, who in 1941 while in Division B went through the season unbeaten in both League and Cup. When Bankfoot and Saltaire had met in 1940 a certain young man, J.C. Laker, scored 101 not out in Saltaire's total of 254 for 5 wickets. Jim Laker topped the Saltaire batting averages in 1940 his thirteen innings bringing an average of 30.81 each. When the 1941 season came Pope took 69 wickets at 6.49 and

---

Bradford Cricket League
Priestley Cup Competition
Season 1941

Presented to _Herbert Pedley_

As a memento of the

Saltaire Cricket Club

Winning Both the Championship of
DIVISION "B" & The PRIESTLEY COMPETITION

The SALTAIRE Club did not lose a match during the whole of the Season, and secured the highest number of points ever achieved by one Club in any Season

RECORD

LEAGUE	CUP FINAL
Won 17	Saltaire 102 runs
Lost 0	Undercliffe 44 runs
Drawn 1	
Points 52	

President _W. N. Foster_

Hon. Treasurer _Hugh B. Robson_

Hon. Secretary _F. M. Watmough_

Copson 59 wickets at 6.59 each, while poor Laker, who would make a name for himself worldwide as one of the finest off-spinners, could get little bowling. He did however get a lengthy spell against Great Horton but cut it short himself by taking 5 for 37. Saltaire's League and Cup double came without a century maker, Crossley with 94 v Bradford and Spencer 99 v East Bierley almost getting there. There was however nothing wrong with their batting talents and when 273 for 6 was scored against East Bierley, Crossley, Spencer and Copson (67) all topped fifty. Then in a 212 all out score againsg Lightcliffe, Spencer, Wilson and Townsend all earned a collection and made 170 runs of that total between the three of them. Six times in the League and once in the Cup a side was dismissed for under 50 runs by Saltaire and with 17 victories and one draw in 18 League games a new record points total was also reached.

The Townsend mentioned earlier was in fact Leslie Fletcher Townsend, a man who had played 4 Test Matches, 446 First Class matches and had scored 233 runs in a County Match innings. Les, born in 1903, had one or two odd facts in his early days with Saltaire. In 1941 his only two fifties were both against Lightcliffe, both undefeated. The following year he only topped fifty twice again and neither was in league games. He had 82 not out in round one of the cup v Farsley and then 60 in the semi-final against Lidget Green. His best bowling was also reserved for the Cup when he had 5 for 22 in the Final, enabling Saltaire to retain the trophy.

Fletcher did perform well in league games in 1943 when Saltaire were top once more. Here was batting to rely on and although Pope and Copson had left the Club, Tom Goddard and Bill Voce had arrived to help him. Goddard was not available regularly. Eccleshill, against whom he had a hat-trick in his 4 for 4 and Brighouse against whom he took 9 for 19, no doubt wished he had not been available at all. Incidentally while Goddard was doing the hat-trick for the Saltaire 1st XI v Eccleshill, Alf Burgoyne was also taking one for the Saltaire 2nd XI v Eccleshill in the reverse fixture. His was a hat-trick in a 5 for 7 return. Idle hit 93 runs off Bill Voce at Saltaire and 48 in the return at Idle but Bill did have 8 wickets and 4 wickets respectively to compensate.

While all these 'stars' were bringing in the crowds, taking all the headlines and indeed winning most trophies, Saltaire had, in 1943, a batsman who averaged 27.38 from 15 innings and who became one of the best of all Bradford League openers, though never to reach County status, Leonard Ratcliffe. In 1940 Len scored 135 not out for Queensbury against East Bierley and ended the season with over 600 runs at 43.00. After one more year at Queensbury when his fortunes declined, he signed for Saltaire, stayed seven seasons and then completed his Bradford League days with eight years at Bankfoot. Radcliffe was steady, difficult to remove and not often dismissed in the fifties. Once he got there he really set his stall out for the second fifty. It is said that the finest innings Leonard Radcliffe played was in 1953, in a Priestley Cup game at Salts. His 112 not out was the highest Cup score of that season and I have it on very good authority that he came off soaked to the skin with perspiration looking all the while as if he'd been for a dip in the River Aire which flows at one side of the Salt's ground.

Spen Victoria won the Division B title in 1943 and it really surprised no one. Following relegation in 1942 the club had signed Arnold Hamer, George Pope and Arthur Booth whilst retaining Clifford Sykes, who despite 'the drop' had made five scores between 58 and 62. During the championship campaign of 1943, Hamer exceeded fifty only once, though he went well over the top with 106 not out when playing Lightcliffe. Sykes once and Pope once were the only other half century makers which was not too surprising when you realise Farsley (24), Lightcliffe (28), East Bierley (40), Farsley (44, Priestley Cup) and Bankfoot (45, also in the cup) failed to total fifty. There was a hat-trick for Booth v Pudsey St. Lawrence and at the seasons end Pope and Booth shared 147 wickets.

The surprise came when not only were they able to march into Division A and go to the 'top', they completed the double with four large cup wins. Arnold Hamer scored over 600 League runs to average 40.33. Pope with 67 wickets at 11.22 and Booth with 61 wickets at 12.95 dispelled all doubts by those who claimed that Division A would find them out. After all why should it have done so? George Pope had first played County Cricket in 1933 when he was 22 years old. His Bradford League performances were instrumental in keeping him in County Cricket for a further three years after the War and in 1947 George made his Test Debut for England at Lords against South Africa. His most satisfying of all round performances in the Bradford League was probably his 76 runs and 6 for 36 which won the 1944 Priestley Cup Final. Arnold Hamer became only the third player to score 1,000 runs in a season and created a new league record with 1106 runs. This was in 1949 whilst with Pudsey St. Lawrence. He then went on to an eleven year career with Derbyshire which commenced in 1950. While Hamer was not exactly noted for quick scoring, at Yeadon in 1945 he was dismissed with the score on 120, having made 110 of them. He returned to play in the League during the sixties, with his original club, Spen Victoria, and won the League batting averages in 1963 with an excellent 73.73 average.

Prior to the 2nd World War only Barnes and Grimcliffe had taken as many as 4 wickets with successive balls but in 1941 Constantine, 1943 Ellis Robinson and 1945 Tom Goddard were able to perform this same feat. Whilst on the subject of bowling, in 1944 David Taylor became only the second person to take 'all ten' in 2nd XI cricket. Taylor took 10 for 12 which still remains the best 2nd XI bowling feat. Bankfoot were the luckless victims and when George Roberts, on April 30th 1949, became the third player to take 'all ten' his 10 for 61 also came for Bowling Old Lane and once again against Bankfoot. After Taylor and Roberts, another Bowling Old Lane 2nd XI player should be mentioned. Playing against Lightcliffe in July 1944, opening batsman Creasey was brought on to bowl with Lightcliffe 88 for 7 chasing Old Lane's 129. His first ball took a wicket, as did his second and also his third. Three balls only and a wicket with each one—a rather special hat-trick.

Wicketkeeping must have been of a very high standard during the War years. A look at the laurels for 1944 shows Freddie Beaumont of Spen Victoria, top of the tree but just take a look at those who followed, George Dawkes, Ken Fiddling, Arthur Wood, Denis Smith, George Duckworth, Don Brennan and Arthur Fagg to name but a few. Idle were lucky to have Ken James, the New Zealand Test keeper for one match when usual keeper Rishman was not available. James took one catch and was no doubt brought to Idle for the game by 'Stewie' Dempster.

There have not been too many New Zealanders in the Bradford League but during the Second World War, Leslie Bulcock and C.S. Dempster were two who played with distinction. Bulcock was an all rounder playing first at Bingley in 1936/37/38. The all rounder tag was ably illustrated by his 1938 averages. Fifth in the batting with an average of 41.35 from 579 runs and also fifth in the bowling with 45 league wickets at 11.57. After missing 1939 he played for Windhill in 1940 taking 47 wickets and scoring 378 runs. Bulcock joined Baildon Green in 1942, a season in which he took 8 for 20 v Eccleshill. One year later there was a slight improvement on this with 8 for 19 at Queensbury. Having performed a hat-trick for Bingley v Bowling Old Lane in 1937, made 107 and 82 in two games v Idle in 1938 and finished second in the League averages in his first season he certainly made his mark. Stewie Dempster left his, all over the world. He was not of great stature, rather a stocky chap who in play rarely lifted the ball. He played ten Test Matches, a hard hitter with no respect for reputations. It was he who once hit five fours off Billy Quaife in an over at Quaife's beloved home ground of Edgbaston. Dempster joined Idle for 1945 and soon realised the size of his task. At East Bierley, Idle were faced with a total of 176 and they only obtained a draw at 138 for 8, due mainly to a fine knock of 90 from Dempster. In his next innings at home to Great Horton he again made 90 but after Idle declared at 197 for 5, Horton romped home by seven wickets. He followed these two scores with a 73 at Bingley, yet this third consecutive fifty still brought no joy as Idle facing 227 for 4 dec managed only 161. Dempster could have been rather relieved he had to leave Idle before the season's end, his twelve innings having provided an average above thirty.

When Dempster made his 73 at Bingley the home team's top scorer was Miles Coope who made 119 towards the Bingley total. Playing in 1945 Coope hit a sensational fifty against East Bierley. Now Bierley were not just to suffer at the hands of Coope that year for in game eleven they were at Home to Bankfoot. With one draw and nine defeats in ten previous games Bankfoot staggered to 65 for 8 when their no. 10 batsman Lawrie Dobbie went to the wicket. Fifteen minutes later Bankfoot had added a further 57 runs with Dobbie reaching his fifty in a whirlwind 14 minutes. This was a league record at the time. When he was finally out he had scored 55 in a stand of 57, exactly fifty of those runs coming in boundaries (five sixes and five fours). Bierley won by six wickets and the Bankfoot innings of 128 was the third match in a row that wicketkeeper Crick had not conceded a bye. Dobbie's fifty in fourteen minutes was beaten in 1949 when Geoff Hitchenor reduced the time to 13 minutes, for Baildon v Lidget Green, then in 1950 Miles Coope, for Salts against Eccleshill also had a fifty in 13 minutes. The innings to end them all came in 1945 by Miles Coope for Bingley against Bierley. In this instance one must remember that overs in those days were 'eight ball' overs. It seems the time spent finding the ball may have stopped it being the fastest ever fifty, but Coope reached this figure in two consecutive overs. Here's how . . .

    Off Barlow . . . 0 0 6 6 4 4 4 1 = 25
    Off Govier . . . 6 0 0 6 6 0 6 1 = 25

As can be clearly seen, he did not score from five deliveries out of the sixteen received. Note also he not only 'pinched' the strike at the end of the first over but at the end of the second also, on reaching fifty. Coope went on to total 102 runs.

Born in Gildersome Coope qualified for Yorkshire but just maybe he played across the line too often and his county career was to be with the more cavalier county of Somerset. He played for Spen Victoria from 1940, joined Bingley for 1943 and then moved to newcomers Salts for their first season in 1946. It was 1954 when he rejoined his first club Spen Victoria and having made a 'ton' for them in each of his first two seasons (40/41), made a century for them in each of his last two seasons, 103 v Lightcliffe in 1954 and 120 not out v Windhill in 1955. Alas Miles Coope died in 1974 aged only 56.

Another hard hitting batsman, who could bowl a bit too, but who like Coope died tragically early was Charles Harris. C.B. was born in December 1907 and sadly left us before his 47th birthday. It was Harris who first greeted fielders and umpires alike with, 'Good morning fellow workers'. It was he, who finding the light far from playable went out to bat at the fall of a wicket with a torch (switched on I presume) and took guard at square leg. His Bradford League days consisted of three war years with Yeadon beginning in 1943.

His first brought early confrontations with other big hitters. Playing against Bingley he batted at No. 5 making 73 out of a total of 158. Bingley in reply made 50 for 3 when rain ended play and their 'big man' Coope was ominously on 35 not out. Then a visit to Windhill where Learie Constantine and Les Ames were in opposition. Harris came out of that one well too, for Ames made 1 and Constantine 7. Windhill totalled 153 and then unleashed Copson, Constantine and Alf Pope. Harris made 85 not out having opened, seeing his side home by three wickets. His 1943 average of 32.80 increased to 34.50 in 1944 when he gained a losers medal in the Priestley Cup Final. There were two more medals for him in 1945. This time his side won the Priestley Cup and his 14 innings with an average of 53.11 gave him top spot in the League averages. In addition to this he had Cup scores of 76 not out, 50 not out, and 62, this last score being in the Final. Charles Harris, like so many more, brought to the City of Bradford, cricket of the highest standard and nowhere else in the country was there such a galaxy of stars nor such an array of talent to be seen.

Perhaps however there is one man more than any other that followers were grateful to in the war years, F.M. Watmough. After acting as Assistant Secretary to H.L. Walker in 1931, Mr Watmough took over, in charge, for 1932 and continued until handing over to W.W. Snowden in February 1951. What endeared Watmough most was his Bradford League Bulletin. Due to the shortage of newsprint in the war full scores could not be published in certain papers, so he brought out a weekly Bulletin with full scorecards, Leauge tables and some comment. Many of these were sent away, throughout the world, for the benefit of servicemen. These bulletins were much sought after by Bradford League players and supporters alike, in fact so keen are people to hang onto ones they have, a full set will be rare should anyone possess them all. So popular were they that they continued for three years after the war had finished.

Looking back at the war years, great names roll off the tongue almost as easily and as often as runs from the bat of Len Hutton. There are others too, stars of a different kind. On 4th

September 1943 Eric Brook took 4 for 32 for Bankfoot v Great Horton and then scored 54 runs out of a total of 93. Brook was a 'star' but in another field. Although he starred for Bankfoot that day his main talent was football which he played at the very top level with Manchester City (Division One) and England. Then there was another 'star', a man who batted at No. 10, scored one run, took a catch and ended a great career aged 71 years young. On the last day of the 1943 season Ernest Holdsworth played for Bowling Old Lane at Queensbury, his team won by 46 runs and his catch dismissed the home teams top scorer John Bailey who had made 27. It was at the age of 43 that Ernest Holdsworth had made his Bradford League debut, in Bowling Old Lane's first league season of 1915. Never in his wildest dreams would he have imagined an appearance 28 years later to become the oldest player to turn out for any Bradford League club. Stars certainly do come in all forms.

THE BRADFORD CRICKET LEAGUE IN WAR TIME

PROMINENT PLAYERS FOR SEASON 1942

Baildon Green – F. Dennis (Ex-Yorks), H. Fisher, G. Dawson.
Bingley W.W. Keeton (Notts), K. Fiddling (Yorks), G. Carter, L. Powell, *G.L. Majors and *R.T. Bryan (both Kent, have promised to assist when duties permit).
Bowling Old Lane – J. Parkinson, J. Lightowler.
Brighouse – F. Woodhouse, A. Coxon.
Eccleshill – Ellis Robinson (Yorks), *G. Cox (Sussex), *G. Duckworth (Lancs), T.R. Barker, A. Davison.
Farsley – Freddie Wharton, L.H. Towers.
Idle – F. Berry (Surrey), R.B. Rae, S. Rishman.
Keighley – E. Paynter (Lancs), E.A. Martindale (West Indies), D. Booth.
Lidget Green – A. Dyson (Glamorgan), *P.A. Gibb (Yorks) when duties permit, B.P. King (Worcs), G. Lavis (Glamorgan), A. Bastow.
Pudsey St Lawrence – J. Brewin, G. Dawson.
Lightcliffe – A. Topp, A. Hartley.
Queensbury – G. Senior, W. Johnson, L. Whitham, Oliver Glover.
Saltaire – G.H. Pope (Derby), L.F. Townsend (Derby), J.S. Douglas (Yorks).
Spen Victoria – W. Barber (Yorks), E. St. Hill (West Indies), *F.T. Prentice (Leics) when duties permit, S. Render.
Undercliffe – A. Wood, M. Leyland, T.A. Jacques (all Yorks), G.W. Brooke (Worcs).
Windhill – D. Smith, W.H. Copson, A.V. Pope (all Derby), J.S. Buller (Worcs).
Yeadon – J. Smith (Middlesex), J.A. Swift.

* Denotes Amateur

Great Horton, East Bierley and **Bankfoot** were all amateur.

1944 WHEN THE STARS WERE BRIGHTLY SHINING

FIRST TEAM BATTING AVERAGES
Qualification – 10 innings – average 25

	Ins.	N.O.	High Ins.	Total	Avge.
J. Bailey (Eccleshill, Hampshire)	12	4	84	482	60.25
L. Hutton (Pudsey S.L., Yorks)	14	3	101*	620	56.36
J.V. Wilson (Undercliffe)	16	3	132*	676	52.00
A. Wood (Undercliffe, Yorks)	15	2	88	593	45.61
A. Mitchell (Bowling O.L., Yorks)	16	3	105	573	44.07
E. Paynter (Keighley, Lancashire)	17	3	101*	611	43.64
W.A. Shackleton (Bowling Old Lane)	14	5	67*	365	40.55
A. Hamer (Spen Victoria)	17	2	82	605	40.33
L.E.G. Ames (Windhill, Kent)	13	1	89	472	39.33
H. Taylor (Lightcliffe)	11	2	109*	337	37.44
A. Hartley (Lightcliffe)	15	4	87*	404	36.72
W. Barber (Brighouse, Yorks)	16	1	91	544	36.26
A.H. Dyson (Lidget Green, Glamorgan)	16	3	115*	468	36.00
W.W. Keeton (Bingley, Notts)	14	1	98	465	35.76
C.B. Harris (Yeadon, Notts)	11	3	69*	276	34.50
G.V. Gunn (Keighley, Notts)	14	1	91	426	32.76
L.F. Townsend (Undercliffe, Derbyshire)	16	6	73*	326	32.60
D. Smith (Lidget Green, Derbyshire)	15	0	97	468	31.20
A Coxon (Brighouse)	16	2	93	423	30.21
G. Dawson (Pudsey St. Lawrence)	16	1	78*	452	30.13
F. Dennis (Undercliffe)	12	3	50*	270	30.00
K. Warnett (East Bierley)	14	1	73*	359	27.61
D. Hill (Great Horton)	16	4	61*	330	27.50
H. Fisher (Yeadon)	15	3	53	330	27.50
J. Speak (Farsley)	14	0	120	381	27.21
G.H. Pope (Spen Victoria, Derbyshire)	12	1	75	283	25.72
H.H. Daphne (Farsley)	12	1	79	281	25.54
L.J. Farmer (Windhill)	10	4	42	152	25.33
G. Smithson (Queensbury)	17	1	52	405	25.31

FIRST TEAM BOWLING AVERAGES
Qualification – 30 wickets

	O	M	R	W	Avge.
H. Fisher (Yeadon)	162.7	43	350	57	6.14
J. Smith (Yeadon, Middlesex)	182	34	411	54	7.61
J. Ellison (Pudsey St Lawrence)	163	20	602	72	8.36
L. Powell (Bowling Old Lane)	218	44	603	69	8.73
W.H. Copson (Saltaire, Derbyshire)	230	36	676	76	8.89
T.A. Jacques (Undercliffe)	158.6	25	449	49	9.16
G.H. Pope (Spen Victoria, Derbyshire)	241.3	34	752	67	11.22
A. Calvert (Idle)	216.7	13	707	62	11.40
J. Lawrence (Bingley)	183.2	21	696	60	11.60
S. Render (Bankfoot)	173.4	22	564	48	11.75
T.B. Mitchell (Lidget Green, Derbyshire)	145.5	18	568	55	11.96
C. Gladwin (Lidget Green)	152.2	29	433	36	12.02
A. Hartley (Lightcliffe)	115.2	10	448	36	12.44
E. Achong (Windhill, West Indies)	217.4	39	710	57	12.45
A. Booth (Spen Victoria)	243.5	37	790	61	12.95
G. Senior (Queensbury)	140.1	25	515	38	13.55
H.H. Daphne (Farsley)	105.3	5	478	34	14.05
O. Glover (Queensbury)	219.7	11	877	62	14.14
A. Bastow (Lidget Green)	153.1	21	472	33	14.30
A. Coxon (Brighouse)	218.3	33	738	51	14.47
J. Bailey (Eccleshill, Hampshire)	111.1	10	498	33	15.09
A.V. Pope (Baildon Green, Derbyshire)	221.7	30	707	46	15.36
F. Hollingsworth (Idle)	140.2	11	563	35	16.08

KEIGHLEY CRICKET CLUB v WINDHILL C. CLUB

PLAYED AT LAWKHOLME LANE on 31st JULY 19 43

INNINGS OF WINDHILL

	BATSMEN	HOW OUT	BOWLER	TOTAL
1	CUTMORE J.	LBW	MARTINDALE	18
2	KIPPAX H.G.	LBW	MARTINDALE	9
3	POPE A.V.	b	MOULE	54
4	AMES L.E.G	c GUNN	MARTINDALE	55
5	SMITH D.	c SEABROOKE	MARTINDALE	16
6	ROBINSON N.	b	JEFFERSON	6
7	WATSON	b	JEFFERSON	11
8	BAILEY	b	JEFFERSON	24
9	MAWSON	NOT	OUT	0
10	FARMER	NOT	OUT	1
11				

EXTRAS 8
TOTAL 202 FOR 8 WKTS.

	BOWLERS	OVERS	M'DNS	RUNS	WKTS	AVGE
1	MARTINDALE E.A			72	4	
2	PAYNTER E			28	0	
3	MOULE J.			61	1	
4	JEFFERSON H.			33	3	

INNINGS OF KEIGHLEY

	BATSMEN	HOW OUT	BOWLER	TOTAL
1	PAYNTER E.	b	POPE	86
2	GUNN G.V.	LBW	POPE	50
3	MOULE J.	NOT	OUT	6
4	MARTINDALE E.A	b	POPE	1
5	PARTRIDGE	NOT	OUT	2

EXTRAS 12
TOTAL 157 FOR 3 WKTS.

	BOWLERS	OVERS	M'DNS	RUNS	WKTS	AVGE
1	COPSON W.H.			49	0	
2	POPE A.V			32	3	
3	MAWSON			35	0	
4	WATSON			19	0	
	KIPPAX H.G.			10	0	

UNDERCLIFFE CRICKET CLUB v BOWLING OLD LANE C. CLUB

PLAYED AT INTAKE ROAD ON 12th AUGUST 1944

INNINGS OF UNDERCLIFFE

	BATSMEN	HOW OUT	BOWLER	TOTAL
1	LESTER E.	c CREIGHTON	APPLEYARD	72
2	WILSON J.V.	c LIGHTOWLER	APPLEYARD	19
3	WOOD A.	b	APPLEYARD	2
4	TOWNSEND L.F.	b	APPLEYARD	5
5	DENNIS F.	c LIGHTOWLER	APPLEYARD	27
6	SEFTON	NOT	OUT	41
7	JACQUES T.	c SHACKLETON	POWELL	8
8	JOWETT	NOT	OUT	16
9				
10				
11				

EXTRAS 9
TOTAL 199 FOR 6 WKTS. DEC.

BOWLERS

	BOWLERS	OVERS	MDNS	RUNS	WKTS	AVGE
1	POWELL L.			96	1	
2	APPLEYARD R.			69	5	
3	FORDE			14	0	
4	CREIGHTON C.H.			11	0	

INNINGS OF BOWLING OLD LANE

	BATSMEN	HOW OUT	BOWLER	TOTAL
1	MITCHELL A.	NOT	OUT	58
2	SHACKLETON	b	DENNIS	8
3	BUTLER	c JOWETT	DENNIS	30
4	HELLEWELL C.	c WOOD	DENNIS	1
5	FORDE	c JOWETT	TOWNSEND	11
6	CREIGHTON CH	b	JOWETT	6
7	PRIESTLEY	NOT	OUT	5
8				
9				
10				
11				

EXTRAS 14
TOTAL 133 FOR 5 WKTS.

BOWLERS

	BOWLERS	OVERS	MDNS	RUNS	WKTS	AVGE
1	JACQUES T.A.			41	0	
2	DENNIS F.			28	3	
3	JACQUES T.			23	0	
4	TOWNSEND L.F.			6	1	
	JOWETT			5	1	

FINAL LEAGUE POSITIONS

1940

Division A
	P	W	D	L	Pts
Windhill	18	14	3	1	45
Bowling Old Lane	18	10	5	3	35
Keighley	18	8	6	4	30
Baildon Green	18	7	6	5	28*
Bingley	18	8	4	6	28
Brighouse	18	6	7	5	26*
Spen Victoria	18	6	2	10	21*
Great Horton	18	4	4	10	17*
Lightcliffe	18	3	5	10	14
Bradford	18	2	2	14	8

* signifies extra point added for a tied game.

Division B
	P	W	D	L	Pts
Lidget Green	18	14	2	2	45*
Undercliffe	18	14	2	2	44
Idle	18	11	1	6	34
Eccleshill	18	9	2	7	30*
Queensbury	18	7	3	8	24
Farsley	18	6	3	9	21
Saltaire	18	6	3	9	21
Pudsey St Lawrence	18	6	2	10	20
East Bierley	18	5	3	10	18
Bankfoot	18	1	1	16	4

* signifies extra point added for a tied game.

Batting Averages
1. E. Paynter (Keighley)   74.28
2. W. Barber (Brighouse)   59.62
3. W. Place (Keighley)   57.30

Bowling Averages
1. T.A. Jacques (Undercliffe)   79 wkts @ 8.53
2. E. Lodge (Lidget Green)   54 wkts @ 10.00
3. G. Pope (Lidget Green)   88 wkts @ 11.01
4. A. Booth (Bowling Old Lane)   89 wkts @ 11.11
5. G. Brooke (Eccleshill)   87 wkts @ 11.70
6. L. Constantine (Windhill)   76 wkts @ 11.80

1941

Division A
	P	W	D	L	Pts
Windhill	18	10	3	5	33
Idle	18	9	5	4	32
Spen Victoria	18	8	5	5	29
Bingley	18	8	2	8	26
Brighouse	18	6	8	4	26
Undercliffe	18	7	4	7	25
Lidget Green	18	6	3	9	21
Bowling Old Lane	18	5	5	8	20
Keighley	18	6	2	10	20
Baildon Green	18	4	5	9	17

Division B
	P	W	D	L	Pts
Saltaire	18	17	1	0	52
Great Horton	18	10	3	5	33
Bradford	18	10	2	6	32
Pudsey St. Lawrence	18	9	3	6	30
Farsley	18	8	3	7	27
Bankfoot	18	7	2	9	23
Queensbury	18	7	1	10	22
Lightcliffe	18	6	3	9	21
Eccleshill	18	3	4	11	13
East Bierley	18	1	2	15	5

Batting Averages
1. E. Paynter (Keighley)   52.37
2. W. Barber (Brighouse)   50.28
3. W.A. Shackleton (Bowling Old Lane)   40.07

Bowling Averages
1. A.V. Pope (Saltaire)   69 wkts @ 6.49
2. W.H. Copson (Saltaire)   59 wkts @ 6.59
3. R.B. Rae (Idle)   72 wkts @ 7.43
4. W. Johnson (Queensbury)   33 wkts @ 10.72
5. G.H. Pope (Lidget Green)   68 wkts @ 11.22

1942

Division A
	P	W	D	L	Pts
Lidget Green	18	12	4	2	40
Windhill	18	11	5	2	38
Saltaire	18	9	5	4	32
Idle	18	8	4	6	28
Undercliffe	18	8	4	6	28
Bingley	18	7	6	5	27
Brighouse	18	4	5	9	17
Great Horton	18	3	5	10	14
Spen Victoria	18	3	4	11	13
Bowling Old Lane	18	2	4	12	10

Division B
	P	W	D	L	Pts
Keighley	18	12	4	2	40
Eccleshill	18	9	4	5	31
Yeadon	18	9	4	5	31
Lightcliffe	18	9	3	6	30
Baildon Green	18	8	4	6	28
Queensbury	18	7	5	6	27*
Farsley	18	6	6	6	24
Pudsey St. Lawrence	18	6	4	8	22
East Bierley	18	3	3	12	12
Bankfoot	18	0	5	13	6*

* Bankfoot and Queensbury each awarded an extra point for a tied game.

Batting Averages
1. E. Paynter (Keighley)   138.55
2. C. Sykes (Spen Victoria)   46.55
3. H. Fisher (Baildon Green)   44.40

Bowling Averages
1. A. Bastow (Lidget Green)   63 wkts @ 6.96
2. H. Fisher (Baildon Green)   52 wkts @ 8.03
3. W.H. Copson (Windhill)   66 wkts @ 8.42
4. G.H. Pope (Saltaire)   64 wkts @ 8.80
5. T.B. Mitchell (Lidget Green)   78 wkts @ 8.94
5. Jim Smith (Yeadon)   53 wkts @ 9.00

1943

Division A
	P	W	D	L	Pts
Saltaire	18	10	6	2	36
Windhill	18	8	7	3	31
Eccleshill	18	9	2	7	29
Keighley	18	8	4	6	28
Bingley	18	6	8	4	26
Brighouse	18	5	7	6	22
Lidget Green	18	5	4	9	19
Undercliffe	18	4	7	7	19
Yeadon	18	5	3	10	18
Idle	18	4	4	10	16

Division B
	P	W	D	L	Pts
Spen Victoria	18	13	4	1	43
Pudsey St. Lawrence	18	11	3	4	37*
Baildon Green	18	10	4	4	34
Bowling Old Lane	18	9	5	4	32*
Great Horton	18	5	7	6	22
Lightcliffe	18	5	5	8	20
Farsley	18	5	4	9	19
Queensbury	18	3	7	8	16
East Bierley	18	3	5	10	14
Bankfoot	18	1	6	11	9

* Pudsey and Bowling Old Lane each awarded an extra point for a tied game.

Batting Averages
1. G. Cox (Brighouse)   52.00
2. E. Paynter (Keighley)   45.30
3. L. Hutton (Pudsey St. Lawrence)   45.07
4. H. Fisher (Baildon Green)   36.16
5. W. Barber (Brighouse)   34.58

Bowling Averages
1. A. Booth (Spen Victoria)   78 wkts @ 6.58
2. G.H. Pope (Spen Victoria)   71 wkts @ 7.40
3. L. Powell (Bowling Old Lane)   68 wkts @ 8.02
4. E.P. Robinson (Eccleshill)   51 wkts @ 8.58
5. L. Hutton (Pudsey St. Lawrence)   43 wkts @ 8.97
6. S. Render (Pudsey St. Lawrence)   34 wkts @ 9.08

1944

Division A

	P	W	D	L	Pts
Spen Victoria	18	11	4	3	37
Lidget Green	18	9	6	3	33
Eccleshill	18	8	4	6	28
Pudsey St. Lawrence	18	8	3	7	27
Saltaire	18	8	3	7	27
Windhill	18	7	6	5	27
Baildon Green	18	6	4	8	22
Bingley	18	5	5	8	20
Brighouse	18	3	5	10	14
Keighley	18	3	4	11	13

Division B

	P	W	D	L	Pts
Yeadon	18	13	5	0	44
Undercliffe	18	13	4	1	43
Bowling Old Lane	18	10	4	4	34
Great Horton	18	7	5	6	26
Queensbury	18	6	4	8	22
Lightcliffe	18	5	7	6	22
Bankfoot	18	5	3	10	18
Idle	18	4	3	11	15
Farsley	18	4	2	12	14
East Bierley	18	1	7	10	10

Batting Averages

1 J. Bailey (Eccleshill) 60.25
2 L. Hutton (Pudsey St. Lawrence) 56.36
3 V. Wilson (Undercliffe) 52.00
4 A. Wood (Undercliffe) 45.61
5 A. Mitchell (Bowling Old Lane) 44.07
6 E. Paynter (Keighley) 43.64

Bowling Averages

1 H. Fisher (Yeadon) 57 wkts @ 6.14
2 J. Smith (Yeadon) 54 wkts @ 7.61
3 I. Ellison (Pudsey St. Lawrence) 72 wkts @ 8.36
4 L. Powell (Bowling Old Lane) 69 wkts @ 8.73
5 W.H. Copson (Saltaire) 76 wkts @ 8.89
6 T.A. Jacques (Undercliffe) 49 wkts @ 9.16

1945

Division A

	P	W	D	L	Pts
Undercliffe	18	10	4	4	34
Pudsey St. Lawrence	18	10	3	5	33
Saltaire	18	7	7	4	28*
Yeadon	18	7	6	5	27
Baildon Green	18	7	5	6	26
Windhill	18	7	4	7	26*
Lidget Green	18	6	6	6	24
Eccleshill	18	4	6	8	18
Spen Victoria	18	3	8	7	17
Bowling Old Lane	18	3	4	11	13

Division B

	P	W	D	L	Pts
Bingley	18	14	3	1	45
Keighley	18	10	6	2	36*
Farsley	18	8	5	5	30*
Lightcliffe	18	8	5	5	29
East Bierley	18	8	3	7	28
Brighouse	18	6	5	7	23
Queensbury	18	6	4	8	22
Great Horton	18	6	3	9	21
Bankfoot	18	3	1	14	10
Idle	18	1	5	12	8

* Each awarded an extra point for a tied game.

Batting Averages

1 C. Harris (Yeadon) 53.11
2 W. Barber (Brighouse) 53.07
3 L.F. Townsend (Undercliffe) 52.80
4 L. Hutton (Pudsey St. Lawrence) 50.55
5 E. Paynter (Keighley) 47.25
6 W.W. Keeton (Bingley) 39.54

Bowling Averages

1 J. Lawrence (Bingley) 69 wkts @ 6.50
2 R.B. Rae (Bingley) 51 wkts @ 8.13
3 A.V. Pope (Lidget Green) 62 wkts @ 8.95
4 T.W. Goddard (Keighley) 61 wkts @ 9.06
5 H. Fisher (Yeadon) 48 wkts @ 10.35
6 L.F. Townsend (Undercliffe) 37 wkts @ 10.54

Bingley (Div 2) did not lose a match until a home game on the last day of the season. Idle (Div 2) had only one win and that was away from home. They gained only one point in their last ten matches.

Chapter Six
County Connections

One of the finest relationships enjoyed by the Bradford League Clubs is that which it shares with the First Class Counties. It has been a two way satisfaction with players graduating to the First Class game after learning their trade within the League, but it is also a place where First Class cricketers have not hesitated to play, at times when County Cricket has been disrupted or when they needed practice, or a high standard in which to end their careers.

In the first decade of Bradford League Cricket the likes of Major Booth and Abe Waddington were playing at County level and in the Bradford League whenever the occasion demanded. As soon as County Cricket was suspended during World War One the cream of England's cricketers streamed northwards.

As expected many Yorkshire players turned to the Bradford League, Percy Holmes, Herbert Sutcliffe, John Newstead, Schofield Haigh, Emmott Robinson were some. The journey from the south and midlands brought amongst others, Bill Hitch, Jack Hobbs, Frank Woolley, Charlie Parker, Charlie Llewellyn, Sydney Barnes, J.W. 'Young Jack' Hearne and James Seymour.

Extra sparkle was added to the strongest league in the land and the boast soon to be made 'The Strongest League in the World' was not an idle one. Matches threw up some interesting confrontations between players who used to be colleagues.

In the England side of 1912 against Australia you would find Hearne, Woolley, Hobbs, Gunn, Hitch and Barnes and all six were opposed to each other in the Wartime Bradford League fixtures.

Just as all Bradford League clubs had their County men, so each County was represented apart from Glamorgan who remained that way till Arnold Dyson came to Lidget Green in 1940, scoring 72 in that seasons Cup Final.

In the First World War the benefits of having Test and County players to such a large extent are obvious. Fine players bring top class cricket and pass their knowledge on to the up and coming players, leading to better future cricketers.

With crowds as they were, all clubs were getting in gate receipts, sufficient to pay their 'Stars' without financial troubles. It suited everyone, the Bradford League Handbook for 1916 records that, 'the 1915 season will ever be remembered as being the most seriously critical and exceptionally successful we have ever experienced'.

There were a few who felt, as in other parts of the country, that cricket should have been curtailed. The League Management Committee had serious misgivings, deliberating long and hard before deciding to go ahead with competition as usual. Many thousands of people would testify that the League was right and at a time of great trouble, temporary respite was provided which was not available elsewhere, at least to this standard, and in many towns and cities not at all. Wartime Bradford League was a successful period for all concerned.

Two items from those days which may surprise are that the bottom five had to apply for re-election and that the matches started at 2.30 pm and 2.15 pm in September. This is compared with 1 pm today. Maybe their was less worry about bad light appeals in those days, players played more for the love of the game than for the importance of winning or losing.

Businessmen in the area were not slow to capitalise on having star players close at hand. Sports and Pastimes, a Cheapside sportshop in the City advertised a bat which will drive farther than any other bat and will not sting. It was the type used by Jack Hobbs they said. No wonder he did so well if it was his bat which determined how far he drove a ball and not The Master himself. It must have been a real challenge to the ordinary club cricketer to pit his wits against the best of the day.

For the record here are a few selected players and details of their best Bradford League performances. The selection is made from only those who played during World War One, as part or all of their Bradford League career.

Sydney Barnes (Saltaire)
Best batting – 168 v Baildon Green, in the Priestley Cup 1918.
Best bowling – 10 for 14 v Baildon Green, 1915 (inc 5 wkts in 5 balls)

Schofield Haigh (Keighley)
Best batting – 86 v Bowling Old Lane, 1919
Best bowling – 5 for 7 v Bingley, 1919

J.W. Hearne (Keighley)
Best batting – 80 v Bankfoot, 1917
Best bowling – 5 for 34 v Low Moor, 1917

Bill Hitch (Eccleshill)
Best batting – 99 v Idle, 1918

Jack Hobbs (Idle)
Best batting – 132 v Saltaire, Priestley Cup 1917
Best bowling – 9 for 39 v Saltaire, 1916

Percy Holmes (Great Horton)
Best batting – 100* v Eccleshill, 1918

Charlie Llewellyn (Undercliffe)
Best batting – 75* v Farsley, 1920
Best bowling – 8 for 40 v Bankfoot, 1918

Charlie Parker (Windhill)
Best bowling – 9 for 31 v Bowling Old Lane, 1917

Emmott Robinson (Keighley, Bankfoot and Pudsey St Lawrence)
Best batting – 96 for Pudsey v Bowling Old Lane, 1919
Best bowling – 9 for 29 for Bankfoot v Keighley, 1917

Abe Waddington (Crossley Hall and Laisterdyke)
Best bowling – 8 for 27 for Laisterdyke v Bingley, 1912
            Also had 8 for 28 for Laisterdyke v Undercliffe, 1915

Frank Woolley (Keighley)
Best batting – 126 v Saltaire, 1920
Best bowling – 7 for 16 v Lidget Green, Priestley Cup 1916

Figures given as best bowling are determined by the highest number of wickets taken in an innings. In the case of Frank Woolley for example, whats to say that his 7 for 16 was any better than his 6 for 2 against Farsley in 1919. What constitutes 'Best' is of course very debatable according to one's school of thought.

After the First World War many players stayed in the League while others returned to help their club when County duties permitted. Some who had not played in the wartime were attracted too, so that it was not all oneway traffic. The names may not have been as well known but the talent was still there.

Farsley for example signed a player many readers may not have heard of, Alan Turner. Yet Turner had played for Yorkshire in 1910 – 11 and either as opener or middle order batsman was good for 600 – 700 runs per season. Turner almost reached a century in his first season with Farsley making 96 against Eccleshill but made no mistake in 1922 scoring 128* v Saltaire, the Club which he batted through against in 1921 making 55* against the Saltaire attack which contained Sydney Barnes. Turner had played County Cricket before moving into the League, but the 1920s saw appearances of those who were to move the other way.

Arthur Mitchell was probably the most famous who moved to the 'big time' having started in the League soon after the war. Mitchell started at Tong Park, his first half century coming in 1921 against Bowling Old Lane. One year later he joined Barnes at Saltaire and in 1925, despite not having a century (99 v Windhill almost got him there) he had a batting average of 81.12 and topped the League averages. Mitchell from his league beginnings went onto a County career of

FIXTURES, 1911.

First Eleven.

Date	Name of Club	Where Played	Result
Apr. 8	Opening Match	home	
15	Idle	home	
17	E.M.—Windhill	away	
22	Bradford	home	
29	1st R C.—Queensbury	away	
May 6	Shelf	home	
13	Eccleshill	home	
20	Saltaire	away	
27	Undercliffe	away	
June 3	Lidget Green	home	
5	W.M.—Great Horton	home	
6	W.T.—Bingley	away	
10	Queensbury	home	
17	**2nd Round Cup**		
24	Lidget Green	away	
July 1	Undercliffe	home	
8	Saltaire	home	
15	**3rd Round Cup**		
22	Bingley	home	
29	Great Horton	away	
Aug. 5	Shelf	away	
7	B.H.—Semi-Final C.		
12	Bradford	away	
19	**Final Cup**		
26	Queensbury	away	
Sept. 2	Windhill	home	
9	Eccleshill	away	
16	Idle	away	

Captain: W. G. Bateman.
Vice-Captain: A. Budd.

Bankfoot Cricket Club.

(Members of the Bradford Cricket League.)

PATRONS :—

John Greenough, Esq.
Arthur E. Greenough, Esq.
John Gray, Esq.
Walter Wood, Esq.
Irvine C. Woodhead, Esq.
Thurston Bolton, Esq.
Coun. Albert Cowling, Esq.
Mrs. Mark Shaw,
Fred Burnett, Esq.
Walter Clough Pearson, Esq.
Harry Carter, Esq.
Mrs. Thomas Lightowler.
Alfred Gaunt, sr., Esq.
Angus Holden, Esq.
George Jackson, Esq.
William Wilkinson, Esq.
T. E. Sykes, Esq.
James Clayton, Esq.
Arthur M. Sutcliffe, Esq.
Joshua M. Sutcliffe, Esq.
Joe Day, Esq.
Charles Scofield, Esq.
Edmund Muff, Esq.
Harry Shaw, Esq.
James Sharp, Esq.
Messrs. Mitchell Bros.
Coun. G. Wilkinson, Esq.
Albert Weatherhead, Esq.
John Townley, Esq.
Tom Riley, Esq.
J. H. Macqueen, Esq.
E. F. Holdsworth, Esq.
Walter Gray, Esq.
J. H. Thwaite, Esq.
Firth Cordingley, Esq.
Harry Ben Wood, Esq.

(26) Name *Mr. James Mitchell*
Address *Laisterdyke.*

Subscriptions due on or before May 31st.

LIST OF OFFICERS FOR 1911.

President: JAMES OGDEN, Esq.

Vice-Presidents:—
Mr. Seth Barraclough.
Mr. W. G. Bateman.
Mr. Squire Wilkinson.
Mr. Harry Worsnop.
Mr. Amos Lindley.
Mr. Thornton Muff.
Mr. Sam Throp.
Mr. Squire Mackay.
Mr. James Mitchell.
Mr. Harry Rowley.
Mr. Chas. E. Thwaite.
Mr. Sam Howsen.
Mr. Edmund Barraclough.
Mr. Arthur Greenroyd.

Mr. A. Budd.

Committee:—
Mr. John Wm. Barker.
Mr. Ernest Thornton.
Mr. Arthur Sykes.
Mr. Ronald Wilkinson.
Mr. Smith Ainsworth.
Mr. Peter Sykes.
Mr. Arthur Gray.
Mr. Albert Shackleton.
Mr. James Fletcher.
Mr. James Normington.
Mr. Tom Lightowler.
Mr. James Priestley.

Chairman of Committee:—Mr. Arthur Gray.
Hon. Treasurer:—Mr. Edmund Priestley.
Hon Sec.:—Mr. Allen Burnett, 6 White Lane, Wibsey.

League & Cup Representatives—
Mr. Tom Lightowler, Mr. Ernest Thornton.

Ground: Pearson Road, Odsal.
5 Minutes Walk from Bankfoot Tram Terminus
Headquarters—Fox 4 Hounds, Odsal.

ADMISSION : NON-MEMBERS, 3D.

General Meeting., October 27th, 1911.

Membership—April 1st, 1911 to March 31st, 1912.

An autographed photograph of Jack Hobbs, taken on the Idle Cricket ground and presented by the great cricketer to Mr J.J. Booth (at the time Bradford League President).

Bankfoot – 1917/18 (Record breaker Wilf Payton 2nd from left front row)

Brighouse CC – 1925 – Taken before start of first game in the Bradford League. Caps specially presented for the occasion. Cup at the front is the Bower Cup won the year previously in the Halifax Section of the Yorkshire Council. Back (l to r) W. Palfrey (Comm), J. Ingam (Comm), H. Naylor (Pro), F. Whiteoak, Mr Briggs (President), S. Whittles, M. Stott, F. Cardwell (Comm). Middle – F. Gibson, T. Bates (Pro), H.N. Wood, G. Brearley (captain), H. Outram, L. Brown (Pro), A. Fell (Pro). Front – H. Goulding, F. Barker

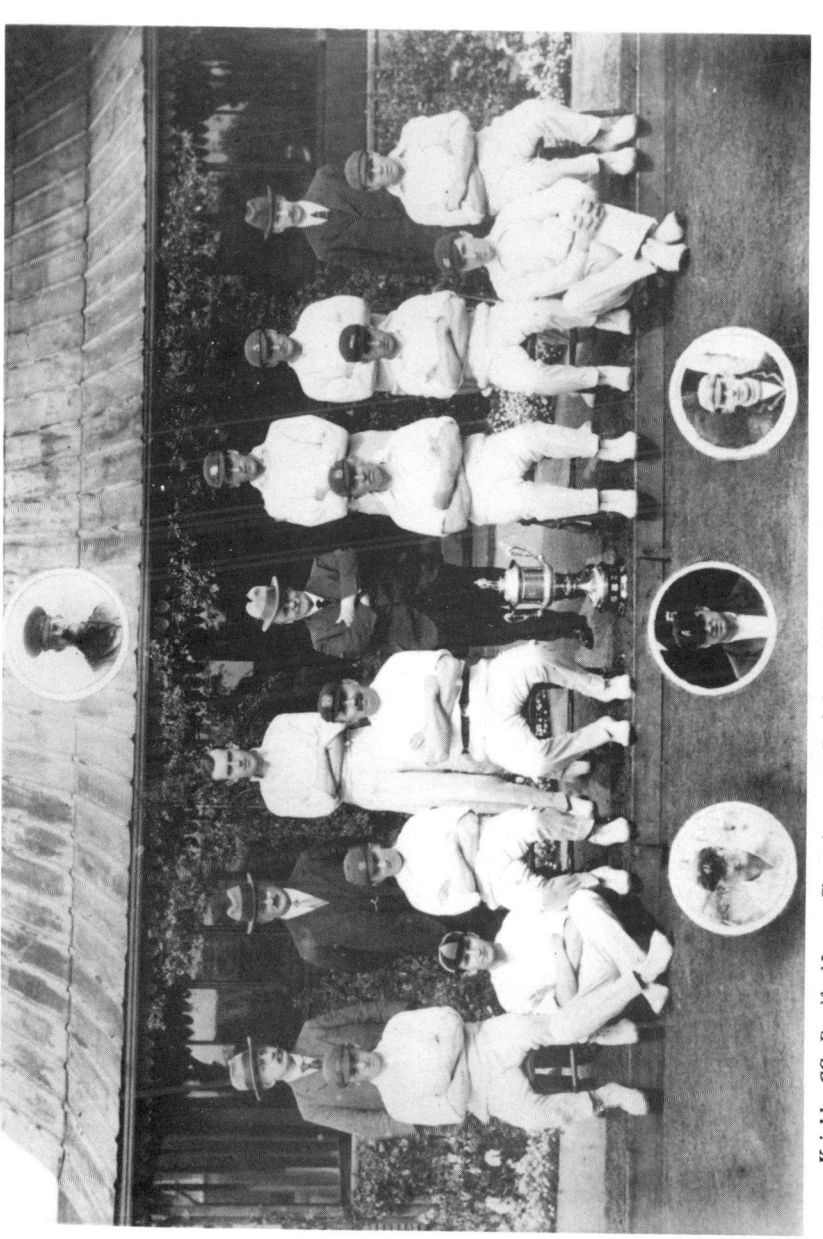

Keighley CC – Bradford League Champions 1919 – Back (l to r) J.W. Carruthers (Treas), F. Smith (Sec), G. Crawford, J. Ickringill (Chairman), F.E. Woolley, J. Seymour, S.M. France (scorer). Front – W. Holden, Jas Lang, H. Haigh, W. Morley, F. Horner, D. Roebuck, H. Robson, J.J. Williams. Circles – Top – G.C. Foulds, Bottom – Willis Walker, Scoofield Haigh and Jack W. Hearne

Windhill CC – *(mid 1920s)*

Windhill – *Cup winners 1925*
H.C. Robson (captain)
Taken on the bowling green at Bradford Park Avenue. The cricket and football stand can be seen in the background and part of the pavilion in the foreground.

Saltaire CC – 2nd XI Champions 1928 – Photograph taken at Keighley 8 Sept 1928

Saltaire CC – 1933 – Back (l to r) Fred Gawthorpe, W. Farndale, J.H. Ellicott, George Kennie, T.A. Jacques, Harry Lee, Herbert Pedley, George Hayley (Captain), Johnny Basham, Titch Crowther, Stanley Brown

*Herbert Sutcliffe (Left) and
Percy Holmes going out to bat.*

Fred Root (Bowling Old Lane)

Undercliffe CC – Champions 1935 – Back (l to r) H. Marsh (Hon Sec), G.C. Johnson, E. Lodge, H. Bailes, E. Lamb, H. Ainley, E.G. Crofts, F. Wellock (Scorer). Front – C Topham (President), I.B. Dibb, J. Asquith, J.E. Jowett (captain), T.A. Jacques, F. Crossley, T. Tunnicliffe (Hon Treas)

Undercliffe – Priestley Cup Winners 1938 – Back (l to r) F. Wellock (scorer) L. Brame, T.A. Jacques, B. Topham (Chairman), J.S. Lund, H. Jackson, T. Illingworth (Secretary). Middle – E. Smith, L. Potter, A. Sharpe, L. Phillips (Captain), F. Wharton, L. Smith, F. Lees. Front – N. Windle (wicket-keeper), H. Stone

Willis Walker (Keighley and Nottinghamshire)

The Master

Saltaire CC – 1st XI 1941 Division B and Priestley Cup Winners – Back (l to r) S. Crabtree, W.H. Copson, G.A. Wilson, A.V. Pope, F. Earnshaw, H. Pedley, H. Ogden (scorer), J.M. Crossley, J.C. Lee, L.F. Townsend, G. Birbeck (President), G.B. Haley (Captain), J.H. Roper (Vice-President), A. Spencer

Baildon Green CC – 1944 – Back (l to r) Dean, Davison, Hudson, Thompson, Burnet (captain), Sutcliffe, Pope (A.V.) (Derbyshire). Front – Henry, Robson, Crowther, Bulcock

Yeadon CC – 1944 Division B Champions and Cup Finalists – Back (l to r) B. Dean, G.T. Dennison, J. Moorhouse, K. Ellison, A. Maud, G. Hardcastle, C.B. Harris (Notts), D. Bateson, J. Illingworth, S. Howard, G. Carter. Front – J. Swift, J. Smith (Middlesex), H. Hutchinson, L.G. Berry (Leics), H. Fisher (Yorks)

Spen Victoria – Double Winners 1944

Yeadon CC – *Juniors 1948 – Champions of the Airedale Junior League. Brian Close (captain) (age 17 years) middle of front row.*

Saltaire CC – *1949*

Lightcliffe CC – *Park Avenue Cup Final v East Bierley, August 1950, last season before overs limit. Back (l to r) A. Hartley, J.T. Newsholme, D. Hirst, M.S. Woodcock, A. Smith, B. Webb, J. Barritt. Front – A. Clarke, R. Hirst, H. Aspinall, R. Booth, D.G. Mallinson*

Action shot of Brighouse v Queensbury. Queensbury are batting, Terry Webster is bowling and Alec Higson is keeping wicket.

Towmson bowled by Burkinshaw (wk Brian Snook)

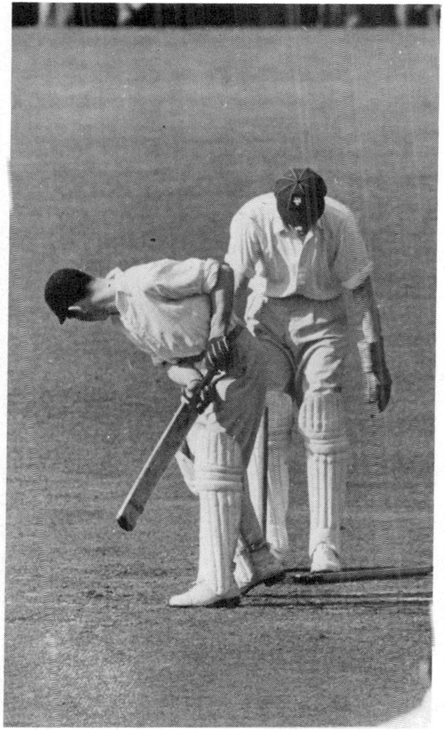

R. Long bowled by Burkinshaw

The final victim also bowled Burkinshaw

1952 Cup Final, Baildon v Keighley

Wilf Burkinshaw's hat-trick, all clean bowled

Baildon CC – 1952 Cup and League Double Winners – Back (l to r) B. Snook, E. Hitchenor, L. McLean, J.R. Burnet (Captain), G. Moore, P. Robson, D. Dobson. Front – W. Burkinshaw, G. Dean, T. Tetley, W. Ellis

Bradford CC – 1953 Cup Winners – Back (l to r) A.M. King, J. Clapham, M. Holdsworth, K. Woodward, J.L. Cheetham. Front – P. Ibbotson, M. Riley, P. Hutton (Captain), E. Barraclough, H.V. Douglas, B. Clough.

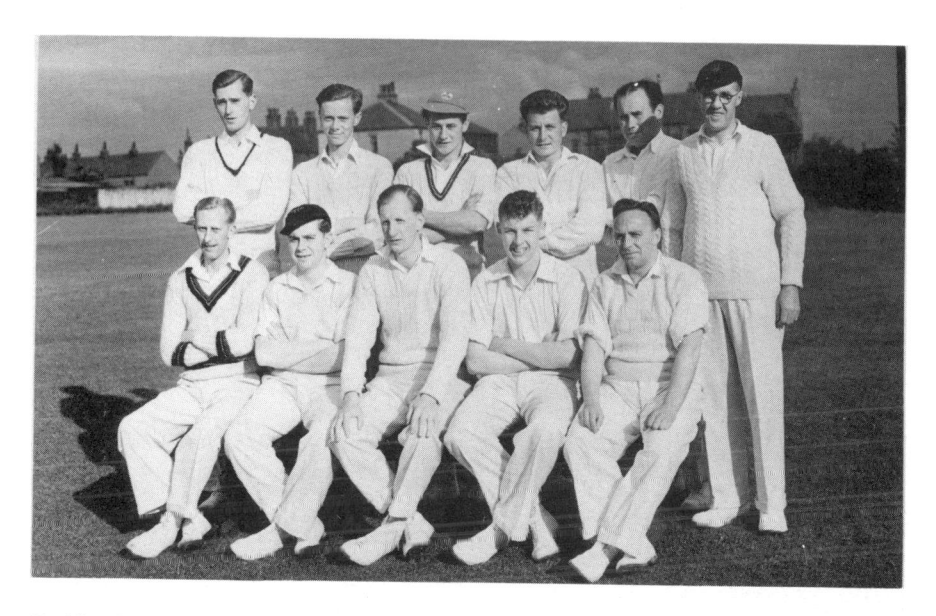

Bankfoot CC – *2nd XI, Priestley Shield Winners 1954* – *Back (l to r) D.W. Greenwood, D. Pickles, N. Holmes, B. Tordoff, J. Fitzpatrick, C.A. Hodgson. Front – R. Cragg, M. Irving, S.C. Cowman (captain), G. Thompson, G. Roberts*

Great Horton – *1955*

Spen Victoria CC – 1958 – Back (l to r) Denis Rhodes, Stuart Platt, Eric Fisk, Percy Watson, David Firth, Les Walker. Front – Alan Carter, Trevor Wood, Harry Hoyle (Captain), Bill Brown, Geoff Brown

East Bierley CC – 1959 – Taken at Blackpool CC (Stanley Park) for a mid-season friendly. Back (l to r) – Malcolm Smith, Norman Kitson, Gordon Phillips (captain), Terry Gunn (wk), David Field, David Reynard. Front – Harry Waterhouse, Derek Tordoff, Tony Rowe, Michael Collins and a 15 year old Brian Lymbery.

401 matches, playing six times for England. When his first class career was over, Mitchell did not forget his roots and returned to give fine service to Baildon Green, Bowling Old Lane and Undercliffe. Arthur Mitchell is one of few men who have batted through a complete innings which he did oddly enough in his first season, 1921, for Tong Park against Keighley, scoring 48*.

The most famous names from the 1930's to move into County Cricket were Len Hutton and Brian Sellars. Most schoolboy cricket fans, home and abroad, know that Len Hutton started out at Pudsey St. Lawrence. Brian Sellars commenced Bradford League life at Keighley making his first fifty (57 in fact) in 1925 as a youngster against Great Horton. In 1931 he hit 104 against Bradford in the Priestley Cup. In three seasons commencing 1929 Brian scored 1434 runs in League games at an average of thirty and it wasn't long after that he found himself a regular First Class player going on to make 334 Yorkshire appearances with fifteen seasons as the Yorkshire captain.

The Bradford League breeds not only fine cricketers but first class captains also. Since World War Two, Ronnie Burnett, Raymond Illingworth, Brian Close, Vic Wilson, David Bairstow and Phil Carrick have captained Yorkshire, each having an amount of success. From little acorns etc.

During the Second World War the League continued its attraction, not only by its continuance but by providing wickets not far removed from County standard. Once more the crowds flocked in, this time to see the likes of Cyril Washbrook, Eddie Paynter, Tommy Mitchell, Les Ames, Len Hutton, Tom Goddard, Arthur Wood, Cliff Gladwin, the brothers Pope (George and Alf), James Bailey and Bill Copson to name but a few.

Once more the standard was extremely high and Counties need have no fears that players would not stay in practice for when 'normal' cricket was resumed. Spectators were spoiled for choice with such an array of stars to watch, but when County Cricket re-commenced the County Clubs were ever grateful and regularly supplied second teamers to Bradford League games to (a) assist them with learning their trade and (b) as a thank you for the Leagues assistance during the war years, for providing the countries 'Best' with regular top class matches.

Picking two games at random from the war years — a cup-tie between Keighley and Saltaire, had a scorecard showing Keighley all out for 77 runs. This despite having in their ranks Eddie Paynter (8) Ted Lester (18) George Gunn (2) and Tom Goddard (15). Saltaire won by eight wickets, their matchwinners being Alec Coxon (4 for 32) and Bill Copson (6 for 45). What thrills the likes of those players provided. A typical match of the period in the League was Lidget Green v Idle from July 1943. Lidget batted first making 199-6 before declaring. They had County players in Phil King, who played for Worcestershire before the war and Lancashire after. King made 113* in this match, his opening partner Arnold Dyson making just 11, but the ex-Glamorgan man proved himself on other days. Idle got within seventeen runs before being all out. They had James Bailey (Hampshire) and Les Berry (Leicestershire) to open for them but it was ex-Test bowler Tommy Mitchell in this game with 9-90 who brought Lidget the points.

Most games would contain approx. five players with County experience. Since the war many Counties have benefitted from Bradford League players. It's no good saying that Yorkshire has missed home grown talent for its simply a case of they can't accommodate everyone. Gordon Barker was one who escaped, in the mid-fifties, and went off to join Essex, but look at Yorkshire's batting at the time and you'll realise there was no place for him, however talented. Jim Laker escaped to Surrey and we all know what he did there, but he too was trying to get into County Cricket when Yorkshire had some fine spinners at a time when Laker was inexperienced.

Obviously the Yorkshire Club has benefitted most from the production line that is the Bradford League. In the other direction maybe Derbyshire have been keener than most to see their players getting Bradford League experience. David Smith, Les Jackson, Ashley Harvey-Walker, Jim Brailsford, John Harvey and many others have enjoyed this experience and profitted from it, in many cases other than just financial.

To make a list of all players with County and Bradford League experience would take a book in itself but there is no doubt that the League have gained much from having County players come to Bradford and the Counties have gained much also from the best breeding ground in the country.

An up to date illustration of County Connections shows that in 1988 a Yorkshire team could include, Ashley Metcalfe, Martyn Moxon, Kevin Sharp, David Bairstow, Phil Carrick, Phil Robinson, Neil Hartley, Peter Hartley and Chris Pickles all of whom learnt their trade in the League. The 'Uncapped' colts like Simon Kellett, Chris Shaw, Paul Booth, Phil Berry, Neil Nicholson, Bradley Parker, Paul Grayson, Jamie Robinson and Phil Anderson are all playing in the League.

Bill Athey is with Gloucestershire, Tim Boon, David Ripley, Nick Cook, Les Taylor, Neil Mallender, Roy Piennar and others are scattered throughout the Counties after Bradford League beginnings.

When Worcestershire played in the Nat West Trophy Final at Lords, in September 1988 they had Steven Rhodes, Richard Illingworth and David Leatherdale who all commenced their careers in the Bradford League.

Yorkshire sides have been known regularly in the past and particularly in the 1970's and 1980's to field teams which included eight, sometimes nine, players, all with Bradford League experience. Long may it remain so.

Chapter Seven
Magic of the Priestley Cup

In whatever sport, there is always extra interest when Cup time comes around. The Bradford League is no exception. Although there was no such competition in the League's inaugural season, the year of 1904 brought the first Priestley Charity Cup Competition (to give it its full name). It has been a most popular event for players and spectators ever since.

The Cup, given by Alderman W.E.B. Priestley, was for clubs in the Bradford District to compete for annually, but the trophy was to be owned by the Bradford League and should the League ever cease, the trophy will be the property of the Governors of Bradford Royal Infirmary. In 1904 the Cup was taken on a tour to all four villages competing in the Preliminary Round, and then displayed in the window of a City Centre Jewellers, Manoah Rhodes, until the Final. Lidget Green were to play hosts to this first Priestley Cup Final, and Allerton and Shelf were in opposition. Alas this was rather a one sided affair. Allerton who batted first making 202 of which opener William Robertshaw scored 112, batting through. In reply Shelf were never in it and had slumped to 77-7 when play was ended by bad weather so it was not until Wednesday evening that the game could end. A fresh wicket had to be cut too to allow the match to conclude, and only twenty deliveries were needed for Allerton to take the last three wickets and with them the Cup. Alderman Priestley's wife presented the Cup to the Allerton skipper, Wilkinson. While they were never to win the trophy again and are now no longer competing for it, the club are at least remembered as the first winners.

Another side no longer in the League reached the Finals of 1905 and 1906, Clayton, and batting first on both occasions made totals of just 122 and 79 to be beaten by Saltaire and Great Horton respectively. In 1907 a record, albeit an unwanted one, was created which still stands. That of the lowest total in a Priestley Cup Final. Windhill and Bankfoot were in opposition and batting first Windhill made a disappointing 129, yet they won by 102 runs as Bankfoot could muster just 27. It was Windhill's third Bradford League season, and in their first they took part in one of the most amazing of Priestley Cup ties. Playing against Laisterdyke in their first ever cup-tie, Windhill bowled out Laisterdyke for just 29 and lost. Laisterdyke were winners by three runs, and after this 1st round knockout Windhill were also knocked out at that stage the following year. So 1907 was the first year they'd even reached Round Two. They had only one run to spare over Great Horton in their 1907 semi-final before facing Bankfoot. Halliday was their star in that Final with 6-14.

After their one run semi-final defeat Great Horton hadn't long to wait for a Final appearance. In fact three years in a row they took part in it, beating Lidget Green in 1909 by 7 wkts, and losing to Undercliffe in 1910 by 118 runs. For their third successive Final Windhill were their opponents. Great Horton batted and totalled 262 but Windhill had no answer to J. Parkin who took 5-11 and Great Horton won by a massive 166 runs.

A new name appeared on the Trophy in 1912, Idle, who had a comfortable eight wicket margin over Undercliffe (58 all out) but 1913 and 1914 belonged to Bradford.

The League were to lose Bradford and its Park Avenue ground during the war, but before it was requisitioned, Bradford beat Great Horton by 80 runs in 1913 and retained the Cup, the first club to do so, with a 61 run margin over Windhill. Playing for Bradford was the father of J.M. Kilburn, (then just four years old) who became Senior Cricket Correspondent for the Yorkshire Post in 1934. He went on to write, The Official History of Yorkshire CCC 1924 – 39 and various other books, never forgetting his first taste of spectatorship at Bradford League games.

Windhill were to be runners-up for the third time in five years when, in 1915, they met, "new sensation" Bowling Old Lane. In their first season they reached the Final and were Champions for a unique double. Old Lane's Cup exploits started with Undercliffe whom they beat by three

51

THE FIRST PRIESTLEY CUP FINAL – 1904

ALLERTON v SHELF

INNINGS OF ALLERTON

	BATSMEN	HOW OUT	BOWLER	TOTAL
1	WILKINSON W.	c SWITHENBANK	BATES	7
2	ROBERTSHAW W.	NOT	OUT	112
3	TWYFORD N.	b	BATES	4
4	WILKINSON E.	ST. SWITHENBANK	FIRTH	2
5	STUART DR.	c & b	HIRST	1
6	WILKINSON H.	LBW	HIRST	5
7	ILLINGWORTH J.	b	HIND E.	40
8	KNIGHT E.	LBW	HIND E.	4
9	GIRLING A.	b	HIND E.	2
10	DODSON S.	HIT. WKT.	FIRTH	10
11	VARLEY L.	b	FIRTH	3

EXTRAS 12
TOTAL 202 FOR 10 WKTS.

INNINGS OF SHELF

	BATSMEN	HOW OUT	BOWLER	TOTAL
1	SWITHENBANK S.	b	WILKINSON E	22
2	FIRTH N.	c VARLEY	ROBERTSHAW	28
3	HELLINGS S.	c ROBERTSHAW	GIRLING	2
4	SYKES T.	LBW	GIRLING	0
5	BATES A.	b	KNIGHT	16
6	HIND E.	NOT	OUT	5
7	PETTY E.	c STUART	WILKINSON H	2
8	HIND A.H.	b	WILKINSON H	0
9	ROBINSON E.	c VARLEY	GIRLING	0
10	HIRST E	b	WILKINSON E	0
11	KELLETT	b	WILKINSON H	0

EXTRAS 4
TOTAL 79 FOR 10 WKTS.

52

wickets with 90 from the bat of Charles Grimshaw. In the Second Round there were fine performances for Bowling Old Lane by Fred Popplewell 97* and A. Emsley 56 backed up with 5-23. I mention those two first so they are not overshadowed by what comes next. Old Lane totalled a magnificent 455 and Charles Grimshaw scored 230, a record which still stands as the highest individual innings in a Priestley Cup tie. In the semi-final Grimshaw made 72* and batted through as Saltaire were beaten by 53 runs. Ernest Holdsworth, who later became the oldest first team Bradford League cricketer (aged 71), took 5-13 in Saltaire's reply. When Windhill were dismissed for 107 their only chance was to dismiss Grimshaw very very early, they failed and he scored 71* as Bowling romped home by 10 wickets. In four cup-ties Grimshaw scored a total of 463 runs for only twice out. Average 231.50. Quite startling. After a victory over Queensbury by 155 runs in 1916 Old Lane lost their first ever cup match to Undercliffe by 8 wickets, who proved too good and then went onto face Tong Park in two consecutive Finals, winning both.

Prior to 1918 there had only been one close Final that being Saltaire's eight run margin over Clayton in 1905. Saltaire were again in the Final of 1918 which was to prove the closest of all. Read what the Pudsey and Stanningley News had to say about the tied Final and the replay.

REMARKABLE CRICKET
Saltaire v Bankfoot – Match ends in tie
£400 gate – £40 collection for Firth

The Priestley Cup Final at Park Avenue on Saturday had more than a passing interest for Pudsey cricketers by the fact that Bankfoot, who were meeting Saltaire, were themselves beaten by Pudsey Britannia in a league fixture the previous week, while in the Cup semi-final the 'Footers' got the best of Pudsey St Lawrence in an encounter at Lidget Green which will be remembered for many a long day.

The tussle on Saturday ended in a tie. Saltaire leading off with a score of 99, made in two hours and forty minutes and the total was equalled by Bankfoot just as twilight was setting in. The crowd numbered 13,500 and the receipts amounted to £406, against £190 taken at last years Final – the previous best. It is many years since such a sum was taken at Park Avenue, even in a County match.

Both sides were indebted largely to one batsman for the totals they compiled. Firth, for Saltaire and Shackleton for Bankfoot, opened their respective innings and each 'got his eye in' as the phrase goes, before the effects of the roller had worn off the wicket. Of the two performances Shackleton's appealed more to the imagination. It was freer from blemish to start with, for Firth was badly missed in the slips when he had made 13 and his innings would have terminated at 36 but for a misunderstanding between the fieldsmen as to who should go for a proffered catch on the leg-side. Shackleton who had to hold his end up against twenty one overs sent down by Barnes, some of them when the wicket was at its worst, gave no real chance in his 47 and his innings was played when his side had their backs to the wall – just the circumstances that appeal to a Yorkshire crowd.

There was another point in which Bankfoot showed to better advantage and that was in the brighter character of their batting. They got their runs off 42 overs whilst their opponents required 60. What the match lost in spectacular interest was compensated for in the fighting finish. Firth batted two hours and five minutes for his 53 runs and on completing 50 the usual collection was made and it yielded £40 which is of course a record. All went well with Saltaire until they passed the 70 mark with two wickets down, Firth and Outram having got a fine start with 34 for the first wicket. There was another good stand by Firth and Moody who took the total from 44 to 76 for the third wicket, although the last named batsman was something of a passive resister, staying half an hour for 9. When he left things began to happen, Nutter and Fell carrying all before them. Nutter, who bowled brilliantly, but without a trace of luck, had three

BANKFOOT CRICKET CLUB v SALTAIRE C. CLUB

PRIESTLEY CUP FINAL. PLAYED AT PARK AVENUE ON SAT. 17th AUGUST 1918

Innings of SALTAIRE

	BATSMEN	HOW OUT	BOWLER	TOTAL
1	FIRTH M.	st. LAMB	FELL	53
2	OUTRAM R.	c BOTTOMLEY	TASKER	13
3	BARNES S.F.	c NUTTER	FELL	4
4	MOODY W.	bowled	FELL	9
5	SEDGWICK H.	c. LAMB	NUTTER	2
6	FEATHER H.	NOT	OUT	3
7	SWITHENBANK S	bowled	FELL	5
8	SMITH C.	c. TASKER	NUTTER	0
9	EASTWOOD C.R.	c. KITCHINGMAN	NUTTER	0
10	SLACK J.	c LAMB	FELL	4
11	WHITELEY P.	LBW	NUTTER	3

ATTENDANCE — 13,500
EXTRAS 3
TOTAL 99 FOR 10 WKTS.

Innings of BANKFOOT

	BATSMEN	HOW OUT	BOWLER	TOTAL
1	SHACKLETON E.B.	NOT	OUT	47
2	PAYTON W.	RUN	OUT	10
3	NUTTER R.	c WHITELEY	BARNES	0
4	SPRING A.W.	c SMITH	BARNES	4
5	BOTTOMLEY M.	c WHITELEY	BARNES	3
6	KITCHINGMAN J.	c WHITELEY	BARNES	3
7	LEACH P.	c SLACK	BARNES	0
8	LAMB J.	c FEATHER	BARNES	1
9	TASKER H.	c EASTWOOD	BARNES	11
10	RENTON S.	c SLACK	BARNES	5
11	FELL A.	bowled	SLACK	11

GATE RECEIPTS — £406.
EXTRAS 4
TOTAL 99 FOR 10 WKTS.

FALL OF EACH WICKET (Saltaire): 34 | 44 | 76 | 79 | 89 | 90 | 91 | 91 | 96 | 99

FALL OF EACH WICKET (Bankfoot): 20 | 20 | 26 | 35 | 39 | 39 | 41 | 62 | 78 | 99

BOTH TEAMS AWARDED WINNERS MEDALS

BOWLERS	OVERS	MD'NS	RUNS	WKTS	AV'GE
1 R. NUTTER	25.3	8	36	4	9.00
2 A. FELL	24	6	42	5	8.4
3 H. TASKER	6	3	9	1	9.00
4 A.W. SPRING	5	0	9	0	—

BOWLERS	OVERS	MD'NS	RUNS	WKTS	AV'GE	
1 S.F. BARNES	21	4	50	8	6.25	inc 'HAT TRICK'
2 H. SEDGWICK	15	2	35	0	—	
3 J. SLACK	6	2	10	1	10.00	
4	—					

BANKFOOT CRICKET CLUB v SALTAIRE C. CLUB

REPLAYED — PRIESTLEY CUP FINAL. PLAYED AT BOWLING OLD LANE ON MONDAY 19th AUGUST 1918

Innings of BANKFOOT

	BATSMEN	HOW OUT	BOWLER	TOTAL
1	SHACKLETON E.B.	bowled	SLACK	29
2	PAYTON W.	bowled	BARNES	16
3	NUTTER R.	bowled	SEDGWICK	6
4	SPRING A.W.	c FEATHER	SEDGWICK	9
5	BOTTOMLEY M.	c SLACK	SEDGWICK	0
6	RENTON S.	c SEDGWICK	BARNES	11
7	TASKER H.	c WHITELEY	BARNES	0
8	LAMB J.	c SWITHENBANK	BARNES	3
9	LEACH P.	bowled	SEDGWICK	4
10	POLLARD A.E.	NOT	OUT	8
11	FELL A.	bowled	BARNES	2

ATTENDANCE — Approx 11,000 (10,069 PAID)
EXTRAS 1
TOTAL 89 FOR 10 WKTS.

Innings of SALTAIRE

	BATSMEN	HOW OUT	BOWLER	TOTAL
1	OUTRAM R.	bowled	SPRING	37
2	FIRTH M.	bowled	POLLARD	15
3	MOODY W.	c LAMB	NUTTER	9
4	SEDGWICK H	NOT	OUT	9
5	BARNES S.F.	NOT	OUT	16
6	SWITHENBANK S			
7	FEATHER H.			
8	EASTWOOD C.R.	D.N.B.		
9	SLACK J.			
10	WHITELEY P.			
11	SMITH C.			

GATE RECEIPTS — £235
EXTRAS 5
TOTAL 91 FOR 3 WKTS.

FALL OF EACH WICKET (Bankfoot): 24 | 31 | 41 | 41 | 71 | 71 | 75 | 75 | 86 | 89

FALL OF EACH WICKET (Saltaire): 28 | 49 | 72

BOWLERS	OVERS	MD'NS	RUNS	WKTS	AV'GE
1 S.F. BARNES	19	6	43	5	8.6
2 H. SEDGWICK	15	4	34	4	8.5
3 J. SLACK	7	2	11	1	11.0
4	—				

BOWLERS	OVERS	MD'NS	RUNS	WKTS	AV'GE
1 R. NUTTER	14	1	28	1	28.00
2 A. FELL	8.1	1	22	0	—
3 A.E. POLLARD	9	4	22	1	22.00
4 A.W. SPRING	4	0	13	1	13.00

54

catches missed off him in the slips and yet had a return of 4 for 36. Fell a cunning left-hander with good command of length, taking five wickets for 42.

When Shackleton opened Bankfoot's innings against Barnes and Sedgwick their policy was just the reverse of that of Saltaire for they went for the runs while the wicket was newly rolled. Twenty were on the board in ten minutes when Payton, the Notts cricketer, was run out by a gross want of judgement and thereupon other wickets fell so rapidly that 7 were down with only 41 scored. Three of these were taken in consecutive deliveries by Barnes. Kitchingman being snapped up at the wicket and Leach at slip, while after a stoppage for rain Lamb put the ball into the hands of short-leg when Barnes resumed. Barnes' performance met with a big ovation and £9 was collected for him.

Then came Bankfoot's revival. Tasker staying 35 minutes and helping the score to 62. Renton 'stuck it' gamely for half an hour while the score mounted to 78 and later, Fell who seemed the coolest player on the field, with two fours to the leg of Barnes brought the scores to 96. Thus four was required to win when Shackleton faced Slack, the slow left-hander, and a two to leg added to the excitement. A powerful straight drive would probably have won the match for Bankfoot but the ball struck the opposite wickets and only a single was run.

This brought the game to a tie and Fell was bowled by the very next ball, Shackleton thus batting through the innings. Barnes took 8 wickets for 50 runs. Sedgwick met with no success, while Slack took 1 wicket for 10 runs. The wicketkeeping of Lamb on one side and Whiteley on the other were outstanding features of the game.

Under the exceptional circumstances the Executive Committee decided on Saturday night that the players of both teams should be presented with medals.

THE REPLAY
(Monday at Bowling Old Lane)

The second meeting of the teams aroused almost as much interest as Saturday's game.

The attendance on Monday on the Bowling Old Lane ground was about 11,000 of whom 10,069 paid for admission, and the gate receipts being £235. The aggregate attendance for this year's Final is thus 25,000 as compared with the previous record of 16,000, whilst the total receipts stand at £641, the best figures previously being £190.

The game ended in a rather easy win for Saltaire by seven wickets. Batting first Bankfoot took two hours and ten minutes to compile the modest total of 89 and were lucky to make so many, for Shackleton, who was top scorer with 29 was missed no fewer than four times. For Saltaire, Sedgwick and Barnes bowled finely, the former being the better of the two on this occasion and, but for lapses in the field, would have had the best bowling figures in the match.

The best batting in the match was displayed by R. Outram for Saltaire. Going in first Outram was third out with the total 72 his share being 37 made in 79 minutes. He might have been stumped when one, off Fell, but afterwards batted well. Barnes batted well and had the satisfaction of making the hit which won the Cup for his side. Saltaire knocked off the runs in just an hour and a half.

The above is an account taken from the *Pudsey and Stanningley News*, of the 1918 Priestley Cup Final – the only Final to end in a tie.

Pudsey St Lawrence reached their first Final in 1919 but Undercliffe kept them 39 runs adrift. After failing to reach one hundred in their previous three finals, Bankfoot reached the 1920 Final and not only failed again to total one hundred but took part in the shortest ever final. They already had the lowest total of 27 and batting first against Bowling Old Lane only just managed to pass that by three runs. Bowling Old Lane reached 30 without loss and the total playing time was just 1 hour 28 minutes, a Final record which still stands. After four unhappy attempts at winning a final, between 1907 and 1920, Bankfoot although having unbroken league membership have never been back. In fact since the First World War they have not even reached the semi-final.

One of the greatest shocks in a final came in 1921 when Keighley were not expected to be a match for Saltaire, Barnes and all. Before the Final was reached there was a record partnership when G. Lawrence 113* and A. Cansfield 63 took part in a ninth wicket stand of 188 for Idle v Low Moor, 79 for 8 became 267 all out but actually the 79 would have been enough, for Vickerstaffe took 6 for 18 and Idle won by 226 runs. Proud of that they then succumbed themselves by 265 runs to Bowling Old Lane. Yet it was Keighley v Saltaire in the Final and Saltaire batting first made 157. With Barnes in their side it was expected to be enough, but this was the one match in nine years when Barnes failed. The match belonged to Herbert Haigh. Firstly he took 5 for 34 in the Saltaire innings and then made 70* as Keighley triumphed by nine wickets. The wicket which fell was that of H. WHitham but he had made 62 before it did, when Keighley were almost home. On route to the Final Keighley had dismissed Tong Park for a paltry 14 which equalled the lowest score in the competition, made by Greengates against Windhill in 1907.

A record last wicket partnership which has stood the test of time came in 1922 when J.E. Nixon 164* and J. Berry 46, put on 163 for Laisterdyke v Eccleshill in round one. Saltaire again reached the Final and once more were runners up, this time Bowling Old Lane scored 23 runs too many. After record breaking stands in 1921 and 1922 the hat-trick was completed in 1923 when H. Taylor 119 and A.E. Lashbrooke 113 put on 184 for the second wicket in the Bowling Old Lane v Windhill second round match. As you may expect Old Lane won, moving on to the Final where Idle (161-7) just pipped them by three wickets.

The first side to score over 300 in the Final was Lightcliffe who did so in 1926, not bad for your first final appearance. They batted first and were indebted to three players, Sam Cadman, former Tong Park and Yorkshire star who made 103*, Ronnie Somers scored 55 and F.T. Poole who made 69. With Hirst taking five wickets, Lidget Green's reply ended at 183. What was even more remarkable than that 316 total was the aggregate Lightcliffe total in their four Cup games. In addition to the Final they scored 331 v Bradford in the semi-final, following 156 v Saltaire and 268-7 v Windhill in earlier rounds. Their 1,071 total from four rounds was a new record. Despite their high totals the margin of victories leading to the Final had only been 20 runs, 3 wickets, and 4 wickets respectively. After a margin of 133 runs over Lidget Green in the Final, an easy win was expected in 1927 when the first round draw threw up the same opponents. Lidget Green however gave a much improved performance though Lightcliffe eventually got through by just ten runs. There was another side making its first final appearance in 1927, Queensbury. In 1922 they had been semi-finalists when Bowling Old Lane beat them by 17 runs. By a strange coincidence in 1927 Queensbury had a first round win against Bowling by the same seventeen run margin. When Windhill totalled 297 in the semi-final Queensbury were not expected to progress beyond that stage, but led by 83 from the captain T.G. Dobson they reached 298 for 6 qualifying to meet Saltaire.

Now Saltaire had two fine bowlers in J.R. Hartley, and T. Mawson. In the semi-final they had a 204 run margin after making 280. A spirited Queensbury effort in the Final was not enough, Saltaire 153-6, winning by four wickets. Bowling Old Lane in 1928 became the first losing side to top 200 in the Final. Batting first they made 243 after which Bingley replied with 244-8. However a book could be written about the Cup Competition that season alone. If Old Lane had an unwanted record of the highest losing score in the Final that year, they were pleased with two other records they created. Firstly their 486 was the highest total in the competition so far, and in that total, which came against East Bierley in the semi-final, five Bowling Old Lane batsmen topped fifty. G. Kennie (77), H. Parkinson (55), H. Elam (90), G. Southall (58) and H. Watson (66). However of these five only one, Southall with sixty two managed a good score in the Final. If 1920 was the shortest Final played, 1928 was certainly the longest. Due to continual bad weather this final took fourteen days to complete. It ended just two weeks after it began. Bowling Old Lane were runners-up in both 1928 and 1929 and this was part of a sequence which began with being beaten finalists in 1923 and continued to 1965, when in nine final appearances during those forty-three seasons, all nine were lost.

Just two years after Bowling Old Lane's 486 in a Priestley Cup-tie, Saltaire broke it by two runs. It was a first round match and in the Saltaire 488 run total no less than 210 came from the willow of F. Stead. Replying to that mammoth total, Keighley actually passed 400 losing by only 85 runs. A match aggregate of 891 with Butterfield (79), Taylor (58), Burton (70) and Gilson (68) all making half centuries in Keighley's spirited reply. Ironically their top batsman that season A.B. Sellars was alas unable to make a significant contribution in this one. Somewhat surprisingly Saltaire lost in round two to East Bierley (by three wickets). Bierley went onto the Final where Idle beat them by six wickets but a whole year was to pass before the semi-final and final were played. So bad was the 1930 weather that the semi's were left over, giving Idle a chance in 1931 to win the 1930 final and be knocked out of the Cup in the same year. Its rather strange that Idle won four cup matches and only three league games for the 1930 season, but as two of these cup-ties were played in 1931 we must be careful not to say they had more cup wins than league wins in the same year.

In the second Priestley Cup Final played in the year of 1931, the rightful one this time, the trophy was back at Undercliffe after a fine final. Batting first Undercliffe scored 184, Bailey Dibb top scoring with 61. Old Lane replied with 171 and Undercliffe triumphed by thirteen runs perhaps thankful that Charles Grimshaw did not play in the Final, having taken 71* and 7 for 49 against them in the league that year. You had to feel sorry for Old Lane now in a permanent "bridesmaids dress". Grimshaw did play in 1932 when Keighley were in opposition. He took 6 for 94 as Keighley made 200 and then scored 55 before Old Lane fell just three runs short, another heartbreak. So near, yet so far. East Bierley came very near in 1933 too, failing only by five runs, chasing an Undercliffe total of 251. This 1933 Undercliffe triumph was their seventh, first winning in 1910. After three close Finals, margins widened, 69 runs for Bradford over Bowling in 1934, 44 runs for Keighley who had suspended against Great Horton in 1935, and 32 runs for Spen Victoria who also suspended in 1936, Lightcliffe being the opposition. Spen were in the 1936 Final mainly through a fine half century from Arnold Robertshaw in the semi-final triumph over Eccleshill. Lightcliffe returned to win the 1937 final by 74 runs despite a cup final hat-trick from J. Petts. Only once before (S.F. Barnes in 1918) had this feat been performed.

At this time, it paid to bat first but when Windhill did so in 1938 they reckoned without Sandy Jacques. Windhill all out 99 were only the second side for eighteen years to fail to raise three figures. Jacques took 9 for 30 which remains the best bowling performances in a Priestley Cup Final. Undercliffe had a little struggle losing six wickets before winning. Two rather unexpected finalists in 1939 were Eccleshill and Spen Victoria. Only four runs had separated Spen from Old Lane in the semi-final, while Eccleshill had only beaten Idle by the same four run margin in round two. In the league, Eccleshill won only four games, yet they won all their cup-ties and when chasing Spen's 197 found the men for such an occasion in T.R. Barker (71) and H. Hardcastle (116*) who put on 188 for the first wicket. When Barber was out Eccleshill were just ten runs from victory, and duly won by nine wickets. It was their first cup final win. Bonny cup fighters Undercliffe were back in 1940, Idle (by six wickets), Keighley (by 46 runs), Queensbury (by seven wickets) and Windhill (by five wickets) were beaten on route to a final meeting with Lidget Green. Undercliffe suspended at 153-8 and had no need to go in again, as Sandy Jacques added 8 for 55 to his 9 for 30 two years earlier, and Lidget were all out three runs away from making Undercliffe bat again.

In 1941 Saltaire were all out 102 (Jacques 6 for 37) and another Undercliffe win was looking very likely. They had a fine side too, Vic Wilson made 159* v Bingley in the semi-final when Undercliffe totalled 326. Freddie Wharton had five wickets in the semi and also in round two against Windhill when a record £135 gate was taken. Les Phillips and Arthur Wood, along with Jacques, made Undercliffe a formidable side, but needing only 103 to win, they were never in it, with Bill Copson taking 6 for 30 Undercliffe were all out 44. The Club had met their match as Saltaire with a team of, J.C. Lee, A. Spencer, A.V. Pope, L.F. Townsend, G.A. Wilson, J.M. Crossley, G.B. Haley, W.H. Copson, H. Pedley, F. Earnshaw and S. Crabtree completed the Cup and League Double (Division Two Champions).

In 1942 Saltaire still had Pope but A.V. had become G.H. as the second of the three Pope brothers replaced his older brother. Playing for Saltaire in 1942 Cup (second round) against

Yeadon, GEORGE POPE OPENED THE BATTING. WHEN THE SCOREBOARD SHOWED 67 FOR 0 THERE HAD BEEN NO EXTRAS, AND ONE OPENER HAD NOT SCORED. POPE HAD ALL 67 TO HIS NAME, THE FIRST SIXTY SEVEN ON THE BOARD. When he was out at 78 for 3, he had scored 75 of them. Saltaire beat Yeadon by three wickets going onto a Final against Windhill where Leslie Townsend took 5 for 22 to dismiss a Windhill side for a disappointing 94 which Saltaire comfortably knocked off.

The 1943 Final had the added attraction of Len Hutton, for Pudsey St Lawrence, who had yet to win the trophy and were in only their second Final in 25 years. Pudsey had been taken close in their early rounds. First Queensbury, who lost by only three runs, with George Hutton being the Pudsey "star" scoring 86*. Lightcliffe were beaten by 32 runs but this needed a great performance from Len Hutton who took 6 for 36 after Roland Parker had top scored with 57*. The Hutton brothers saw the back of East Bierley by thirty eight runs when Len made 51* and George 53* before suspension. Prior to the Final, Pudsey had a shock when Squire Render was unable to play through injury and a second team player T. Lowe was drafted in. Batting first Pudsey made 149 with Len Hutton scoring 64. In reply Brighouse only managed one more than Hutton himself and as Pudsey won by 84 runs it was largely due to that second teamer Lowe who took 6 for 24. A great day for him in such illustrious company.

After all his fine performances in 1942 in the Cup, George Pope was to the fore again in 1944. By now he was at Spen Victoria and if ever a man dominated a final, Pope did so in 1944. Yeadon were the victims as Pope first of all scored 76 out of 151-8 susp. and then he took 6 for 36 in a Yeadon reply of 79 all out. Yeadon (runners-up in 1944) and Pudsey (winners in 1943) met in the Final of 1945. Yeadon were in the Final by way of victories over, East Bierley, Lidget Green, and Spen Victoria. They had Charles Harris of Notts, James Cutmore of Essex, and Horace Fisher of Yorkshire in their side. Pudsey had the Hutton brothers and Arthur Vickers, but it was Yeadon who triumphed comfortably by sixty one runs.

Eccleshill reached the 1946 Final and by now had among their ranks Sandy Jacques who in three previous Cup Finals with Undercliffe had taken 23 wickets. Jacques wasn't the only bowler Baildon had to worry about for in the semi-final that "cricket conjurer" Johnnie Wardle had mesmerised and tantalised the Great Horton batsmen as only he could. Wardle had finished with 6 for 12 guiding his side safely into that final. Batting first Eccleshill reached the suspension point of 150 with seven wickets down, and could have gone in again, but Sandy Jacques was at it again, taking wickets in a final had become almost a habit it seemed as he took 5 for 47 and Baildon were all out 125.

In four final Jacques had taken a total of 28 wickets. That is 7 per innings, at a cost of just 6.04 runs each. A tremendous feat by a tremendous and much respected man.

Records tumbled once more in the 1947 Final when Yeadon opposed Salts. Now we had the highest number of runs in a Final as Yeadon made 365 and Salts 307 in reply. A young Dennis Bateson scored 90 for Yeadon and Joe Lodge made the highest individual cup score of the season with 133. The Salts reply contained 87 from Newall and 69 from Firth, but in a match where batting shone it was ex-Hunslet and Australian rugby player Arthur Clues who had the last word taking six Salts wickets for 84.

The uncertainty of cricket helps make it the great game it is. The Priestley Cup over the years has contained many "Tales of the Unexpected". Fifty years ago Les Phillips made 79* for Undercliffe against Pudsey (1938 semi-final) and no one topped that score in the whole of that season's competition. Perhaps the 124* by Eddie Paynter for Keighley v Salts in the 1948 competition was not unexpected, but in 1949 a youngster at Farsley scored 148* against Pudsey. He was 16 years old when the innings started and 17 years old when it finished having celebrated his birthday on one of the days during which the game took place. His name, Raymond Illingworth. It was 29 years before anyone beat that individual score in a Priestley Cup match and we all know what a fine player and captain of his country that young lad became. Tom Falkingham and Jim Illingworth put on an unbroken 180 for the sixth wicket in the Final of 1949 for Yeadon against Farsley. They came together with the total 21 for 5 and Yeadon supporters fearing the worst. It brought them victory too—by one run batting second. That all

SPEN VICTORIA CRICKET CLUB v YEADON C. CLUB

PRIESTLEY CUP FINAL PLAYED AT PARK AVENUE ON 16th SEPT 1944

INNINGS OF SPEN VICTORIA

	BATSMEN	HOW OUT	BOWLER	TOTAL
1	SYKES C.	LBW	SMITH	0
2	HAMER A.	LBW	SMITH	17
3	MELLING F.	c HARRIS	SMITH	28
4	POPE G.H.	c BATESON	SMITH	76
5	WATERHOUSE H.	b	MAUD	4
6	STEAD C.	LBW	SMITH	2
7	WATERHOUSE A.	c HARRIS	FISHER	1
8	ROBERTSHAW A.	b	SMITH	1
9	CARTER N.	NOT	OUT	11
10	BEAUMONT F.	NOT	OUT	2
11	BOOTH A.	D.N.B.		1

EXTRAS 9
TOTAL 151
SUSP. FOR 8 WKTS.

	BOWLERS	OVERS	MDNS	RUNS	WKTS	AVGE
1	SMITH J.			51	6	
2	MAUD			28	1	
3	FISHER H.			63	1	
4						

INNINGS OF YEADON

	BATSMEN	HOW OUT	BOWLER	TOTAL
1	HARRIS C.B.	c WATERHOUSE H.	POPE	1
2	BERRY L.G.	c WATERHOUSE H.	POPE	6
3	MOORHOUSE J.	c SYKES	POPE	0
4	SWIFT J.A.	c WATERHOUSE	POPE	4
5	FISHER H.	c MELLING	BOOTH	41
6	BATESON D.	LBW	POPE	0
7	ELLISON I.	st BEAUMONT	BOOTH	12
8	ILLINGWORTH J.	c POPE	BOOTH	0
9	HUTCHINSON A.	c WATERHOUSE	BOOTH	8
10	SMITH J.	NOT	OUT	3
11	MAUD A.	c CARTER	POPE	0

EXTRAS 4
TOTAL 79
FOR 10 WKTS.

	BOWLERS	OVERS	MDNS	RUNS	WKTS	AVGE
1	POPE G.H.			36	6	
2	BOOTH A.			39	4	
3						
4						

came about because of the suspension rule where teams can suspend and go in again batting last having also batted first, if it makes sense.

In 1950 Lightcliffe met East Bierley in the Final and suspended at 154-4 and then bowled out Bierley for 153, winning by one run though of course Lightcliffe could have gone in again. It was an excellent performance by Lightcliffe for they were a Division Two side. Queensbury were no match for Idle in the 1951 Final though with the help of George Senior, Laurie Powell, Jack Moule, Alwyn Gossop, Jim Chatburn and Derek Keeton, Queensbury reached 169. Idle's reply saw Wilf Horner (83*) and Les Horsman (78*) at their very best and a nine wicket win ensued. Horsman spent his winter months in the number 5 shirt for Bradford Park Avenue in Division Three (North). That meant Centre Half in those days, but there was nothing half measure in his cricket and I'm sure quite a few opposing Centre Forwards knew how 100% he was. On the way to that Final an Idle batsman got his name into the record books with the fastest century in the Priestley Cup history. Norman Kitson blasted 100* in the second round out of a total of 304-5 dec. His 'ton' took him just 43 minutes.

Baildon won the Cup in 1952 and as they also completed a Championship hat-trick that season, it can be seen they had a fine side. In the Final they were represented against Keighley by Dobson, Robson, McLean, Hitchenor, Burnet, Dean, Ellis, Snook, Burkinshaw, Moore and Tetley. Batting first Baildon scored 233 for 7 declared, the suspension rule having been done away with. Dennis Dobson made 53. Keighley's reply ended at the dreaded 'Nelson' (111), not the first time that figure was a total in a Priestley Cup Final. Wilf Burkinshaw became only the third player to perform a hat-trick in the Final during the Keighley innings. The first to do so was Syd Barnes in 1918, while Petts performed his for Great Horton in 1937. Following the Burkinshaw hat-trick there were two more in the Final within seven years. Percy Watson for Spen Victoria in 1956 and Derek Webster for Salts in 1958. Then in the last thirty years, none, leaving Barnes, Petts, Burkinshaw, Watson and Webster the only five.

In the 1956 competition Yeadon were moving steadily at 49 for 1 against cup holders Lightcliffe. Half an hour later they were all out, having lost their last nine wickets for 9 runs. Wilcock finished with 6 for 12 and Hartley 4 for 6. Lightcliffe romped home by six wickets having given a lesson in how to keep the pressure on once you get on top. In the third round there was yet another amazing collapse and this time it was Lightcliffe themselves who were on the receiving end of it. Playing against Spen Victoria, Lightcliffe were 65 for 5 chasing only 89 to win. They were all out 65, their last five wickets failing to produce a run as Percy Watson took four wickets in an over. Fact is certainly stranger than fiction. Lightcliffe were only in that third round because of a two run margin against Baildon in round two. When the two sides met in 1957 that margin became a tie and a replay was needed before Baildon progressed in round two. The 1956 Final between Spen and Pudsey looked as if it may produce a 'sting in the tail' for after Watson's hat-trick in Pudsey's 152, Spen were 107 for 9 when Alan Carter and Tony Heaton started accumulating runs. They added 24 and Pudsey were obviously getting a bit concerned. This became great relief when leg spinner Eddie Leadbeater had Heaton caught by Roland Parker, giving Pudsey a 21 runs victory.

The thrills continued unabated in 1957. In Round One Yorkshire Colts Skipper Ronnie Burnet led Baildon to a first round win, while Bradford's Eric Barraclough had to contend with the noise from 62,000 at Odsal for a Rugby League Final as he hit fourteen fours and two sixes across the way at Bankfoot where Bradford won by 147 runs. The Yorkshire Post referring to a "brilliant run out by Kong of Bankfoot's Radcliffe". It was a source of dressing room amusement that Tony King be so referred to, as he wasn't all that large. It reminds me of a report I once sent in to The Spenborough Guardian which was hand written. My reference to a superb catch taken ankle high a yard in from the boundary, was printed as "a yard in from the Laundry". Never again did I submit written reports.

The cup draw of 1957 brought Idle against Great Horton and when it was played Idle topped Division One and Great Horton were at the foot of Division Two. A good chance for a shock but Idle were too good to slip up in that one, and after Great Horton, with 56 from Spittlehouse, ended on 128, Idle quickly knocked them off with only Rowbottom (56) dismissed. The *Yorkshire*

Post printed it as 'Ro Botham', maybe they had a crystal ball into the future for I.T. Botham was just eighteen months old at the time.

Those midweek evening cup matches have now been replaced by Sunday matches. Only do we see mid-week cricket now in cup-ties if rain interferes on a Sunday, but some of those night games threw up extra interest simply because of the length of time between innings, or when the end of play left intriguing situations. Take the 1957 cup-tie between Bingley and East Bierley. Batting first, Bingley scored 158 of which Kilvington made 47 and Norman Kitson had 7 for 76. An average score to ponder twenty four hours. In reply East Bierley were still needing 67 to win with only three wickets left but Malcolm Smith stood firm, made 43 not out and guided his team to a two wicket win. Bierley moved into the semi-final where they dismissed Salts for 112 (Billy Rhodes, father of county keeper, Steve, made 31). In reply East Bierley strolled home by seven wickets with Terry Evans making 57 not out, and helping the club reach its third Priestley Cup Final. Waiting for them in 1957 were Bradford. They had beaten Baildon in the other semi-final when Joe Phillips, with only 66 runs in six league innings, hit 85 in a Bradford total of 245 for 6, too many for Baildon who were without Burnet and Moore who were playing for Yorkshire Colts against Cumberland. Losing out on your Yorkshire Colts by having to continue on successive evenings, was something certain sides disapproved of, thus causing a division of opinion about night matches. Each had their own interest very much at heart and it was clear to see which sides approved and why.

The inter-divisional fixtures were in operation during the 1957 season so Second Division East Bierley, by a strange coincidence, were able to tone up for their cup meeting with Bradford, by playing an inter-divisional fixture against local rivals Spen a few days before the Final. How well they did too. Bierley making 253 for 9 declared and bowling out Spen for just 126. Bradford had been warned. The Final was one of the best of Post War Years. Bierley rose to the occasion. In the face of some fierce bowling from Bob Platt and Mel Ryan, they managed 162 and that great enthusiast for sport, Brian Redfearn, was top scorer with 42. Bradford's reply was steady rather than spectacular and when play ended for the day Bradford needed 75 in 17 overs with eight wickets left. Brian Bolus was 53 not out and Derek Blackburn had a single.

On resumption, twelve runs came from the first two overs upon which "Bierley's Douglas Jardine" took over. No disrespect intended, to Bierley skipper Gordon Phillips who then moved his fielders to the leg side. It was a "seven-two" field and bowlers bowled to their field. Wickets were taken, runs were hard to come by, but his great effort failed as Bradford got home in the penultimate over with a four from Harry McIlvenny. Another great Priestley Cup tie had ended.

The first round of 1958 brought about some close games. Bradford with 45 from Phil Sharpe and 37 from Jackie Birkenshaw beat Undercliffe by ten runs. Lightcliffe all out 90 where Dennis Bateson had taken six wickets beat Saltaire by six runs, Brian Whitham had taken six for the home side. Idle beat Bowling Old Lane by twenty two runs and Bankfoot all out 115 beat Windhill by twenty one. Yeadon beat Farsley by one wicket and East Bierley, with Mick Collins the star, restricted Bingley to 92-7 (Collins 5-23) and then won by five wickets.

In the second round Bankfoot knocked out Pudsey on their own ground by two runs, while both the 1957 finalists, Bradford (at home to Lightcliffe) and East Bierley (at Eccleshill) surprisingly went out. Potential shocks always add extra excitement to Cup games. There was a thrilling finish at Eccleshill in Round Three when, replying to the home sides 123, Yeadon were 119 for 9 with one over remaining. With the second ball of the final over Miles was LBW to Phil Roantree (match winner with 7 for 57) and a four run win placed Eccleshill in the semi-final.

In the semi-final they were opposed by Salts who totalled 200 for 6 declared. Owing to holidays Eccleshill were without certain recognised first teamers. Bill Ellis, better known for his bowling, opened the Eccleshill batting with a seventeen year old third teamer, Jack Gledhill. They had a stand of ninety-two. However Ellis was out for 80, Gledhill for 29 and Salts entered yet another final, their third in eleven years. In their previous two they'd topped 300 and lost, this time 136 for 2 was enough to beat Lidget Green with ease.

I am sure its pleasing to all sports fans when the trophies are shared around a bit. The Priestley Cup has never been dominated by one club and often a ten year span will see at least eight different sides taking the spoils. 1958 was the first year that six ball overs had been used in the League bringing them in line with cricket in many other parts of the Country. Having been brought up on six ball overs it would be wrong of me to draw comparisons, though eight ball overs must surely have been more strain on the bowler. The Bingley v Eccleshill first round tie of 1959 was one of the few times a side batting second had gone too slowly and not made use of its eleven members. Needing 201 to beat Bingley, the Eccleshill reply ended at a rather strange looking 189 for 4. On the same day Chris Balderstone, now "a man in a white coat on the County scene", scored 79 for Baildon but his side were knocked out by Queensbury. It was Queensbury who provided the shock of the season by knocking out holders Salts in round two and by six wickets no less. Idle put paid to Queensbury in round three and reached the semi-final to play Bradford, Bob Beanland a seventeen year old schoolboy playing for Idle witnessed his first three colleagues dismissed for three and went to the wicket when the fourth man fell at 32. He then blitzed his way to 106 in 104 minutes as Idle recovered to 215 for 9 declared. They looked to have the match well in hand until Donald Longbottom (40*) and Harry McIlvenny (24*) used some 'long handle' as the match appeared to be slipping away and turned it completely around. A four wicket win for Bradford.

The second semi-final was equally as exciting. Farsley all out for 117 fought back brilliantly to reduce Bowling Old Lane to 3 for 4, then 21 for 6 and 50 for 7, before Alan Dimbleby and Peter Bretherick put on 68 to take their team to victory. The value of this partnership can be clearly seen as it followed seventeen wickets going down for just 167 runs. So two sides who came back from the dead, would meet in the 1959 final.

The Bradford/Bowling Old Lane Final at Park Avenue in 1959 would I feel cater for all cricketing tastes. Batting of excellent quality came from Tony King (57), Eric Barraclough (79) and Claude Helliwell (25*) as Bradford totalled 198 for 7. Harry Rider with 3 for 41 in 13 overs and Malcolm Shackleton with 2 for 51 in fourteen overs had pleased many with his line and length deliveries. In Old Lane's reply opener Brian Clough playing against his old club reached 50 before Claude Helliwell had him caught behind. Then 53 year old Jack Douglas who had lost none of his old guile kept the batsmen tied down for long periods, taking 2 for 57 but more importantly bowling twenty two overs, five of which were maidens. He was largely responsible for Bowling being restricted to 178 for 8. That was twenty runs short, and speaking of twenty runs, Alan Dimbleby made twenty for Old Lane batting at number five before being run out. His brother Keith went in at number seven also made twenty, and was also run out.

Both Bradford and Bowling Old Lane made great openings to their 1960 Cup campaign. Bradford amassed 248 for 7 and beat Pudsey by 94 runs, while Old Lane, with 98 from Barrie Jenkinson, thrashed Farsley by 136 runs with Harry Rider taking 7 for 17 in Farsley's all out total of 54. Dennis Leng with 8 for 51 put Old Lane out for another year helping Idle beat them in round two despite a great effort from John Walker who had seven Idle wickets for 63 runs. The second round game between Lidget Green and Salts in 1960 contained two record breaking partnerships. Firstly the opening partnership record was broken by Bernard Ellison and Jack Lees who made 119* and 93 respectively, putting on 213 before Lees was dismissed. Lidget ended at 226 for 1 at the end of their 50 overs and many neutrals wondered whether too much caution had been shown. Indeed it had for in reply Salts raced to 227 for 4 with eight overs left, and their record breakers were Alec Hodgson and Horace Barber who put on 124 runs for the fourth wicket. The previous best for that wicket was 104 dating back to 1951, also by two Salts batsmen. Salts were also in good form with the bat in the next round scoring 270 for 9 and beating Bingley with ease.

The star of that third round was one of the first West Indian fast bowlers the League had seen. There had been Achong, Constantine, St Hill and Minott but in 1960 it was Norman Steadman and his 6 for 15 brought East Bierley a win over Queensbury with only a total of 96 to defend. Bradford put paid to Bierley's chances in the semi-final and faced up to Saltaire in the Final. Although a Division Two side Saltaire had knocked out their local rivals Salts who were in Division One, in the semi-final.

Unfortunately, 21 year old skipper, Adrian Gray was unable to bring the best out of Saltaire in the Final and they were soundly beaten. Not that I am in any way criticising Gray who was a fine skipper and worked wonders for Saltaire at times. This time they were beaten by a much better side and if the winners were odds on before the match started, they were at incredibly shorter odds soon after, for Blackburn and King took part in an opening stand of 89 in 70 minutes. King who was dismissed in Bateson's first over scored 101 in 80 minutes. Bateson bowled well as always, his reward being 7 for 91 in 21 overs. W.E.N. Holdsworth the Bradford paceman had the last say, with 8 for 52, and Saltaire were a disappointing 112 all out.

The 1961 Final was in complete contrast. No large innings, a real struggle for supremacy by both teams (Keighley and Bowling Old Lane) but a quite magnificent Final, for its nailbiting finish and its closeness throughout. Bowling Old Lane made only 126 but it contained a spot of amusement when Jackie Hill asked for a runner, play was suspended while the runner padded up and what seemed like an eternity ended with ironic cheers as he emerged from the pavillion. Hill was then out next ball. Keighley's reply was one of those special innings which stands out years later. Good batting, tight bowling and fine fielding. Their was much Keighley relief as Fielding made the winning hit for a two wicket win. Their application brought a just reward. The crowd was just under 5,000 which compared disappointingly with 5,577 the previous year.

Bradford were back in 1962 and opponents East Bierley came under great criticism for only making 186 for 3 at the end of their fifty overs. Many said with seven wickets to fall the total should have been higher. I agree. Lewis Pickles hitting the ball with great vigour and Eddie Slingsby put on 148 for the first wicket before Mike Fearnley had Slingsby caught by Derek Blackburn for 57. Lewis Pickles was run out for 96 trying to push the score along but with seven wickets still to fall after 50 overs, Bierley had a disappointing total. Bradford's reply was halted at 31 for 0 after fourteen overs, but when it continued the following night there was always going to be only winner, Bradford. The match was a personal triumph for skipper Derek Blackburn who was in his last season as Bradford captain. His captaincy and 89 runs playing a vital part, in this tenth Priestley Cup win for the club. This overtook the nine they previously shared with Undercliffe.

In 1963 we heard the first shouts for Sunday Cricket and it came from the Queensbury Club. They suggested this should be possible only by agreement between the two participants thus allowing those who disapproved to continue with night matches. As most readers will be aware it found favour and was eventually adopted and now all Priestley Cup ties are on Sundays, weather permitting.

Bradford were back in the Final in 1963 and their opponents were Farsley. Now this was a real surprise. In round three Farsley had met Division 1 leaders Pudsey, while they themselves had not won a league match so far. With 6 for 53 and 37 not out from J.T. Bairstow, Farsley scraped home by two wickets. A semi-final against Brighouse gave Farsley's Geoffrey Hirst chance to play against the side he used to captain. His score of 54 will have pleased him against his old team mates, but Farsley's score of 134 for 9 in fifty overs is hardly one likely to win a semi-final. Yet win it they did, another example of what application can do, and it brought Farsley into a match which local papers said would surely give Bradford yet another Final victory. Bradford 118 all out, Farsley 119 for 3 tells its own story. In a fifty over cricket match anything can happen, and most times 'anything' does.

Lightcliffe met East Bierley in the 1964 Final, as indeed they did in the 1950 one too. The result was the same, a Lightcliffe win, but whereas in 1950 it was a comfortable six wickets this time it was a nailbiting twelve runs with Bierley's last pair at the wicket. Lewis Pickles now with Bierley scored 122 against Bradford in the semi-final, the highest individual score of the season, but took away a losers medal as Lightcliffe won for the third time in three appearances since 1950, under the same captain, Herbert Aspinall, now their highly-rated secretary. That marvellous Idle side of the mid-sixties fought its way to the Final of 1965 against Bowling Old Lane. Round one brought a three wicket win over Bradford, and after such a hard won victory, against top class opponents, the bye they were given in round two had been earned. Dick Sherred took 6 for 51 and John France hit 51 as Bingley were sent packing in round three and in the semi-final against Lightcliffe Dick Sherred's 7 for 54 provided a thirty run passage to the Final.

The Final belonged almost entirely to Ken Hill and John France. They had a record breaking fourth wicket partnership of 159 which started when Idle were tottering at 33 for 3. It ended at 192 when France was bowled by Malcolm Naylor (what a steady bowler he could be on his day). Hill ended 62 not out and Idle at 192 for 5. It was a match of injuries, Malcolm Naylor stayed on with a bruised foot, paceman Harry Rider of Old Lane went off with a muscle strain as did Ken Woodward the Idle skipper. Old Lane's reply of 55 all out was the lowest total for fourteen years. It was also a tribute to the bowling of Ian Leng, Dick Sherred and Malcolm Swift and some fine captaincy from Ken Woodward. This Final was also famous for the rape which took place on the field of play. An Idle batsman was the victim I believe as he was 'raped' on the pads. Hmm. It was viewed by a few thousand people too. Misprints in newspapers now and then do add a little bit of humour to the game. Not that I ever felt there was a shortage of it in Bradford League circles.

Once more a first round meeting brought together a match between the previous years finalists. Idle and Bowling Old Lane had a much closer game than the 1965 Final. In fact it couldn't have been much closer. Old Lane once more collapsed this time for 71 and Dick Sherred had just two wickets with brother Martin the other eight. The Old Lane got among 'em making Idle fight very hard. If it hadn't been for Stuart Herrington's 29* I doubt if Idle would have seen round two, as it was they beat Old Lane by two wickets. While all this was going on there was a sending off at Windhill. It took place in the Priestley Shield (the 2nd XI cup competition). While Keighley 1st XI were beating Windhill by five wickets, second teamer G. Needham refused to bowl from one end of the Windhill ground saying it was unsuitable for his type of bowling. Skipper Kedward sent Needham off and Keighley who had won the Priestley Shield the year before were knocked out. Geoff Needham duly apologised to Mike Kedward when called before the Keighley Committee to explain his conduct and although in his 'teens' he acted like a man, albeit in retrospect and the matter was forgotten with Needham giving his assurance such action would not be repeated.

Idle, who in 1966, were in the middle of a hat-trick of Championship Titles and who were also Cup holders, got their marching orders in the 1966 third round at Bingley. Stylish, classy, extremely talented, say what you will it all applies to Ken Standring who in this match scored 32 runs and took five Idle wickets as Bingley triumphed by 49 runs. The semi-finals brought Laisterdyke face to face with Eccleshill and Bradford had home advantage against Bingley. Sunday play was in operation in 1966 for the first time and the semi's were played on consecutive Sundays. This was ideal for all those wanting to see both. Laisterdyke entered their first Final thanks to Jack Hainsworth, who was carried from the field shoulder high after the semi-final victory. When Eccleshill had made 216 for 6, Hainsworth took 3 for 43. He followed this with fifty in 46 minutes, his next 44 in 25 minutes leaving him 94* as Eccleshill were beaten by six wickets. Hainsworth and Harold Gill who opened, put on 77 before Gill was out for 59. There was 40 from Goolam Abed and this was the sort of team performance to concern the Bradford and Bingley lads who watched it.

The following Sunday there was no play due to rain, which meant that Bradford would be without Derek Blackburn when the match got under way on the Monday night. Bingley batted and met Mike Fearnley at his deadliest. There was an encouraging 29 from David Batty, but all else failed and Bingley were all out 67. (Fearnley 6 for 26). What a shock Bradford were to get in reply. Ken Standring took five wickets for four runs in six overs and the home side slid to 18 for 6. Then came a stand of 29 between Bulman and Burnett (Tony) but Bradford still needed fourteen with their last pair at the wicket. Last man Mike Harrison chanced his arm and made all fourteen, his last two scoring shots being boundaries. Fortune favoured the brave yet again, but how Bingley fought.

A somewhat fortunate Bradford found the Final much easier in which Laisterdyke did not do themselves justice. All out 92 they failed by 66 runs. The Final had been arranged for August Bank Holiday Monday and one of the Umpires chosen was to be the Rev. Robert Burd (no relation to Harold, in fact its spelt differently). Alas the Final was postponed to a Sunday when the Rev. Burd was therefore no longer available to officiate.

Rain ruined most of the cup-ties in the first round of the Priestley Cup in 1967 and caused Undercliffe some problems. Had the match at Spen gone ahead they could have called upon County players Les Jackson, David Smith, Alan Ward, Jim Brailsford, Ashley Harvey-Walker and Roger Wrightson. The match was moved to the following Monday but realising in time that David Smith would not be available for the Monday fixture he went to Undercliffe to make an appearance in the Priestley Shield match which was played in considerable drizzle for the most part and Smith perhaps not too unexpectedly scored an unbeaten century. When the First XI match was eventually played Undercliffe were able to call on Jackson, Brailsford and Harvey-Walker but found Percy Watson (7 for 59) too strong and were all out 107 losing by 67 runs. 1967 was notable for the first appearance of two teenagers, and not late teens either. A fifteen year old David Bairstow and fourteen year old Phil Carrick, little did we realise the heights those two would reach in future years.

An early 'star' in the 1967 competition was Brian Askham of Eccleshill who after three rounds had taken twelve wickets for a total of 118 and led his side to three victories. In the semi-final Askham and his team faced Bradford. Replying to Bradfords 183 (Askham 1 for 54) Eccleshill were going smoothly at 45 for 1. Then in ten overs they scored only six runs slumping to only 53 when the sixth wicket fell. Askham and Emsley thereafter made a tremendous effort, Askham finished with 52* and Eccleshill reached 171 for 8 and caused many hearts to flutter before Bradford went to their fourteenth Final. Despite an innings of 90 from Yorkshire Colt Barry Leadbeater, Bradford could not stop Bingley winning the Cup for the first time since 1928. Jack Roe and Ken Standring shared a second wicket partnership of 108 and Bingley declared at 219 for 8. It was Standring again with the ball who had Bradford struggling, their last eight wickets fell for just 18 runs, with David Batty (5 for 68) lending excellent support.

After losing all nine Finals in which they appeared between 1923-65 Bowlng Old Lane reached the 1968 Final and actually won. It was obviously a popular victory apart from opponents Saltaire, yet even they I suppose would have agreed if they had to lose it, it would be better to lose to Old Lane who were deserving some Cup success after all their tears and heartbreak. It was close too, just eighteen runs at the end in a match where neither side managed at any time to look really on top.

Bingley having won in 1967 missed out in '68 but were in the next three finals. In 1969 they won easily (9 wickets chasing Spens 109). One year later they lost easily, all out 44 batting first and a performance to forget. When they met Spen again in a repeat of the 1969 Final, they soon had the initiative whipping Spen out for 119. However this time Spen were made of sterner stuff and made Bingley fight every inch of the way. Seven wickets were taken before Bingley finally reached 123 to win. In fairness they only like to win in an odd year, 1967, 1969, 1971, they forgot themselves in 1978 but since then have had two more odd wins in 1979 and 1987.

Undercliffe won the Priestley Cup in 1972, 74 and 1975 making up for a lapse that went back thirty two years. In the third of these Undercliffe passed 230, only the second Club to do so since 1952. There was an outstanding performance in the second round match between Pudsey St Lawrence and Hartshead Moor in 1975. Keith Smith (109*) and Tony Page (80*) put on 160 for the fifth wicket, a new record for the competition. Smith's 109 was the highest individual score that year. Idle's win by 65 runs in 1976 was a little unexpected for they had struggled a little in previous rounds. A win over Lightcliffe was by just four runs and Undercliffe ran them quite close in the semi-final before Mike Bailey with 5 for 60 ended any nonsense as far as Idle were concerned. With 82 from Brian Lymbery and 72 from Tony Moore, Idle were always in the ascendency in the Final with Bingley and it was this same Tony Moore who helped create the sensation of the 1977 competition.

Playing against Cleckheaton in the second round of 1977 Tony Moore and Malcolm Mawson put Idle in the record books again with a first wicket stand of 273. It is the highest stand for any wicket in the Cup and Moore ended up 183 not out. The highest individual score not only of the season, but since Stead's 210 in 1930.

A new name went on the trophy in 1977, however, when the winners were Manningham Mills. Lightcliffe provided the opposition in an open Final, with no side really favourites over the other. Batting first Lightcliffe made a creditable 192, Martin Radcliffe scoring 72. Manningham's reply owed a lot to Phil Sharpe's 97, though as Manningham triumphed by four wickets it would be wrong not to mention the part Richard Noble had played with 5 for 70. Manningham were doing a Bingley appearing in the Final only when it was an odd year. This they did in 1975, 77 and 1979 and in 1979, their third final, it was Bingley 'the odd specialists' whom they met. That Bingley triumphed over Manningham Mills was due largely to a knock of 119 by Neil Hartley to add to his 97 in the previous Final. Mills couldn't quite fathom the leg spin of David Batty who finished with 7 for 57 leaving Manningham Mills 87 runs short. The finalists met in the second round of the following year and Manningham gained revenge by one wicket in a real nailbiter, (John Harker 28*). It was felt throughout the League that to beat Manningham you had to get Phil Sharpe early, well that certainly helped, but it was easier said than done. When he made 114* in round three, Laisterdyke were bewitched, bothered and bewildered. In the semi-final he made 57 against East Bierley who, batting first, were all out 184. Paul Topp who had bowled Sharpe, came on for a second vital spell and bowled Swallow who had made 55. Mills were 167 for 5 with three overs left. Phil Taylor took two wickets keeping his cool, to swing the game in Bierley's favour but John Wilde struck a six and when the final over started Mills were 178 for 7. Just seven needed. A leg bye came from the first delivery and after not scoring from the second, Wilde managed a boundary from the third, but was out to the fourth ball and when David Jay was bowled by Taylor first ball it left one to tie, two to win and only one delivery left. Paul Harrand made some contact and he and Noble set off as if pursued by something terrifying and scraped a single bringing the scores level and forcing a replay. Bierley did get rid of Sharpe cheaply in the replay, for eighteen in fact, and his club totalled 168. When Bierley reached 138 for 3 they had only six overs left at which point Murphy Walwyn took over, taking 26 from an over by Don Wilson. In fact when he drove a six for the game winning shot, his last 32 had come in just seven scoring strokes and East Bierley were in the Final.

It was Undercliffe who were successful in 1980 the thirteenth time they had carried off the Trophy, Bierley never really got to grips with them. Openers Page (29) and Coates (20) had them off to a steady start followed by Crossland (21) and then Ray Peel 76*. A total of 195 for 7 didn't look a great deal but only Chris Broadby the Tasmanian with 27* and Phil Taylor with 26, both lower order batsmen, showed signs of staying there long. Undercliffe's Steve Sylvester, though he batted (1), was unable to bowl because of a badly injured thumb but in a depleted Undercliffe attack John White 'the old stager' shone with 5 for 43 in twenty overs. East Bierley would be disappointed to end at 163 for 9.

In 1981 Bierley were back in the Final. This time Farsley were in opposition but they were swept aside. After seven previous finals (all lost), East Bierley at last got their hands on the Trophy. One hour after the tea interval you wouldn't have given much for Bierley's chances. Having made 195 for 5 they couldn't part Farsley openers Mark Brearley and Billy Holmes. Both passed fifty and with all wickets standing Farsley needed only 82 when the scoreboard stood at 114 without loss. It was at this point Paul Topp struck, bowling Holmes, his next delivery had Steve Wundke leg before wicket but still Farsley looked well on top (if you'll pardon the expression). When Brearley was stumped, again off the bowling of Topp and Tony Lush run out for none, panic set in. Topp took three more wickets, skipper Taylor took three and Farsley were all out for 158. What a fightback by Bierley and not surprisingly Paul Topp (6 for 44) won the Man of the Match Award.

Playing in the Priestley Cup competition of 1982 was one of cricket's greatest leg-spinners, at any level. Abdul Qadir. In round one against Spen Victoria he scored 19 and took 5 for 10 in six overs as Spen were dismissed for 73. In round two v Undercliffe, Qadir hit 12 in his teams 150 for 8 declared. In the Undercliffe reply he'd bowled one over costing a single when the Hanging Heaton captain David Garner wanted Abdul to change ends. Abdul who had taken seven wickets the day before from the end at which he was bowling, refused to do so and was taken off. His action cost his side the match as they lost by two wickets. After taking the step of suspending Qadir for three games the Club were quite rightly praised for their action, and eventually Qadir's contract was cancelled by mutual consent. Undercliffe, no doubt glad to have Abdul's aid towards their victory, profited by going all the way. Pudsey St Lawrence and East Bierley provided the two hardest opponents they could have been drawn against but they came through with flying colours thanks to Richard Coates' fifty against Pudsey and Deryck Crossland's 61 against Bierley. Les Bradbury took 3 for 67 in 25 overs v Pudsey and David Dobson 5 for 42 in the semi.

Opposition in the Final was surprisingly provided by Eccleshill. They had faced Yorkshire Bank in the semi-final and a century by Marsden Claughton (with two fingers strapped together because of a chipped bone) put Bank on top as they reached 196 all out. When Eccleshill had made only five runs from their first eight overs not many expected them to triumph. Des Wyrill (46) and Wayne Giebel (36) gave matters a turn for the better but with twelve overs left Eccleshill were 128-5. Peter Vallance with a quickfire thirty made it all possible and amidst great excitement Barry Firn and Peter Haslam obtained twenty-eight runs in the last five overs, with Firn hitting the winning boundary from the third ball of the final over. Another semi-final to store away and recall during long winter evenings. Having obtained their winning runs at 8.30 pm in that semi-final, Eccleshill wisely chose to bat first in the Final. After ten overs Dave Hallett and Brian Shirley had scored fifty without loss, but soon after both were removed by Les Bradbury, Des Wyrill took over making 68. After his departure, Peter Vallance thrashed 52 not out, so that despite some economical bowling from David Dobson (1 for 26 in 10 overs) and Les Bradbury bowling through (25-3-103-3) Eccleshill reached a highly respectable 234-5 dec.

Undercliffe also had fifty for the first wicket before Crossland was out to Robinson for 33. At the half way stage the scoreboard read 94-1 and the scene was set for the onslaught. The fact that Undercliffe failed (all out 198) was due in no small measure to the bowling of Andy Wilsdon and Mick Robinson. Robinson with 4 for 61 in 22 overs was deservedly named Man of the Match.

Eccleshill had risen once more to the occasion gaining their third Priestley Cup Final win. It was far removed in both time and result from that day in 1928 when these same opponents, Undercliffe, had dismissed them for 19.

Farsley spent all 1983 in the lower half of Division One yet when it came to the Cup they managed to get their 'big guns' together and mount a challenge which took them to the Final. A bye in round one helped, followed by victory over Undercliffe which was a real team effort, Brian Bolus (29), Mark Brearley (42), Peter Vallance (42) and David Brown (23) making runs whilst Brian Hird (4-47) and David Atkinson (2-17 in 9 overs) did their stuff with the ball. There was a fine 63 from Chris Gott against Bingley in round three but he needed assistance from Kevin Sharpe (34), Brian Bolus (32) and Ashley Metcalfe (36) to help Farsley to a winning total.

In the semi-final Ashley Metcalfe blazed away for 134* and Keighley needing 244 tried extremely hard reaching 212 all out. Yorkshire Bank who would end the year as Champions were perhaps favourites, though that would be based on League form. This 1983 Final was another highly entertaining affair. Batting first Yorkshire Bank had 37 on the board in eight overs, Marsden Claughton (whom I could watch all day when he's batting) scored 83 and Graham Boothroyd, although taking sixty-four minutes for his 22 runs saw the Bank to 223-5 in their fifty overs. Claughton's dismissal was to a brilliant catch on the boundary by Hird and from that point Farsley moved slowly towards victory. Bolus and Metcalfe had thirty on the board in six overs and when Bolus went at sixty-four having scored 26, Ashley Metcalfe and Tim Boon put on 136 for the second wicket. Farsley were coasting home but we had the added thrill of a close finish when, three times, Mike Smith at long-on took catches from Metcalfe, Boon and Gott, all off John Hespe. With five wickets down Farsley needed twelve runs from the last three overs. David Ripley and Jonathon Brearley, both teenagers at the time, steadily took Farsley home from the fourth ball of the final over. There had been just that little doubt all through as to whether they would fall short. Ashley Metcalfe for his 122 was Man of the Match.

Keighley reached the Final of 1984, it was their first since 1961 though a first round bye obviously helped. Holders Farsley bit the dust in round two while against Manningham Mills the margin was only five runs and Mills had to contend with Ray Illingworth who took 3-29. Stan Caines certainly caned Keighley for 76 in round three but his Queensbury team-mates were only able to add 100 more and with fifties from Mark Sample and Peter Bickley, Keighley strolled into the semi-final by seven wickets. Pudsey St Lawrence and Spen Victoria barred the way of Keighley and East Bierley to a meeting in the Final but both managed it, though with only 155-8 on a good wicket Keighley were always struggling as East Bierley having won their first Priestley Cup Final in 1981 duly won their second.

There was a new name in the Final of 1985, Hanging Heaton, but they very nearly didn't get past the first round. Playing Baildon, Hanging Heaton chased 131-9 and had their last pair at the wicket needing two to win with one delivery remaining. A single was managed to bring the scores level and a replay was needed. There was no scare in the next round as Chris Pickles took 6-34 and Heaton lost only one wicket in beating Drighlington. While that was going on, Undercliffe scored 249-6 with David Dobson (89*) and 56 from Asad Rauf. They too had their sights set firmly on yet another Final appearance. Having ended their second round match at 111-1 Hanging Heaton reached 111 again in the quarter-final, this time all out against Second Division Great Horton. A big shock was on the cards until Harry Atkinson (3 for 25 in 20 overs) assisted by Roger Braithwaite brought about a collapse and Great Horton failed by eleven runs. With a tied match and that narrow win Hanging Heaton were living dangerously. Batting first in the semi-final and all out 106 against favourites Farsley, their Cup campaign had surely come to an end. Harry Atkinson and Roger Braithwaite thought differently, backed up by some safe catching (Ronnie Hudson took four catches) Farsley were dismissed for just 84. The second semi-final was even closer with Yeadon needing just five to win off the last over and two wickets remaining. A single and two run-outs left them tantalisingly short, with Undercliffe the victors.

Not often have Priestley Cup Finals been anything but exciting and the Undercliffe v Hanging Heaton was no exception. A superb 91 from Roy Spencer and a patient 50 from Peter Ingham gave Hanging Heaton 208-5. With Undercliffe 51-2 in reply play was ended for the day leaving an intriguing situation. When play resumed, former Leicestershire player, Peter Booth steadied the innings and added forty-six with Asad Rauf. David Dobson gave hope with 26 but when he was run out Undercliffe were left without experienced batting at one end and though Booth had 70 not out they finished twelve runs short. It would be fairer to comment on the all round Hanging Heaton performance than on any shortcomings Undercliffe may have had, for when two good teams meet it is often not a disgrace to lose. Harry Atkinson bowled through and his 25 overs brought 5 wickets for 77 runs.

The thrills brought by Hanging Heaton in the 1985 Final were equalled, if not bettered, in 1986 when they returned to retain the Cup. In round one Hanging Heaton amassed 293-4 off the unfortunate Yeadon attack. Peter Ingham (73), Chris Pickles (67), Ronnie Hudson (56), Simon Lax (43*), Chris Lethbridge (41). Five men went to the crease and no one had less than forty-one runs. Yeadon, despite 64 from Pat Fordham, had no answer as Lethbridge, Braithwaite, Plant and Pickles bowled Hanging Heaton into the next stage of the competition. Second division Hartshead Moor put up a brave show restricting Heaton to 187, Chris Leathley's 37 being top score. Roger Braithwaite kept Hartshead well away from that with 6-26 and they fell at 114.

A quarter-final match against Idle looked as if it may prove Heaton's undoing. Batting first they were 23-4 and struggling. Somehow they managed to set Idle 168 to get, with Kevin Plant showing earlier batsmen the way with 50 not out. Idle reached 19-5 and never recovered. While Hanging Heaton were in this encounter Second Division Eccleshill were creating a shock at Farsley. Eccleshill with 73 from David Riley and 49 from Gordon Ibbotson totalled 244-6 and they bowled extremely well to keep Farsley to 210.

Most betting men would have picked Pudsey and East Bierley to win the 1986 semi-finals, yet neither did so. Ronnie Hudson had one of those innings, which puts him a class above many others, ending on 92 when Mark Greatbatch caught him off Peter Graham. Chris Leathley added 69 and with helpful contributions all round, Hanging Heaton finished their allotted overs at 272-6. In reply Pudsey had a steady start with openers Greatbatch (45) and Dracup (80) preparing the way for a late chase. However it never really came, no one else stayed long enough and they, disappointingly for their large following, concluded at 215-7. East Bierley meanwhile were victims of another Eccleshill surprise. Batting first they were all out 118, with four wickets for Raper, three for Akhbar and two for West. Dave Hallett was an Eccleshill hero with 35 not out but it needed six runs from last man Nigel West to take Eccleshill through.

So the scene was set, big hitting Hanging Heaton against the underdogs and real surprise packets. Now there have been some magnificent innings on Priestley Cup Final day over the years but I doubt if there was a better innings than that played by Ronnie Hudson against Eccleshill. His twenty fours and eight sixes helped him to total 152* and Eccleshill stared 290 in the face in 50 overs if they wanted to win. They made a brave effort and at the half way point were 117-4 but they didn't have a Ronnie Hudson. In fact only Hanging Heaton have one of those. Surely they broke the mould after creating this fellow and it was to no ones surprise that the Man of the Match Trophy, in Hanging Heaton's 115 run win, was given to Ronnie Hudson.

Before the 1987 competition started, Corals Bookmakers ran a book on the season's Priestley Cup. Hanging Heaton were installed as favourites at 5-2, with Undercliffe expected to meet them, at 9-2. Neither however, managed to reach the Final. Hanging Heaton lost to Pudsey St Lawrence and Undercliffe reached the semi-final only to be beaten by Bingley. Bingley v Pudsey was a Final which I am sure would have suited most neutrals, both were in mid-table but Bingley, as would be seen at the seasons end, had nine wins to Pudsey's four and were playing the more positive cricket. It was that bit of extra positive play on their part which won the 1987 Final.

Batting first, Bingley who have never been afraid of playing youngsters if they were good enough, had a low average age but reached 268-3. Lee Hanson (39), Billy Holmes (50), John Goldthorpe (75), James Robinson (50*) and Mark Best (39*) were the only men who went to the crease giving the Pudsey bowlers a torrid time. Although Chris Gott reached 55 in Pudsey's reply, Sean Atkinson, Martin Redhead and Richard Allinson all reached thirty but Pudsey held back that little too long and were all out for 252 with David Batty's leg-breaks bringing 7-115. It was the first time since 1948 a team topping 250 in the Final had lost.

There have not been many disappointing Priestley Cup Finals over the years but it has to be said that 1988 was one of them. Yorkshire Bank had no answer to Pudsey St Lawrence and after totalling only 68 were beaten by 9 wickets. True the damp wicket looked as if it would get easier later, and this made winning the toss very important. Pudsey won it, put Yorkshire Bank in, and then Pete Graham and Steve Rowe with 5-25 and 4-20 respectively, took full advantage. All credit to them for that. Mike Smith gave stubborn resistance staying 18 overs for 5, but only Nigel Leech (16) and Steve Singh (14) made double figures. Pudsey skipper James Dracup was 37 not out in reply leading the club to their 3rd Priestley Cup Final victory. For such a well established club a 3rd win was long overdue, and made up for the disappointment of going close in 1987.

Although some years the weather plays havoc with the Competition, there's a 'Magic' about the Priestley Cup. No boring draws, sometimes a great shock by the minnows of Division Two over the 'big boys' of Division One.

When Alderman Priestley first conceived of the idea way back in 1904 little did he know what he had fathered. Just as it was then, it is now, a Cup that cheers.

Chapter Eight
Star Comments

Here in his own words you will find what the great **SYDNEY F. BARNES** thought about THE BRADFORD CRICKET LEAGUE.

"In May 1915, I saw an advertisement in the Athletic News Annual. *Wanted – a left arm bowler, apply Saltaire Cricket Club.* I applied on the Friday by wire saying, 'Will I do?' S.F. Barnes. A reply came saying, 'Come tomorrow to Bowling Old Lane, Bradford, will arrange terms'.

I went, and thus commenced an engagement which was to last for nine years. They were a very happy nine years and I like to think that my engagement by Saltaire was the start of the Bradford League becoming a power in the cricketing world.

I started quite sensationally by taking eight wickets for eleven runs against Bowling Old Lane, and then 10-14 against Baildon Green. Then the other clubs started. Idle got Jack Hobbs and others followed suit until the climax was reached when Keighley came to Saltaire with a whole team of professionals, including such names as Frank Woolley, Seymour of Kent, J.W. Hearne of Middlesex, Schofield Haigh of Yorkshire, Skelding of Leicestershire, Brookes afterwards of Worcestershire, Herbert Haigh, Moseley, and Hawthorne. Other clubs had such players as Parkin, Llewellyn, Hitch, Billy Cook, Ernest Tyldesley, Emmott Robinson, Cecil Tyson, Sam Cadman, Dexter and Firth of Notts, Frank Field, George Gunn, and many others of, or near to Test Match form. The matches were very keenly and sportingly fought out and afterwards the social side was always very enjoyable. The league management was carried out by a very able and astute body of men, and altogether it was league cricket at its very best. I look back upon my association with the Bradford League with a great deal of pleasure and I hope for, and wish the League continued prosperity.

Thanks for a happy time   S.F. Barnes

Here is what **HERBERT SUTCLIFFE** wrote a few years ago about the Bradford Cricket League. It is as true today as it was then.

'From Land's End to John O'Groats or from Pudsey to Brisbane you wouldn't find a better league than the Bradford League.

For many years it has worthily upheld the finest traditions of our glorious National Game.

Throughout its long history the Bradford League has always aimed to provide excellent grounds thus ensuring for the young player a fine early training on practice and match wickets. No one can deny that the standard of cricket throughout the league has always been of the highest, in fact at one period it almost reached County standard. The success of the young cricketer in highly competitive Bradford League games can be seen in County Cricket throughout the country, for it is a well known fact that the Bradford League has for years been looked upon as a nursery for first class cricket, proof of which lies in the fact that there are so many Bradford League players assisting County Clubs.

Herbert Sutcliffe

Ken Taylor

The Bradford League is to Club Cricket what Lords is to County Cricket and I am pleased that I was fortunate enough to spend my early playing days in that League for if league cricket is played properly (not overs cricket) it is the best grounding any young player can have if he hopes eventually to become a County Cricketer and in this respect the Bradford

League has done more than most by continually providing talented Yorkshire born players for the County team.

I was born in Huddersfield and went to Stile Common School. Wally Heap, an ex-Bradford League quick bowler (at the same time as Alex Coxon) was the Headmaster and I could not have wished for a more enthusiastic and knowledgeable person to start me off on the road to becoming a professional sportsman at both Cricket and Soccer.

Primrose Hill was my nearest Cricket Club and I made my first league apperance for them around 1948-49. Two years later I moved into the Bradford League as the standard of cricket was considered slightly better with four Professionals per club against one in the Huddersfield League.

Most of my playing days in the Bradford League were with Brighouse. Wilf Bottomley was my opening partner and we were captained by Norman Croft who apart from being a very good wicketkeeper found time to encourage and talk to me about the game and I am most grateful for his help during that period.

Brighouse was and probably still is a very good batting track but my first hundred came on a wet miserable afternoon at Eccleshill. I was naturally delighted with my performance but unfortunately the crowd was non existent and I well remember counting my collection which didn't take long for it was 11 shillings and 9 pence. Ten shillings was from the President of the Brighouse CC, one shilling from my father and nine pence came from the crowd. I hope it wasn't a reflection on my batting.

There were a lot of very good players in the League at that time and a few eventually played for Yorkshire, but cricket apart from being the best game in the world is a game where lifelong friendships are made and I'm grateful to Brighouse and the Bradford League for their friendship and for the opportunity to play this wonderful game.

All the best, Ken

Ashley Metcalfe

The Bradford League has always been a great encourager of young cricketers—a stepping stone often to County and International honours. Certainly Yorkshire have benefitted over the years, as have other counties. Farsley CC for example, have produced an enormous amount of talent—Ray Illingworth, Kevin Sharp, Steven Rhodes, Neil Mallender, Tim Boon, David Ripley and myself have all played during the past few seasons. Other clubs are no different. The inevitable result is a particularly strong standard, especially when one remembers that most clubs also employ overseas professionals as well.

Some might say that the standard had declined over the years, but the games constitution has also changed, and in the League's defence, it still consistently produces talented young cricketers with the ability to play First Class Cricket.

Martin Crowe

When the time comes for me sit down and look back over my career in the form of a biography or such I will without hesitation remember clearly the impact my time in the Bradford League had in shaping my future.

After having two successful years with Bradford CC in the Yorkshire League it was with honour that Pudsey St. Lawrence offered me a chance to experience the competitive nature of the Bradford League prior to my Country touring England in 1983.

Despite the fact it rained heavily during my stay at Pudsey the experience gained on playing on sticky wickets against hardened pro's in a competitive environment was invaluable especially now that first class wickets are not covered.

The greatest memory though is the many friendships that I made playing in the League whilst at the great club of Pudsey St. Lawrence.

Fond memories indeed.

Duncan Fearnley

Way back in the early '50s my parents saw some potential in both my brother Michael and myself in our cricket abilities and made us members of our local Bradford League cricket team, namely Farsley. The outstanding highlights in my memory now, after becoming Chairman of Worcestershire CCC in 1986, are every Tuesday and Thursday after school and then after work was to turn up at the Club for practice sessions and then the anxious wait for the selection to go up on the notice board for the weekends cricket. I am sure the discipline and the enthusiasm which came from these early days has rubbed off on my business and cricket career. Both Michael, before he sadly died, and myself tried to put something back into the game we loved. I am glad that my career started in the Bradford League even if the grounds and surrounding areas were not always the best, because there is no doubt in my mind that there isn't a better League in the country.

Mike Bore

Compared to some, my time in the Bradford League was brief but there's no doubt that the experience I gained during two spells in the competition had a tremendous influence on my career.

As a youngster, back in the late '60s, the prospect was daunting when I travelled across from the East Riding to play in what was widely regarded as the best League in the country.

But my mentors in Hull advised me that I must do so in the long-term interests of my career—and how right they were. I learned an immense amount at Bradford, playing under the captaincy of Bob Platt and his guidance pointed me towards a place on the Yorkshire staff.

Some years later, I returned to the Bradford League as pro for Lightcliffe and I remember the 1978 season as one of the finest of my career.

I understand that only the great S.F. Barnes collected more wickets in a season than my 103 and as Martin Radcliffe topped 1,000 runs, it was quite a year for Lightcliffe.

That achivement provided a significant turning-point in my career for after the disappointment of being rejected by Yorkshire, it prompted Notts to offer me the chance to make a fresh start in county cricket.

I've had the opportunity to prove at Trent Bridge that I'm not just a seam bowler or spinner but both and to be involved in one of the finest eras in Notts history—including two Championship successes—has been a privilege and a pleasure.

But I haven't forgotten that I owe a big debt to the Bradford League for helping to make that possible . . . nor will I forget.

Sir Leonard Hutton

I remember my times in the Bradford League with great affection. On my 2nd XI debut at Saltaire, for Pudsey, I batted in short pants at No. 6 and when I went into bat the Saltaire fast bowler slowed down his pace, 'taking pity on the young lad'. Twenty minutes later when I was still there he was back up to full pace trying to dismiss me. So many fine people helped me, like Edgar Oldroyd, while the people of Pudsey have been so good to me and my brothers and of course the St. Lawrence ground will always have a special place in my heart.

Brian Close

My time in the Bradford League was thoroughly enjoyable. I learnt a lot and met some wonderful people such as Stanley Raper who captained Yeadon for three seasons and was most helpful.

I feel it would be better to go back to a system where the onus was on the captains declaration, which would produce more positive cricket. The quality of player who has played and graduated in the League is without question extremely high. I feel the overs system stops players being positive as much as they should be but in the 40's and 50's the standard was without equal.

Alfred V. Pope
Playing in the Bradford League was a great thrill and such a high standard too. My time with Saltaire in the 'boom' years gave us matches against such as Bill Copson, Denis Smith, Learie Constantine, Les Ames, Sid Buller and J.S. Ord. They were happy times and we got good gates. The Windhill side of 1940 and 1941 was the finest club side you could wish for, though every side in the League was so keen to win it was very competitive.

Harold Rhodes
My respect for the standard of Bradford League cricket in the 1970's was very high. At Bowling Old Lane the likes of Jack Hill made you very welcome, and the encouragement given to the side to do well was enormous. One thing which didn't carry any weight was a reputation. Any respect had to be earned, competition was high and it was good grounding for any youngster or second team player from a County. It is easy to see why Yorkshire, has over the years, produced such fine sides.

R.E.S. 'Bob' Wyatt
Though I never played in the Bradford League I did come in contact with many players who did. Bill Voce was a great left hand fast bowler as all cricketers will know. He was also a charming personality. Edgar Oldroyd was a fine No. 3 for Yorkshire and a very good player on a turning wicket. Wilf Payton was a very good player and particularly a good back player. I had several long partnerships with Frank Woolley who was a fine player of all types of bowling. He made all bowling look easy.

Yorkshire in the 1920's and 1930's were a great side, many of whom had come from the Bradford League. I always got on well with them and had a great admiration for them.

And here is what the late Jim Laker wrote in the 1970's . . .

J.C. 'Jim' Laker
Above all things I was grateful to be born a Yorkshireman and decidely fortunate to be given an opportunity to play cricket with Saltaire at the tender age of 15—fantastic years for any hopeful cricketer. An early baptism in the tough competitive atmosphere of Bradford League cricket without question was to stand me in good stead during a career which brought me into conflict with some of the finest cricketers the world has ever seen.

Incredibly over 30 years have passed since I first played, against Baildon Green and how happy I am that I am blessed with a memory which still recalls, a host of memorable matches, but more important still the memory of so many fine league cricketers that I was privileged to play with.

John Harvey
It was during the Winter of 72/73 that I was asked if I would be interested in joining Undercliffe C.C., a club I had heard a great deal about as Derbyshire had for many years a strong link with them.

Having just finished playing first class cricket I was looking to play cricket that would still have a bite to it and I was not to be disappointed when I played for Undercliffe in 1973.

My first game was a great personal success as I scored a hundred with a collection of 97p. Sitting quietly in the dressing room and feeling pretty pleased with myself I was brought quickly back to reality by being told in no uncertain terms that it wouldn't always be that bloody easy. So this was the Bradford League!!

I remember in my third or fourth game getting a thin edge which carried through to the keeper and being on my way to the pavillion before the appeal went up, only to be met by a barrage of abuse in the dressing room about you don't walk till given out etc. etc. After putting over my opinion just as strongly the air was cleared and it was never mentioned again.

During my years with Undercliffe I made many friends both on and off the field and although my visits to Undercliffe are now few and far between I am always given a very warm welcome, which can't be bad for someone South of Watford.

Thomas Alec 'Sandy' Jacques

Between 1933-1947 (inclusive) I played in the Bradford League, for 13 seasons. Being at other clubs in 1934 and 1939, I enjoyed 10 happy years at Undercliffe.

It was an experience and a challenge to play against many internationals and other first class County players. At times my bowling received severe punishment, but the heaviest thrashings my bowling received were from local batsmen. Never shall I forget a superb innings by Willie Sutcliffe who scored 148 for Farsley at Saltaire in 1933, and also in this same season George Senior hit very hard and successfully in a very quickly scored 93 for Baildon Green.

Jack Swift scored heavily on many occasions. He was a splendid batsman who enjoyed a long meritorious career in the Bradford League. Now and again good fortune helped me to get rid of these players before they did too much damage, and as Jack said to me "Where you and I are concerned, we've had it both ways". One day playing against that genial sportsman George Senior, at Undercliffe, George lost his wicket to my bowling in the first over of the match. Later on an off-spinner was bowling and on this day not efficiently in either length or direction. I was fielding on the mid-wicket boudary when George came walking past he said "Sandy you and I reckon to be good pals, but really you've been a bit rotten to me today. I should only want two overs of that stuff for 50 runs and a good collection and here I am helpless to do anything, and all because of you. So we are not on friendly terms for the rest of today. Good afternoon". Well well, Happy days.

Les Ames

My introduction to Bradford League cricket was a rather unhappy affair. I had recently been posted to Harrogate arriving there in August 1942 and within a matter of days Windhill had approached me. I played the following week though a bit worried about my form. I was clean bowled by the late Bill Copson without scoring. This was the least of my worries as I had a call from my Commanding Officer ordering me to report to him immediately.

The interview was short, sharp and startling.

"Who gave you permission to play for Windhill"

"No one, Sir" I replied.

"Don't you know there is a B____ War going on, and you especially as a Junior Officer should be available 24 hours a day. You will not play for Windhill or anyone else without my express permission. Is that understood". "Yes sir". I decided not to seek permission for the rest of that year.

Windhill were anxious for me to play the following year so I summoned up courage to approach the C.O., and this time the interview was more affable, but he made it clear I could play only if there were no RAF games. This included Squadron games where the standard was abominably low.

The Bradford League games I did play were always a rush to get there, and immediately the games were over I had to dash back (CO's orders again). I scarcely knew any of the players, at least not at first, and there was no time to enjoy their company after a game was over. My top score was 118 at Undercliffe but I remember scoring something over 100 at Spen Victoria but before this the two opening batsmen completed 50's and, as was the usual custom a collection was taken. The first 50 brought in £3, the second just under £2 and my century brought in 13s 9d. Obviously it was an advantage to go in first.

Note: (In this innings referred to, Ben Hipkin and Albert Audsley had indeed made 55 and 84 respectively but what Les did not say is that his unbeaten 102 contained 5 sixes and 12 fours and was the fastest ever Bradford League Century. It took just 40 minutes. He then took 3-52 in the Spen reply—in those days George Dawkes kept wicket for Windhill.)

I remember playing with Learie Constantine but he did nothing spectacular. I enjoyed the games in which I played Bradford League cricket though transport to and from games was a bit tiresome and inclined to take the gilt off the gingerbread.

I send my kind regards and best wishes to any readers I played with or against.

Willis Walker

I played for Notts from 1913 to 1937 making 18,259 runs which included 31 centuries, but how well I remember my Bradford League days with Keighley. The following players were playing in the League at the time. Wilf Payton (Notts), Frank Field (Warwicks), Geo Gunn (Notts), Emmott Robinson (Yorks), Arthur Sellars (father of Brian), J.T. Hearne (Middlesex), Fred Barratt (Notts) Alex Skelding (Leics) and George Crawford (Yorks).

When I returned to Notts after playing in the Bradford League I remember on one occasion the rain came down, and the umpires were reluctant to go off. Fred Barratt remarked "I see we are playing Bradford League rules again."

Note At the time of writing Willis Walker was the oldest living first class cricketer, just a boundary away from his 100.

Mark Greatbatch

I first experienced Bradford League Cricket after two Summers with Bradford in the Yorkshire League. I was fortunate enough to play for Pudsey St Lawrence (1984 – 86) who over the years have been a very good club side.

There I experienced three seasons of probably the most enjoyable cricket I have ever played. My team mates and myself were dedicated to producing what we called a 'six points for the lads' every weekend. The team spirit was quite unbelievable, every player working for each other. If someone was having a 'bad trot' we would try and lift that player back up to the standard required.

After the games, in the bar, in my opinion is what won us two League titles and two Yorkshire Champions Cups. Nearly every weekend the first team would spend hours talking about the day's play, the coming games ahead, etc. etc. etc. The whole club was involved, wives, girlfriends, club members, etc. in one thing, Pudsey winning either the League or Cup.

I feel the time I have spent in the Bradford League has made me a better player, a harder player mentally and playing just for the total enjoyment of the game of cricket. Also the friends I have made over the years of playing league cricket in Yorkshire will never be forgotten, for their kindness and friendship.

Les Ames, who shares the fastest League century with George Senior.

Cyril Washbrook

Chapter Nine
A Dose of Salts (1946 – 1959)

Mainly to determine who should qualify for Division One and who should make up Division Two, the 1946 season contained only one division. The top half of the League would figure in the first division and the bottom half in the second for the 1947 season. The reason for this was the vast changes in personnel, with many of the top players going back to County Cricket. A few however, such as Manny Martindale, Eddie Paynter, Miles Coope, Arthur Mitchell and Arthur Wood remained.

Keighley were champions by just one point from Yeadon, yet no side won even half of their fixtures. Bankfoot didn't win any at all, while Pudsey St. Lawrence were unbeaten yet finished only third. The Bradford Club were back in the League and there was a newcomer in Salts C.C. They had very near neighbours in Saltaire who played just across the River Aire in Roberts Park. There is some rather interesting history as to why the Salts Club came into being.

Salts was a Textile Mill founded by Titus Salt who was later knighted. He lived in a large detached house at Lightcliffe. For his 3,000 workers he built the model village of Saltaire with its 4 perimeter roads, 25 streets and 775 houses. Salt who died in 1876 wanted a cricket club, solely for his employees. The result of which Salts Cricket Club was formed, playing in Roberts Park. Sir James Roberts, a former Managing Director of the Mill was the owner of the Park which was officially opened on 25th July, 1871 by Sir Titus Salt. So there was little difficulty in finding a ground or indeed sufficient members. When Salts joined the Bradford League it followed service in The Yorkshire Council, during which time the 'Mill employees only' rule had to be changed due to the decline of the Textile Trade, resulting in less workers to choose from.

When Keighley won the 1946 title it was despite a poor away record, winning only two of their ten away fixtures. In the Priestley Cup, Keighley took a first round knockout from the newcomers, with Salts winning by three wickets—65 runs from Miles Coope and 5 for 65 from Herbert Smith doing most of the damage. These two players aided by Bernard Henry and Jack Firth helped Salts to 5th place in the League thus qualifying for Division One the following season. Undoubtedly the 1947 season belonged to Salts who in only their second season won the League Championship and reached the Priestley Cup Final. Hill's 79 not out v Bingley in 1946 had been the club's highest individual score but in 1947 it was beaten six times with both Giles (127 not out v Keighley) and Coope (120 not out v Bingley) making centuries.

The Salts success story at this point was due to many fine players. Unlike certain seasons in the past when one or two 'stars' were very largely instrumental in gaining success, the Salts side of the late 1940's were teams in the truest sense. All pulled their weight as highlighted by the fact they had in 1947 twenty-three scores above fifty, divided amongst nine of their batsmen. New signing Percy Watson certainly justified his arrival with 59 league wickets at 15.38. This was a wide open season with five clubs in a top of the table race for most of the time. Salts lost four times but were positive and won more games than any other club, making them worthy champs.

In the Priestley Cup, Salts beat off the challenge of Bankfoot (by 5 runs), Bingley (by 5 wkts), Windhill (by 71 runs) and in the semi-final, Pudsey St. Lawrence (by 6 wkts). In the final the Salts attack let them down badly, as Yeadon, who were to take second spot in the League, rattled up a run for every day of the year. Needing 366 runs to win Salts made the most tremendous effort. Firth hit 67 and Newall 87 as they crept ever nearer to what would have been an amazing win. Alas, it was not to be, as their all out score reached a most creditable 307. The total of 672 was a new aggregate record for a Final and no doubt Salts missed J.C. Tennant, who had been their first bowler to take nine wickets in a match, with 9 for 46 against Great Horton earlier in the season. The club had made an early impact in the League and two highly creditable performances among many were the 5 for 19 by Percy Watson when Idle were dismissed for 39 and a 92 not out by Geoff Edrich, one of the four nationally famous Edrich brothers. He assisted Salts (v Great Horton) but was needed by Lancashire after that where he made 322 First Class appearances and was selected to tour India in 1953/54.

Hard hitting left hander Freddie Jakeman joined Salts for the 1948 season and scored three centuries including one in the 1948 Priestley Cup Final. Here again Salts were to top the three hundred mark but Keighley scraped home by two wickets. So Salts for two seasons in succession, made over 300 hundred runs and yet failed to win a Priestley Cup Final. Jakeman's 101, supported by 66 from Walker and 62 from Kitson was followed by another let down from their attack. Salts slipped to 4th but in 1949 they were back as Champions for the second time in three years. The Salts Title in 1949 throws up some interesting facts. Firstly there were six defeats. Now if you don't feel that is unusual please look at the League tables throughout the book and see how many times you can find six defeats by a team winning the Championship. Giles and Henry totalled over 600 runs apiece while Lodge and Firth had over 400 runs each. As well as those four Cliff Kitson also averaged over thirty. In two games (v Undercliffe) Giles made scores of 85 and 103 not out. Twice Percy Watson sent Bingley packing with 5 for 37 in the League and 5 for 24 in the Cup. There were hat-tricks for both Watson (v Windhill) and new signing Joe Lodge (v Undercliffe). Lodge was an all-rounder who had played two games for Yorkshire the previous year. Now he was giving his all-round skills to the Salts Championship challenge and took 50's from Yeadon, Eccleshill and Spen Victoria, as well as providing some fine support bowling. Watson with 63, Fletcher with 44 and Dennis with 35 wickets did most of the 'donkey' work. Thirteen of George Dennis's wickets came in two games against Yeadon, 7 for 16 and 6 for 52, these being the only two occasions he took more than four wickets in an innings.

While Salts did not win the title in 1948, Windhill revived memories of the late 30's with a Championship success. Albert Audsley topped the League batting and Learie Constantine made it a double by winning the bowling. Both Great Horton and Undercliffe won a match more than Windhill, but the Busy Lane outfit were difficult to bowl out and no other club had as many drawn games as the Champions, who had a two point margin at the finish. The next time that Salts slipped (when ten drawn games meant only third spot) in 1950 there was a new champion. Baildon Green, who had often been on the receiving end of hat-tricks, ten wicket feats and big scores. Now at last they had something about which to shout.

Baildon Green came into the League in 1912 and prior to the Division Two title of 1949 had not won anything. The nearest they got was to be runners-up in the 1946 Priestley Cup Final. However in 1950 Baildon Green were Division One Champions. It was appropriate for it was the club's Centenary Year. Despite having had some very fine players before such as Dickie Moulton, George Senior, Ben Hipkin, Horace Fisher, Fred Sinfield, Leslie Bulcock and Alf Pope, none had contributed towards a trophy. When the right formula was found in 1950 it was the lesser known such as Bill Ellis, Albert Audsley and Tom Tetley who bowled sides out cheaply. Geoff Dean, Len McLean, N.O. 'Pat' Robson, Geoff Hitchenor and John Marsland were all heavy scorers. In the Cup 1st round of that year Baildon met Salts, the club that had twice lost cup ties despite making over 300 runs. Against Baildon they again topped the 300 mark, with a mighty 363 but Baildon fell 130 runs short.

With a hundred years and now a Championship behind them Baildon Green decided to drop the word Green from their name and from 1951 they were to be simply known as Baildon. Not that it was a simple thing to beat them, for in 1951 Baildon retained their title. At home to Windhill on Whit Saturday, 12th May, the two highest scores of the day came in that fixture, though neither were centuries. In Windhill's 180 for 8 dec, D. Hanson hit 81 and in the Baildon reply Albert Sykes was still there at the end with 90 not out, when Baildon won five wickets. On the same day Manny Martindale took 6 for 16 for Keighley against Saltaire, who were all out for 58.

One of the most surprising performances that Whit Saturday came from a 37 year old who had been persuaded to return to cricket. Eric Henson was fifteen stone and had played in only two of the previous fifteen seasons. Yet Eccleshill thought he would be ideal, with his left arm spin, to

77

spearhead a promotion push. Undercliffe all out for 74 (Henson 7 for 29) tells only part of the story, for he had two in two and then rapped the batsman on the pads with his next delivery only to hear the sad reply 'not out' from the umpire, on his hat-trick ball.

One week later Manny Martindale, who was player coach at Keighley, scored 101 in 98 minutes but again the headlines came from Baildon. Len McLean scored 130 in their match at Bingley, a score which included ten sixes and nine fours. His first fifty came in 51 minutes but the second in just 17 minutes more, taking him to his hundred in 68 minutes. Centuries by McLean and Martindale that day were joined by a third. Jim Thompson, the 25 year old captain of Pudsey St Lawrence, scored 138 at a run a minute against Yeadon. With Bowling Old Lane 207 for 8 dec tieing with Lightcliffe 207 all out, there was plenty to excite in the month of May 1951. It wasn't restricted just to that month either. In June Yeadon had in their ranks Douglas Verity, the 17 year old son of that great and much lamented Yorkshireman Hedley. Douglas (named after Douglas Jardine) was a promising batsman and made 55 not out against Lightcliffe, which contained six boundaries, leading his side to a 5 wicket win. In June Baildon lost their first match of the season to Great Horton by 6 wickets. Dennis Dobson scored 55 of Horton's runs and the following year was making up for it by scoring runs for Baildon. On the day of that Baildon defeat Ecclesshill made 160 at East Bierley. After trying six bowlers Ecclesshill 'skipper' Ronnie Scarborough brought himself on in desperation. In 4.4 overs he took 5 for 21 and Ecclesshill won by one run. When Bingley met Bowling Old Lane, Jimmy Rigg made a marvellous 140 not out for Bingley, but what appealed to me most about that match was that veteran bowler Arthur Vickers then took eight Bowling wickets for 37 runs which included a wicket in each of seven consecutive overs.

Another feature of the 1951 season was a partnership of 219 runs between Wilf Horner (127) and 16 year old Douglas Padgett (90). This stand took only 140 minutes. Playing for Idle this brought about a ten wicket win and was therefore performed after tea. Before tea however at Spen Victoria, brother Granville Padgett had taken part in an opening stand of 167 with Jack Van Geloven for Lidget Green. In Granville's case it was not enough to bring victory. In July 1951 there was plenty of rain about but although not many games were finished Baildon did beat Salts through some hard hitting by captain Ronnie Burnett who hit 87 in 67 minutes with 66 of these in boundaries beating the rain for a three wicket victory after Miles Coope had scored fifty in 46 minutes for Salts.

When Baildon retained their title in 1951 they had just three points to spare but when they made it a hat-trick in 1952 and completed the double with their first Priestley Cup Final win they were outstanding and there was no one to compare with them. Two league defeats were surprising but not disastrous and in Dennis Dobson, Pat Robson, Geoff Hitchenor and Ronnie Burnett there were four men who could and did score freely. Dobson in fact amassed 980 league runs at 57.65 and with Ellis, Tetley and Burkinshaw sharing almost equally 155 league wickets, it was another superb team effort. True, they had a bye in the 2nd round of the Cup but that probably saved some side from a good thrashing because in the cup campaign Baildon won by margins of 70 runs (v Spen Victoria), 159 runs (v Lightcliffe), 169 runs (v Farsley) in the semi-final and by 122 runs against Keighley in the Final. No side previously had such margins, by more than 120 runs, three times in the same seasons competition. Not surprisingly the Baildon side stayed together for 1953 when Tom Tetley topped the League bowling though the side could not quite make it '4 in 4', finishing 2nd.

Before I come to the sensational conclusion to the 1953 and 1954 Championships let us look at a few other highlights. In 1953 there was a quite remarkable opening to the Keighley v Bowling Old Lane game. The following scorecard will tell its own tale.

Keighley

W.D. Townson c Stocker b Clayton	0
L.G. Skirrow c Padgett b Stocker	0
B. Long b Clayton	0
P. Brooke b Clayton	0
D. Warrington lbw Clayton	0
F. Wellock c Dimbleby b Stocker	0
N. Kitson c Smith b Clayton	20
A. Greenwood not out	17
G. Spencer lbw Stocker	10
F. Clayforth b Clayton	1
A. Hughes b Clayton	2
Extras	11
Total	61

Bowling Old Lane bowling

Clayton 7 for 22
Stocker 3 for 28

Never before have I seen the first six batsmen all fail to score.

Alf Clayton took four wickets in his opening over, including the hat-trick and when Jack Stocker, a speed merchant, started his first over the score was 1 run for 4 wickets, the one being an extra. At the end of his first over the Keighley total stood at 2 runs for 6 wickets. You could say that they had been two eventful overs. Bowling Old Lane won by eight wickets.

On the same day Lightcliffe had five 'ducks' making only 39 runs against Baildon and Pudsey had four men failing to score against Spen Victoria. In fact there was plenty of 'Game Bird' that day because thirty three 'ducks' were recorded in eleven Bradford League games. Ray Marriott making his debut for Spen was responsible for two of the Pudsey 'ducks' in performing a debut 'hat-trick'. Baildon's Wilf Burkinshaw got off to a good start in 1953 with 6 for 14 on the opening day and 5 for 16 (v Farsley) was followed by 6 for 15 against Great Horton. An odd fact about Wilf is that he never played cricket at all until he was 18 years old, only then to help make up a side which was a man short. His left arm slow medium bowling brought him to Undercliffe's notice in 1940 but after one season with them he was dodging the bombs in Malta after being called up. On his return to the area he was told to keep his hand in at cricket for the Army's benefit and so he spent two years at Undercliffe as a professional, subsequently moving on to Eccleshill and Baildon.

The Merry Month of May in 1953 saw another 'all ten' feat when Brian Hall, a fast bowling Yorkshire Colt, took 10 for 52 for East Bierley against Bowling Old Lane. Hall then scored 29 not out as Bierley won by four wickets, reaching 92 for 6. Supporters of Keighley in 1953 needed strong constitutions. On May 23rd, at home to Brighouse they tied at 105 runs each. One week later they had a ten run margin, at home to East Bierley and on the 6th June went to Bankfoot where again they had another tied game. The match at Bankfoot must have been quite thrilling with many fluctuations. Keighley's first eight batsmen all made runs, Wellock 21, Skirrow 32, Greenwood 34, Kitson 38, Long 19 not out, Brooke 13, Spencer 13, to show real consistency towards Keighley's 179 for 7. Bankfoot also got off to a good start, their first three batsmen being Radcliffe 26, Dewhirst 29 and Woodcock 32. Then wickets started to tumble cheaply before Jim Mitchell 20 and Charles Hodgson 38 brought things back to level pegging and became the 12th and 13th players to reach double figures in the match—not a common occurence in league cricket. After they were both dismissed it needed two runs from last man Albert Tetley to bring the scores level before Spencer took his fifth wicket getting Cragg leg before wicket and the match ended with Keighley's second tie in three weeks. The extra point that Brighouse got for the first of these ties made all the difference at the seasons end and gave them the Championship of Division Two, on average over Undercliffe.

The Eccleshill Club, deep in debt, nearly went out of existence in 1953. The fight to save the club, which thankfully succeeded, demonstrated the strength of character of their captain Ronnie Scarborough, a frank outspoken man, who pulls no punches (typical Yorkshireman you might say). Ronnie began playing at Thornbury when he was eleven years old, quite a distinction, and in one spell took four wickets with his first four balls. Educated at Hanson School he continued playing for Thornbury till 1941 when he joined the Royal Air Force. There he played alongside Cyril Washbrook, George Cox, Arthur Fagg, Ellis Robinson and Reg Parkin, son of Cecil. He was asked to captain Eccleshill in 1942 with an instruction to win promotion. He did just that with a little help from his friends, Jack Crapp, George Duckworth, Washbrook, Robinson, Fagg and Parkin. Before the game at Baildon, Scarborough was asked to drop himself down the order due to all the 'stars' in the side. 'Nonsense' he replied, and much to everyones amazement, took a local player in with him to open the innings. Scarborough made 107 with the local also making a good score but the 'stars' failed miserably. The Committee never asked him to move down again. He was much respected at Eccleshill where he stayed until 1957 before spending his last two seasons at Undercliffe. He topped 5,000 runs in the League.

In mid-July 1953, Ken Taylor, then a Yorkshire Colt took his average in six innings to 355. His 103 not out for Brighouse against Eccleshill giving him a total of 355 for just once out. His fielding was quite brilliant and continued to be so throughout his Test and County career. When Bankfoot went to Brighouse it was they who took the eye with an opening stand of 207 from Radcliffe and Dewhirst, but when they met Queensbury they had great difficulty dismissing Queensbury's opening pair, Jim Chatburn and Jack Moule. In the first meeting between the two sides Jim and Jack put on 173 before being parted and when the return fixture came at Queensbury, Chatburn (101 not out) and Moule (75 not out) amassed 187 without being dismissed.

Before the fixtures for the 22nd August 1953 were played, Baildon, seeking a fourth successive Championship, and long time leaders, led the Table from Salts each with two games to play. That fateful day Baildon were all out 106 at Yeadon where Freddie Miles took 5 for 39. Baildon lost by seven wickets. Meanwhile Salts, with 52 from Brian Stott, won by 14 runs at Lidget Green and as a result went top of the League, by one point. There was however one game still to play and Salts would play Queensbury while Baildon would play Lidget Green. On the final day of the season down came the rain, and down, and down, and down. No matches were started that day and the title, by one point, was back with Salts. Simply no chance for Baildon to recover after that Yeadon defeat. It was rather hard luck for Baildon who had once again been a fine side. What happened in 1954 was to be even more heartbreaking.

The season got off to a controversial start with many allegations being made about payment to amateurs. It was a problem that simmered for some years before eventually, (largely through the Pudsey St. Lawrence club) the distinction between professionals and amateurs was abolished. One of the reasons the League had been the strongest in the country was because at a time when the Lancashire League and Central Lancashire League had only one professional, the Bradford League wisely had four professionals per club. With all-rounders mainly being sought in Lancashire the specialists found places in the Bradford League, and with four per club, the strength of the League was unquestioned. A few sides chose to remain all amateur, wise if they could not afford professionals and even wiser if they wished to plough their cash back into their facilities. In my experience of later years, very few clubs overfaced themselves by paying out money they didn't possess.

The individual taking the eye most between 1948 and 1954 was a young Raymond Illingworth. Born on 8th June 1932, Ray was soon justifying headlines, proclaiming a great future. In 1948 he made 148 not out against Pudsey St. Lawrence in the Cup. This of course was for Farsley and at the age of sixteen. By 1952 he had made scores of over fifty against thirteen different clubs. His 162 not out that year against Saltaire helped towards his place at No. 2 in the League batting averages but there were also nine half centuries to go with it. His bowling really came to fruition in 1950 when he took 5 for 14 against Lightcliffe and 5 for 29 against Bankfoot, while in 1952 there were 36 league wickets at 15.53 to go with his 844 league runs, so justifying the all-rounder tag. Well documented elsewhere are his Test and County days, indeed he has written two fine books, but in his late 'teens he gave all his attention to Farsley and now after an illustrious career is doing so again. He has come a long way in the last forty years but thank goodness he hasn't

Lidget Green *CC – Division One Champions 1957) – Back (l to r) Mr W. Haigh (Treasurer), Mr T. Hardman, J. Roe, W. Jamieson (w/k), C. Maston, R. Green, J. Metcalfe, Mr G. Allen, Mr J. Tillotson. Middle – Mr C. Wright, R. Wood (Pro), Mr S. Pickles (President), P. Atkinson (Captain), Mr G. Bowers, T. Shorton, Mr. H.B. Hinchliffe (Coach). Front – B. Topham, R.A. Fisher, B. Jenkinson.*

Farsley 1959 *– Back (l to r) A. Dobson (Scorer), F. Coates N. Pearson, A.D. Webster, B. Claughton, B. Stead, J. Hainsworth. Front – G. Tempest, C.D. Fearnley, M.C. Fearnley, J. Miller, W.N. Wood*

Bankfoot – 1959 – Back (l to r) T. Wilkinson, A. Smith, G. Harrison, K. Hill, J. Metcalfe, E. Hardy. Front – G. Roberts, C. Heap, J. Mitchell, R. Ferguson, H. Hall. (A. Clarke absent due to cartilage operation)

Bowling Old Lane – (2nd Division Champions) 1964 – Back (l to r) H. Elam, A.J.C. Gray, H. Rider, M. Bateson, G. Boothroyd, M. Naylor, B. Bottomley, J. Ward (Scorer), J. Hill. Front – A. Peel, T. Smith, B. Clough (Captain), B. Ellison, J.D. Woodford, M. Waheed

Dent and Moule opening the innings for Queensbury in 1963.
  (Courtesy of Halifax Courier Ltd)

THE STAN LONGBOTTOM TESTIMONIAL MATCH
(by kind permission of the Bradford Cricket League)

The Bradford League XI
versus
The Stan Longbottom XI

at East Bierley Cricket Ground

Sunday, 11th August, 1974

Wickets pitched: 2.30 p.m.

The match ball today has been donated by H. J. Knutton, Sports Outfitters, Bradford, to whom the Stan Longbottom Testimonial Committee extend their grateful thanks.

— SOUVENIR PROGRAMME —

Idle CC – 1965 Division One Champions and Priestley Cup Winners (completed hat trick of Championship wins by also winning Division One in 1966 and 1967). – Back (l to r) S. Smith, F. Sugden, J. France, I. Leng, M. Swift, R. Sherred, M. Reynolds, A. Hogg. Front – L. Horsman, G. Brown, K. Woodward (Captain), K. Hill, D. Hallett

Hartshead Moor CC – 1966 – Back (l to r) Arnold Newsholme, Raymond Hirst, Lloyd Campbell, Bill Brown, Jack Fenton, Geoff Hodgson (wk), Brian Redfearn. Front – Terry Evans, Donald Hirst (Captain), Leonard Squire, Brian Daisy

Vic Wilson (Undercliffe)

Ken Taylor, taken in his Bradford League days. As well as playing cricket for England, Ken was a fine soccer player who once scored 4 goals in a Football League match against West Ham United.

Barrie Leadbeater (now a County Umpire) photographed while with Yeadon in 1980. Yeadon did not win a match, yet Barrie won the League batting averages.

David Batty being presented with the match ball with which he took his 1000th wicket in the Bradford League.

Hartshead Moor – (1972 Division Two Champions) Back (l to r) Peter Squire, Martin Kent, Peter Smith, John Booth, Steven Tart, Alan Greaves. Front – Trevor Holmes (wk), Leonard Squire, Terry Evans (Captain), Mick Holmes, Pat McKelvey

Bankfoot CC – Back (l to r) Ray Hirst, Brian Philmore, Brian Hudson, Roger Verity, John Steel, John Tiffany, Steve Carter, Geoff Scott, Bob Leadbeater. Middle – Eric Wheatley, Dennis Walker, Walt Sheppard, Graham Smith, John Woodford, Alan Hall, Stuart Verity, Ted Senescall, Ian Leng, Ken Hill. Front – Gordon Jagger, Russell Peel, Ken Scott, Herbert Holmes, Alan Clarke (1st XI Captain), Charles Hodgson (Pres), Albert Smith (2nd XI Captain), Jim Burchill, Stanley Demaine, Ronnie Hall, Brian Adamson.
With the Asa Briggs Cup (Div 1 Champs) and Thackeray Cup (2nd XI Div 1 Champs) 1972.

Charles Hodgson (President Bankfoot CC) with the Sir Leonard Hutton Trophy 1972, completed 27 years as President and 49 years with the club in 1988.

Lightcliffe CC – *Priestley Cup Final 1972 at Park Avenue – Back (l to r) Lewis Pickles, Roger Womersley, David Croft, Robert Horne, Peter Booth, Martin Radcliffe. Front – David Roberts, Bruce Deadman, Peter Westerby (Captain), Donald Garside, Nicky Barrett. Note the Park Avenue Football Stand in the background (now demolished).*

Action at Hartshead Moor 1972 (Hartshead Moor v Yeadon)
In their Division 2 Championship winning year. Hartshead's Leonard Squire turns a ball to the legside boundary. Two former Hartshead players in the picture are Stan Longbottom (Wicketkeeper) and Brian Redfearn (slips).

Bankfoot CC – Division 1 Champions 1972 – Back (l to r) Ian Leng, Phil Carter, Stuart Verity, Allan Clarke (Captain) Gordon Bowers (League President), Howard Cooper, Ted Senescall, Brian Hudson, Ken Hill. Front – Raymond Hirst, Chris Metcalfe, John Tiffany, John Woodford

Spen Victoria scorebox

Brighouse pavilion

Lightcliffe CC – The club's centenary side 1975 – Back (l to r) Donald Garside (wk), Andrew Baxter, Richard Elstub, Roger Stead, Nazeer Malik, Martin Radcliffe. Front – Lewis Pickles, Bruce Deadman, Peter Westerby (Captain), Robert Horne, Russell Hutchinson. Scorer Miss Bottomley.

East Bierley CC – (August 1979) – Winners of the Whitbread Village Trophy at Lords Cricket Ground. Back (l to r) Freddie Jones, Barry Hodgkinson, Geoff Fisher, Murphy Walwyn, Neil Helliwell, Paul Topp, Stuart Greenwood, Alan Sanderson. Front – J. Atkinson (Scorer), Brian Nurse, Tony Pickersgill, Phil Taylor (Captain), Claude Defoe, Tony Wilson, John Decent, Stuart Wood.

Bingley CC – 1982 Champions – Back (l to r) Julia Whitehead, Mark Steels, Andrew Arundel, Steve Sylvester, David Smith (wk), David Holden, David Howes. Front – Robin Feather, Billy Holmes, Gordon Ibbotson, David Batty. Phil Padgett receiving Trophy from League Vice President Donald Mallinson.

Manningham Mills CC – 1982 – Back (l to r) A. Storr, J. Slater, R. Noble, A. Clegg, J. Wilde, M.R.J. Veletta (Australia). Front – P. Kellett, D. Jay, P.J. Sharpe (Captain), P. Squires, B. Swallow

East Bierley scorebox

Hartshead Moor scorebox

Raymond Peel, here as an East Bierley player hitting out against Harrogate (Yorkshire League side).

Murphy Walwyn (East Bierley) 1984. Seen here bowling against Hanging Heaton, was one of the League's leading all-rounders having taken "all-ten" on two occasions.

Yeadon CC – 1982 – Back (l to r) J.R. Dale, J.P. Fordham, P.A. Harrand, C.P. Smith, S.P. Rhodes, M.R.B. Lodge. Front – R.K. Illingworth (now Worcs), S.A. Wood, J.W.A. Harker (Captain), G.A. Cope (Yorks), S.A. Atkinson

Keighley CC – Division One 1985 – Back (l to r) L. Selsick, M. Wilson, R. Preston, D. Jacques, S. Humphreys, D. Ash. Front – S. Reape, P. Hartley, J.K. Roberts (Captain), D. Ross, M. Sample   (Courtesy Keighley News)

J.K. Roberts (Keighley) who took all ten wickets v East Bierley in 1985. (10 for 43). Also fielding in the picture is the Yorkshire player Phil Robinson.

Cleckheaton CC – 1984 Young Cricketer of the Year Award. Young Chris Pickles hooking a ball to the boundary.

Donald Mallinson who was made a life member of the League in 1985 presents John Tiffany (Bankfoot 2nd XI Captain) with the 'Day' Cup for Champions of the 2nd Division (2nd XIs) 1987. In the background Mr Charles Hodgson, Bankfoot's long-standing president.

Brian Lymbery, the leading run scorer in the history of the Bradford League.

Australian pace bowler 'Lennie' McKeown who in 2 seasons of Bradford League Cricket with Drighlington (1984) and Farsley (1985) took 166 league wickets at an average of 14.10.

1984 – Steve Rimmington (East Bierley) run out by Steve Rhodes (Pudsey St Lawrence). The latter is now keeping wicket for Worcestershire.
(Photo: Courtesy Cleckheaton Guardian)
(Photograph by Leslie Pratt, Drighlington)

Dermot McGrath joined Undercliffe for 1989 from Manningham Mills. Was voted 'Young Cricketer of the Year' 1987.

finished contributing to the game he loves so well. I doubt if he ever will.

The first few days of the 1954 season saw some very interesting games. Bernard Henry was part of a Saltaire side which was all out for 80 at Park Avenue where Mel Ryan took 7 for 43 for the home side, Bradford. All out for 80 did not stop Henry reaching his fifty with his ten colleagues and extras totalling only 30 between them. Then there was the story of the two 73's in one match, Queensbury v Yeadon. Douglas Verity opening for Yeadon made what I am told was a quite brilliant 73 out of Yeadon's all out total of 107. Queensbury were made to struggle as Yeadon got back into the game only to find Jim Chatburn unmovable as he made 73 not out and eased his team home by just one wicket. Unlucky Windhill had Keighley at 36 for 6 when the rain came down and the match was abandoned while others were being played and points gathered. Bingley were shot out for 83 at Lidget Green when Bill Copson took 4 for 33 and Van Geloven 4 for 40 but Lidget had nine wickets down when they managed to scrape home by the skin of their teeth with Eggett 32 not out. This is the sort of tight cricket everyone loves and the 1954 season was not exceptional. The systems that have been adopted over the years, whether time limits, M.C.C. Rules or limited overs each have had their respective merits.

Personally I would like to see the one point awarded to the team batting second, in a draw, only given if that side was within 25 runs of the team batting first. This I feel would get rid of some of those boring and tedious draws we get when teams chasing a large total have lost a few early wickets. We still plead each year for captains to play the game more positively. Mind you, I am not in favour of Cup Rules applying totally for sometimes there is much merit in a drawn game. On the 20th May, 1954 in Division One, Lightcliffe beat Queensbury by one wicket, Yeadon beat Bingley by one wicket and Pudsey beat Undercliffe by two wickets, yet it is the game at Baildon I would like to tell you about. Salts were the visitors and restricted Baildon to 130 for 8, Ellis and Milner being the main contributors with 35 each. Salts replied with 104 for 6 earning a point for a drawn match batting second. No I am not here complaining about the point that Salts got, simply showing how they got it and how vital it was that they did. The next fixture to refer to is when Baildon went to Bingley in August. By now Baildon and Salts had a big lead in the championship race. Baildon were 36 for no wicket and soon afterwards were 36 for 6 wickets. They had lost six wickets without further addition after a fair opening stand and were then 72 all out. Bingley in reply lost their ninth wicket at 52 and a Baildon win looked likely. Then the score gradually increased until at 71 Bingley lost their last wicket. A one run win for Baildon, but wait, the score books did not tally and after scrutiny by the Umpires it was found a no-ball had not been added and the total was adjusted to 72. So now it was a tie and Baildon had only two points instead of four. The result of this was that on the last day of the season Baildon were four points behind Salts and only a Salts defeat and a Baildon win would give the latter the title and a revenge for the previous year.

On the last Saturday, Baildon duly did their stuff, making 166 for 9 against Undercliffe and winning by 77 runs. Salts only needed a point to be Champions and had dismissed Queensbury for 103. In reply, with the Championship depending on the result, Salts lost by 4 runs. This made Baildon an extremely happy club as they were now level on points. The days events had strengthened Baildon's average whilst diminishing that of Salts. Joy then turned to despair as Salts were still found to have a better average and on that basis Baildon were in second place to Salts yet again. This time it was either a found no-ball or the point Salts gained when pottering to 104 for 6. Either way they had won another Championship, their fourth in eight years.

After the heartbreak of missing out narrowly twice Baildon were relegated in 1955. Small consolation that Salts also had a bad season finishing only three points better. The season started with Keighley bringing back Eddie Paynter to the League. His first game at Bankfoot saw him make 52 out of 102 but his side lost by two wickets. The team of the season was undoubtedly Bradford. Salts seeking to follow Baildon with a hat-trick of Championship wins were all out for 55 to Idle on the opening day without any player getting into double figures. Then when they met local rivals Saltaire in the Inter-divisional fixture they dismissed the Division Two outfit for 100 and a win looked likely till Rhodes 4 for 17 and Thomas 3 for 30 had them all out nine runs short. The Salts run of success was over. Bradford started with a draw

81

caused by rain when they had reached 155 for 4 chasing a target of 215 to win. All other games escaped the rain but Bradford recovered well from this slight setback. They had another too when Joe Phillips dislocated his shoulder but his brother Peter became his replacement for a month. This Bradford side was an excellent all round outfit. At the seasons end the top three places in the League batting averages went to Bradford players, while Kitson with 34.20 and Phillips (twelve innings after his accident) with 35.00 also shone.

The Bradford League has a reputation for positive cricket. Over the years there have been few more positive skippers than Bankfoot's Allan Clarke. Playing at home to Queensbury in 1955 his side needed 152 to win the game but when he went to the crease the scoreboard read 28 for 6. Undeterred he safely guided his side to a one wicket win refusing to accept defeat and making 76 not out in the process. While Clarke was performing his heroics Bradford were chasing 235 at Salts and getting it with four wickets to spare. This was followed by 196 for 2 at home to Lightcliffe and 248 for 2 at Pudsey. However you can of course get too many sometimes and Pudsey replied with 169 for 5 which disappointed many spectators. That 248 made by Bradford reminds me of another day when they made such a total. Reporting on the game for the *Yorkshire Sports,* alas now discontinued, Bradford were 48 for 2 when I rang through my report. At that point half their alloted overs had gone. With only two wickets down the foundation was laid and the next 25 overs saw them add exactly 200 runs, but 248 is hardly a total you would expect when a side was 48 for 2 at the halfway stage. They say that 'fortune favours the brave' and that 1955 Bradford side was certainly full of heroic talent. In mid-June Bradford took part in a marvellous match with Undercliffe, at Intake Road. Undercliffe made 145 which would have been quite a struggle no doubt against the likes of Mel Ryan and Bob Platt. Platt had 3 for 53 and Ryan 6 for 57. In reply Bradford were indebted to Tony King for 78 following 37 from Eric Barraclough but with Cragg taking 5 for 30 Bradford ended at 143 for 9, just two runs short with their last pair at the wicket. On the 18th June 1955 East Bierley were 35 for 8 in reply to Yeadon's 211. Bentley and Naylor, the ninth wicket pair then put on 115 runs for a new League partnership record, they parted at 150, ending 166 all out. Whilst this was going on there was some high scoring at Pudsey. With a collection being taken for 50 runs, the 'hat' went round six times in that fixture. Pudsey had 'earners' in Dobson (86), Parker (76 not out) and Thompson (59 not out). They did not make full use of their batting talents losing only two wickets, ending on 234 for 2. Lightcliffe made better use of their middle order after Hunter (83), Walmsley (72) and Pickard (55) had set the pace and the visitors won by five wickets. Pudsey ended five points behind Bradford, no doubt with regrets that they did not turn fixtures such as Lightcliffe, who were third from bottom, into victories.

The top two in 1955, Pudsey and Bradford, were again the main contenders for the 1956 title, but what an opening day. Champions Bradford were at home to Farsley whom they bowled out for 80. Then got the shock of their lives as Farsley made them fight all the way and nine wickets were lost before Bradford won. Meanwhile Bill Copson took 6 wkts for 3 runs against Brighouse who were all out for 16. What a way to start a season!! The Brighouse top scorer made 5 and seven men failed to score. Keighley only made 93 at home to East Bierley but it was enough to gain victory. On the second Saturday it was again Bradford who where on top before tea, dismissing Bingley for 118, then found it too much and were all out for 80. In game three they managed only 67 chasing Idle's 126. In the meantime Pudsey had three victories, dismissing sides for 78, 75 and 112. This gave them a good early lead over Bradford which proved decisive at the seasons end when Pudsey St. Lawrence had a three point margin. When the two rivals met at Park Avenue, Bradford did not take a wicket for Jim Thompson and Dennis Dobson put on 270 for the first wicket to beat by nine runs the previous record set up in 1919 by Herbert Haigh and W. Morley of Keighley. Pudsey declared at 270 for 0 and although Eddie Leadbeater took six Bradford wickets they cost him 88 runs and Bradford ended at 224 for 7.

On the 28th July 1956 unbeaten Pudsey met lowly Brighouse, the side Lidget Green had dismissed for 16 earlier in the season. Yet lowly though Brighouse were, they broke Pudsey's unbeaten record. Pudsey scored 159 for 9 dec, Brighouse somewhat surprisingly 161 for 4 thanks to Hirst (34), Dickinson (32) and Newsholme (40 not out). After the game apparently the

Brighouse lads warned Pudsey about Copson, as if any warning was needed. 'He'll do you lot like he did us' they bantered. One week later Pudsey were all out 55. Copson did indeed live up to his build up by Brighouse with 6 for 17 and Pudsey lost again, this time by seven wickets. Now we had the return with Bradford and after a long unbeaten run since the seasons start Pudsey lost their third in a row when Bradford whipped them out for 71. The large lead that Pudsey held was down to just three points but after a recovery against Salts by 83 runs those three defeats were only going to be a slight hiccup because they lost only one more that year. You had to look down to eighteenth place in the League batting to find anyone from the Champs, Pudsey. Roly Parker had that spot with an average of 30.60. Despite that record stand of 270 both Thompson and Dobson failed to reach 500 runs, each averaging less than 28. This proves I feel that here again we had a team winning a title rather than one or two individuals.

The Bradford League averages for batting in 1956 was won by Malcolm Woodcock and there were two unusual aspects. Firstly he hit five consecutive half centuries without being on the winning side. On the last day of the season he and Bingley's Jimmy Rigg were in contention. Rigg was averaging 41.73 and on the last day made 65 not out against Farsley, which meant his average had increased to 46.06. Woodcock prior to the last match had 44.38 and his side had dismissed Yeadon for only 80. If Woodcock was dismissed he would have needed 73 to take the crown. This was hardly likely when only 81 was needed to win. If he were not out then he simply had to score 22. In a ten wicket win he finished with 30 not out to gain top spot with 46.69, against Rigg's 46.06. It was as close as two boundaries.

Lidget Green were the slightly surprise packet of 1957. They started the season with a match against the Champions, Pudsey and dismissed them for 57 after Pudsey had been 46 for 4 and after beating them by seven wickets Lidget never really looked back. At the seasons end they had the staggering margin, at that time (until the number of points for a win was increased) of 17 points over second placed Bradford. The win was finalised early and oddly enough came at Bradford, when rain intervened with Lidget 30 for 1 in reply to Bradford's 235 for 5 dec. The Park Avenue clubs failure meant that no one could now catch the runaway leaders. Had Bradford won that game it would have still made no difference as Lidget went on to win their last three matches. Only one defeat befell Lidget that season and there certainly was a tale of the unexpected about it. Lidget, top, met Windhill, bottom and without a win. Both had played six games. Lidget with five wins and a draw, Windhill one draw and five defeats. Here's an example of how unpredictable this great game of cricket can be. Instead of a big win for Lidget, it brought a surprise success for Windhill. Bottom beating top, how often that seems to occur. Lidget were all out for 146 and Windhill won with their last pair at the wicket. I suppose if you must lose it may as well be by the lowest possible margin.

The sting in the tail of that season was an 'all ten' feat on the very last day of the season. Derek Stow (Keighley) taking 10 for 25 against Great Horton. Two other main events of that season concerned a great fightback and a great achievement. The fightback was by East Bierley who beat Bowling Old Lane after being 14 for 7, yes, fourteen for seven. Bowling had scored 102 and Bierley were obviously reeling at 14 for 7, but they were steadied by captain Gordon Phillips, who made 37 not out, East Bierley won by two wickets. I know of no other side who have won a Bradford League match from such a beginning.

The great achievement referred to earlier belongs to Albert Hartley of Lightcliffe. On Whit Saturday, when taking 3 for 45 against Idle, he took his 1,000th wicket to go with the achivement of already having scored 10,000 runs in league and cup. There were no celebrations for it was not known at the time that Hartley had reached that milestone.

Albert Hartley first played Bradford League first team cricket in 1928. He was a fine all-rounder and a loyal servant to Lightcliffe, a club who have been fortunate to have had so many over the years. His thirty year career had many highlights and his 10 for 36 against Keighley in 1952 was obviously one of them. In 1939 he averaged 54.60. During his career he had four centuries and fifty-one half centuries for Lightcliffe and took five or more wickets in an innings on fifty-two occasions. That's some achievement!!! In 1957, his last season, at almost 50 years of age Albert Hartley took 8 for 56 against Brighouse. His left arm spin had been seen in four

Priestley Cup Finals, those of 1936, 1937, 1950 and 1955, the latter three bringing him a winners medal. In the 1937 Final he scored 131. Albert Hartley was very well respected for his cricket ability and equally loved as a man. There are all too few Albert Hartley's around today.

Another man who made a name for himself in that 1957 season was Barrie Jenkinson. As Hartley was leaving the stage, Jenkinson was just entering. Before he'd finished he would win prizes for Batting, Bowling and Fielding in successive seasons and for twenty years give Bradford League followers some real enjoyment. In 1957 Jenkinson was with Lidget Green for whom he made a debut 85 v Salts and 67 not out against Brighouse. In the next two decades he would score centuries for Bowling Old Lane, help Bradford win the Priestley Cup, score heavily for Pudsey and give six years valuable service to Idle. Barrie Jenkinson was a stylist, once described to me as 'a most immaculate all-rounder' and when I saw him make 53 in 1976 for Idle at his supposed career end, it was a perfect example of a top class player. He was still at Lidget when they set about retaining their title in 1958 but had a very early shock when beaten at Farsley by four wickets, despite 59 from Thornton and 31 from Jenkinson. On the same day Keighley beat Bankfoot by one run while Saltaire made 100 for 7 dec and the Old Lane replied with 100 for 6. On the 14th June, Champions Lidget lost 95 to 93 at Lightcliffe. Close matches were plentiful. Lightcliffe went into second spot in the table after that win and Lidget slipped badly down the League, with Bradford taking over as front runners.

When Pudsey were all out for 101 in June 1958, Duncan Fearnley was top scorer with 42. Playing against him his younger brother Mike took 8 for 36 including the hat-trick. Mike was a schoolteacher who became the League's most prolific wicket taker and one of the finest coaches Yorkshire cricket has known. Brother Duncan, currently Chairman of Worcestershire C.C.C. first played Bradford League cricket in 1957 for Farsley. He was a good steady dependable left hander and after one season at Pudsey in 1958 he moved back to Farsley for the next three seasons before having two years at Bradford. Five years away from the League ended with his return in 1969 to Pudsey St. Lawrence with whom he had two more seasons. His four centuries included 158 not out for Bradford against Pudsey in 1963. He added to those centuries thirty scores of fifty and over. His average of 43.08 at Farsley in 1961 caused him to be much sought after, Bradford were the lucky ones and he didn't let them down with his average again over forty, in 1962, his first season at Park Avenue.

It was brother Mike, however, who will be remembered most for his consistency and his ability to use all types of wicket to his advantage. Mike first played Bradford League cricket at Farsley in 1954. He moved to Bradford for the 1962 season with many wickets already behind him. In 1958 there was that hat-trick against Pudsey but he also had hat-tricks in 1960 against East Bierley and 1961 against Lidget Green. He topped the League bowling averages twice and was second on a further occasion. Seven times he played in a Priestley Cup Final but was a winner, rather surprisingly, only twice. Charles Grimshaw had taken 1273 Bradford League wickets but Mike broke that record. Then on a bright sunny day in July 1979 Mike Fearnley collapsed, playing the game he loved so much, on the field in a game at East Bierley for his home town club, Farsley. His death at forty three years was a great shock to all followers of Bradford League cricket. His 1324 wickets will take a tremendous amount of beating and each person that saw him play will have his or her special memories. As for me I will remember seeing Mike in 1972 bowling in two games, each time against the side which ended up as Champions with just three defeats. Two of these were against Farsley who were themselves relegated that year. Mike took 7 for 43 and 9 for 42 in those games and each were displays of intelligent bowling as good as anyone would wish to see. The League has certainly been the poorer for his passing.

While Bradford, in mid-season, took a firm grip on the top place in the League, the Second Division was a great three club battle between Yeadon, Undercliffe and Great Horton. Yeadon did not taste defeat until match fifteen. They did actually wobble in game fourteen when needing 120 to beat Saltaire, playing out for a draw at 61 for 6. In that fifteenth game they met Queensbury who had started the season without a win until game thirteen yet they beat Yeadon by dismissing them for 109 despite 58 from Jim Illingworth and then scoring 110 for 7. Before the season was out Yeadon would taste defeat again, this time on the penultimate Saturday.

They lost by seven wickets to Undercliffe leaving them in third position with one match to play. Undercliffe by beating Yeadon were now top with 46 points. Great Horton were second also with 46 points. Now Yeadon were third with 43 points.

On the final Saturday Undercliffe failed to take the title, when after scoring 112, at Keighley, they managed to get nine Keighley wickets before losing. Great Horton lost the title also by failing to get 126 at Spen Victoria, but held on to take a point with 85 for 8, in the hope that Yeadon lost or in the event of them winning that their own average would be superior. Yeadon did win after being dismissed for only 98 runs, as Bowling Old Lane were beaten by twenty runs. Freddie Miles 3 for 14 and Ken Speight 4 for 29 giving Yeadon a surprise win and an even more surprising Championship, won on average from Great Horton. Remember this was after being three points behind two clubs and all out 98 at tea on the final day of the competition. This really was a victory against all the odds.

Frank Lowson, that stylish batsman returned to the Bradford League in 1959 after his County cricket days had made him an idol of many schoolboys. He returned to play for Brighouse and made 32 on his debut and then 52 in an all out total of 90 at home to Spen Victoria. Frank Lowson was undoubtedly a class batsman, never hurried in his vast range of strokes. His original Bradford League days had been in the company of Bowling Old Lane as a seventeen year old. He had played for them in 1942 and 1943 and then again in 1948 and 1949. His first Bradford League century came at the expense of Lidget Green in 1948. It was an unbeaten 101 which helped him take 2nd spot in the League averages with 47.23. Three times he would finish in second spot and once third showing an amazing consistency. Before he finished at Bingley in 1967, a club with whom he won a cup winners medal, he had become only the fourth player to make 1,000 runs in a season which he did for Brighouse in 1963. Frank's Bradford League days gave him over 7,000 runs in total and many match winning performances. His 1959 return was a happy one for Brighouse who became Champions of Division Two. He made 75 when Saltaire beat Brighouse by 15 runs, 70 not out in a victory over Bankfoot, 94 in a one wicket win at home to Undercliffe and 92 not out at Windhill on the last vital day of the season to give his side the Championship.

This chapter began with the triumphs of newcomers Salts. It went on to show how they twice kept Baildon in second place in the League, once by a point and once on average. In 1959 Salts led the table from Bingley with one match to go. Bingley won by ten wickets at home to Lightcliffe, but it was tears for Salts, for they lost their last match. Once again the title was decided on the last day and once again it did not go to the side leading the table at the beginning of the day. This is, I am sure, how the neutral supporter likes to see the season run, right to the end of the course. The 1950's has been exciting, no team really dominated the decade, and many clubs were capable of winning the Championship but only one could of course and often luck played its part.

The big crowds from the '40's had gone. Television and affordable motor cars meant a changed way of life, but those who paid their money at Bradford League games saw keen quality competitive cricket, the like of which would continue into the swinging sixties.

FINAL LEAGUE POSITIONS

One division only first season after the war

1946	P	W	D	L	Pts
Keighley	20	9	9	2	36
Yeadon	20	8	11	1	35
Pudsey St. Lawrence	20	7	13	0	34
Bingley	20	7	11	2	32
Salts	20	7	10	3	31
Eccleshill	20	7	10	3	31
Spen Victoria	20	6	12	2	30
Windhill	20	7	8	5	29
Great Horton	20	6	9	5	27
Lightcliffe	20	5	12	3	27
Idle	20	5	10	5	25
Brighouse	20	4	12	4	24
Bradford	20	4	11	5	23
Saltaire	20	4	11	5	23
Undercliffe	20	5	8	7	23
Queensbury	20	4	10	6	22
Baildon Green	20	4	10	6	22
Farsley	20	3	9	8	18
Bowling Old Lane	20	3	8	9	17
East Bierley	20	3	8	9	17
Lidget Green	20	3	8	9	17
Bankfoot	20	0	8	12	8

Batting Averages
1 F. Jakeman (Lightcliffe)   49.75
2 J. Crowther (Bingley)   49.30
3 G.F.H. Phillips (Idle)   40.44

Bowling Averages
1 E.A. Martindale (Windhill)   56 wkts @ 9.80
2 T. Tetley (Great Horton)   56 wkts @ 10.14
3 R. Swindall (Brighouse)   51 wkts @ 10.43

1947 Division 1	P	W	D	L	Pts
Salts	22	13	5	4	44
Yeadon	22	12	4	6	40
Eccleshill	22	11	5	5	38
Idle	22	10	7	5	37
Spen Victoria	22	11	4	7	37
Keighley	22	10	4	8	34
Great Horton	22	9	4	9	31
Windhill	22	8	5	9	29
Bingley	22	7	6	9	27
Pudsey St. Lawrence	22	7	3	12	24
Lightcliffe	22	4	2	16	14

Division 2	P	W	D	L	Pts
Undercliffe	22	16	4	2	52
Baildon Green	22	13	3	6	42
Bradford	22	12	4	6	40
Brighouse	22	11	3	8	36
Farsley	22	10	6	6	36
Lidget Green	22	9	4	9	31
Saltaire	22	7	6	9	27
Bowling Old Lane	22	8	2	12	26
Queensbury	22	3	4	15	13
Bankfoot	22	3	3	16	12
East Bierley	22	2	4	16	10

Batting Averages
1 J. Crowther (Bingley)   53.35
2 E. Paynter (Keighley)   47.07
3 D. Fairclough (Queensbury)   46.00
4 G. Curry (Eccleshill)   45.16

Bowling Averages
1 G. Carter (Undercliffe)   94 wkts @ 8.52
2 R. Swindall (Brighouse)   64 wkts @ 9.82
3 W. Burkinshaw (Undercliffe)   78 wkts @ 10.09
All these are Division 2.

Top Division 1 bowler was Learie Constantine of Windhill with 50 league wickets at 12.86.

1948 Division 1	P	W	D	L	Pts
Windhill	22	12	7	3	43
Great Horton	22	13	2	7	41
Undercliffe	22	13	2	7	41
Salts	22	11	3	8	36
Eccleshill	22	10	4	8	34
Spen Victoria	22	10	4	8	34
Bingley	22	10	3	9	33
Idle	22	8	2	12	26
Yeadon	22	7	4	11	25
Keighley	22	6	4	12	22
Baildon Green	22	5	5	12	20

Division 2	P	W	D	L	Pts
Bowling Old Lane	22	15	3	4	48
Pudsey St. Lawrence	22	14	4	4	47*
East Bierley	22	9	5	8	32
Bradford	22	9	4	9	31
Farsley	22	8	4	10	28
Bankfoot	22	7	5	10	26
Lidget Green	22	8	2	12	26
Brighouse	22	6	7	9	25
Queensbury	22	6	5	11	24*
Saltaire	22	6	4	12	22
Lightcliffe	22	6	3	13	21

* Denotes one point award for a tie.

Batting Averages
1 A. Audsley (Windhill)   52.66
2 F. Lowson (Bowling Old Lane)   47.23
3 H.C. Graham (Undercliffe)   46.53
4 F. Jakeman (Salts)   44.35

Bowling Averages
1 L.N. Constantine (Windhill)   45 wkts @ 10.48
2 E. Lodge (Lidget Green)   61 wkts @ 11.21
3 G.E. Govier (East Bierley)   65 wkts @ 11.69
4 T. Speight (Pudsey St. Lawrence)   64 wkts @ 12.45

J.H. Burton (Bingley) who took 101 Division 1 league wickets at 12.89 each, became only the second player after S.F. Barnes to take 100 league wickets in a season.

An odd fact in 2nd XI cricket was that Baildon Green whose 1st XI finished bottom of Division 1 had a 2nd XI team Championship to celebrate. First team bottom – Second team top

1949 Division 1	P	W	D	L	Pts
Salts	22	13	3	6	42
Bowling Old Lane	22	13	2	7	41
Pudsey St. Lawrence	22	12	4	6	40
Windhill	22	11	4	7	37
Eccleshill	22	10	4	8	34
Idle	22	9	5	8	32
Great Horton	22	10	1	11	31
Undercliffe	22	9	3	10	30
Bingley	22	8	3	11	27
Yeadon	22	7	0	15	21
Spen Victoria	22	4	4	14	16

Division 2	P	W	D	L	Pts
Baildon Green	22	14	4	4	46
Queensbury	22	12	4	6	40
Bradford	22	11	4	7	37
Lightcliffe	22	11	3	8	36
Bankfoot	22	10	3	9	33
Brighouse	22	10	3	9	33
Farsley	22	9	3	10	30
Saltaire	22	8	1	13	25
East Bierley	22	7	3	12	24
Keighley	22	6	2	14	20
Lidget Green	22	5	3	14	18

Batting Averages
1 A. Hamer (Pudsey St. Lawrence)   73.73
2 G. Dean (Baildon Green)   52.44
3 R. Giles (Salts)   42.85
4 C. Priestley (Queensbury)   42.64

Bowling Averages
1 C.A. Matthews (Undercliffe)   34 wkts @ 6.88
2 A. Booth (Keighley)   76 wkts @ 10.64
3 L. Powell (Queensbury)   94 wkts @ 11.19
4 A. Hartley (Lightcliffe)   64 wkts @ 12.18
5 A. Tetley (Great Horton)   49 wkts @ 12.85
6 R. Appleyard (Bowling Old Lane)   69 wkts @ 13.43

1950

Division 1

	P	W	D	L	Pts
Baildon Green	22	11	8	3	52
Great Horton	22	10	8	4	48
Salts	22	9	10	3	46
Pudsey St. Lawrence	22	9	8	5	44
Windhill	22	8	8	6	40
Idle	22	7	9	6	37
Queensbury	22	7	8	7	36
Bingley	22	7	6	9	34
Bowling Old Lane	22	5	7	10	27
Eccleshill	22	4	5	13	21
Undercliffe	22	3	8	11	20

Division 2

	P	W	D	L	Pts
Yeadon	22	12	9	1	57
Lightcliffe	22	10	7	5	47
East Bierley	22	9	7	6	43
Bradford	22	7	9	6	37
Farsley	22	7	8	7	36
Brighouse	22	6	9	7	33
Keighley	22	6	9	7	33
Spen Victoria	22	5	11	6	31
Saltaire	22	5	7	10	27
Bankfoot	22	4	8	10	24
Lidget Green	22	3	7	12	19

Batting Averages
1 J. Firth (Farsley) 59.60
2 F.D. Booth (Yeadon) 53.33
3 J.R. Burnet (Baildon Green) 47.60
4 M. Coope (Salts) 44.42

Bowling Averages
1 H. Fisher (Yeadon) 50 wkts @ 9.38
2 D. Waterhouse (Farsley) 55 wkts @ 9.98
3 A. Hartley (Lightcliffe) 50 wkts @ 10.32
4 T. Falkingham (Yeadon) 36 wkts @ 10.61
5 F. Wharton (Yeadon) 57 wkts @ 10.87

Highest Division 1 bowler in averages was Albert Tetley of Great Horton with 37 wkts at 11.91.

1951

Division 1

	P	W	D	L	Pts
Baildon	22	10	10	2	50
Pudsey St. Lawrence	22	9	11	2	47
Great Horton	22	9	7	6	43
Bingley	22	8	9	5	41
Idle	22	9	5	8	41
Salts	22	8	8	6	40
Lightcliffe	22	6	9	7	34*
Yeadon	22	5	12	5	32
Queensbury	22	5	8	9	28
Windhill	22	5	8	9	28
Bowling Old Lane	22	3	8	11	21*

* Extra point awarded for tied game

Division 2

	P	W	D	L	Pts
Keighley	22	11	7	4	51
Bradford	22	10	6	6	46
East Bierley	22	9	8	5	44
Spen Victoria	22	8	9	5	41
Lidget Green	22	7	6	9	34
Bankfoot	22	6	9	7	33
Farsley	22	6	8	8	32
Eccleshill	22	6	7	9	31
Brighouse	22	5	9	8	29
Saltaire	22	5	7	10	27
Undercliffe	22	4	5	13	21

Batting Averages
1 D.L. Kitson (Bradford) 65.93
2 W. Horner (Idle) 53.06
3 J. Moule (Queensbury) 50.00

Bowling Averages
1 B. Hall (East Bierley) 67 wkts @ 11.73
2 W.H. Copson (Lidget Green) 55 wkts @ 12.04
3 E. Lodge (Spen Victoria) 45 wkts @ 12.27
4 P.M. Binns (Keighley) 44 wkts @ 13.07
5 E. Henson (Eccleshill) 30 wkts @ 13.86
6 E.C. Edwards (Keighley) 49 wkts @ 13.89
7 E.A. Martindale (Keighley) 56 wkts @ 14.28
8 H.V. Douglas (Bradford) 78 wkts @ 14.64

Top 8 all from Division 2. First Division 1 bowler to appear in averages was G. Carter (Pudsey St. Lawrence) who took 63 wkts at 14.73.

1952

Division 1

	P	W	D	L	Pts
Baildon	22	13	7	2	59
Lightcliffe	22	10	8	4	48
Pudsey St. Lawrence	22	10	6	6	46
Idle	22	8	10	4	42
Salts	22	8	8	7	39
Bingley	22	8	6	8	38
Great Horton	22	7	6	9	34
Yeadon	22	6	8	8	32
Queensbury	22	5	9	8	29
Bradford	22	4	7	11	23
Keighley	22	3	9	10	21

Division 2

	P	W	D	L	Pts
Lidget Green	22	11	10	1	54
Farsley	22	11	9	2	53
Windhill	22	9	6	7	42
Undercliffe	22	8	7	7	39
East Bierley	22	8	7	7	39
Saltaire	22	8	6	8	38
Bankfoot	22	4	12	6	28
Bowling Old Lane	22	4	12	6	28
Spen Victoria	22	5	7	10	27
Eccleshill	22	4	6	12	22
Brighouse	22	1	9	12	13

Batting Averages
1 W. Horner (Idle) 66.21
2 R. Illingworth (Farsley) 64.92
3 R. Booth (Lightcliffe) 64.50

Bowling Averages
1 W.H. Copson (Lidget Green) 71 wkts @ 9.84
2 H. Hoyle (Spen Victoria) 30 wkts @ 12.33
3 T. Tetley (Baildon) 52 wkts @ 13.40
4 F. Clayforth (Keighley) 55 wkts @ 13.78
5 A. Hartley (Lightcliffe) 60 wkts @ 13.85

1953

Division 1

	P	W	D	L	Pts
Salts	22	11	7	4	51
Baildon	22	11	6	5	50
Bingley	22	9	8	5	44
Lidget Green	22	9	7	6	43
Pudsey St. Lawrence	22	8	7	7	39
Idle	22	8	7	7	39
Lightcliffe	22	8	7	7	39
Yeadon	22	6	7	9	31
Queensbury	22	5	9	8	29
Great Horton	22	4	10	8	26
Farsley	22	2	9	11	17

Division 2

	P	W	D	L	Pts
Brighouse	22	10	9	3	50*
Undercliffe	22	10	10	2	50
East Bierley	22	10	6	6	46
Keighley	22	8	8	6	42§
Bankfoot	22	7	6	9	35*
Bowling Old Lane	22	7	7	8	35
Bradford	22	6	8	8	32
Saltaire	22	6	7	9	31
Windhill	22	5	9	8	29
Spen Victoria	22	4	7	11	23
Eccleshill	22	3	9	10	21

§ 2 pts added for 2 ties by Keighley.
* 1 pt added to Brighouse and Bankfoot, also for ties.

Batting Averages
1 D.E.V. Padgett (Bowling Old Lane) 82.50
2 H. Waterhouse (East Bierley) 62.42
3 W. Horner (Idle) 47.66

Bowling Averages
1 T. Tetley (Baildon) 46 wkts @ 11.06
2 N Kitson (Keighley) 39 wkts @ 12.28
3 W. Burkenshaw (Baildon) 50 wkts @ 12.74
4 W.H. Copson (Lidget Green) 50 wkts @ 12.92

87

1954

Division 1
	P	W	D	L	Pts
Salts	22	12	8	2	56
Baildon	22	12	7	3	56*
Lidget Green	22	10	6	6	46
Bingley	22	9	6	7	43*
Pudsey St. Lawrence	22	9	4	9	40
Idle	22	9	4	9	40
Brighouse	22	8	7	7	39
Lightcliffe	22	7	9	6	37
Undercliffe	22	6	7	9	31
Queensbury	22	4	6	12	22
Yeadon	22	2	8	12	16

Division 2
	P	W	D	L	Pts
Bradford	22	12	6	4	54
Farsley	22	12	4	6	52
Spen Victoria	22	10	7	5	47
Keighley	22	10	6	6	46
Bankfoot	22	9	6	7	42
Windhill	22	7	8	7	36
Bowling Old Lane	22	6	10	6	34
Saltaire	22	6	7	9	31
East Bierley	22	4	9	9	25
Great Horton	22	3	9	10	21
Lidget Green	22	3	9	10	21

Batting Averages
1. H. Halliday (Pudsey St. Lawrence)   60.77
2. L. Horsman (Idle)   57.11
3. H. Waterhouse (East Bierley)   49.59
4. W. Horner (Idle)   47.29
5. W.B. Stott (Salts)   44.53

Bowling Averages
1. G. Bottomley (Lightcliffe)   39 wkts @ 9.71
2. M. Cowan (Bingley)   50 wkts @ 10.40
3. W.H. Copson (Lidget Green)   69 wkts @ 10.71
4. B. Whitham (Bingley)   40 wkts @ 11.20
5. W. Burkinshaw (Baildon)   65 wkts @ 11.91

In Second XI cricket in 1954 there were 2 outstanding sides. Lidget Green won Division 1 with a nineteen point margin, while in Division 2 Keighley were Champions with a 24 point gap over Bowling Old Lane.

1955

Division 1
	P	W	D	L	Pts
Bradford	22	13	7	2	59
Pudsey St. Lawrence	22	12	6	4	54
Bingley	22	11	4	7	48
Lidget Green	22	9	9	4	45
Brighouse	22	7	8	7	36
Idle	22	8	4	10	36
Farsley	22	7	6	9	34
Salts	22	7	4	11	32
Lightcliffe	22	6	6	10	31*
Baildon	22	5	9	8	29
Undercliffe	22	3	5	14	17

Division 2
	P	W	D	L	Pts
Queensbury	22	13	4	5	56
Eccleshill	22	12	3	7	51
Spen Victoria	22	11	4	7	48
East Bierley	22	10	5	7	46*
Bankfoot	22	9	5	8	41
Saltaire	22	8	8	6	40
Bowling Old Lane	22	8	4	10	36
Yeadon	22	8	3	11	35
Windhill	22	6	6	10	30
Great Horton	22	5	5	12	25
Keighley	22	4	5	13	21

Batting Averages
1. E.S. Barraclough (Bradford)   50.46
2. A.M. King (Bradford)   47.80
3. J.D.H. Blackburn (Bradford)   45.82
4. A. Hodgson (Salts)   45.71
5. R. Scarborough (Eccleshill)   45.66

Note: first three all from Champions Bradford. A record.

Bowling Averages
1. W.H. Copson (Lidget Green)   88 wkts @ 8.52
2. D. Bateson (Saltaire)   36 wkts @ 10.00
3. M.J. Cowan (Bingley)   38 wkts @ 10.03
4. C. Helliwell (Queensbury)   70 wkts @ 10.81
5. P. Watson (Spen Victoria)   91 wkts @ 10.86

* The two sides awarded an extra point for a tie are in different divisions. This is because the tie took place in an Inter Divisional fixture.

1956

Division 1
	P	W	D	L	Pts
Pudsey St. Lawrence	22	11	7	4	51
Bradford	22	10	8	4	48
Bingley	22	8	9	5	41
Farsley	22	7	9	6	37
Lidget Green	22	6	12	4	36
Idle	22	6	10	6	34
Lightcliffe	22	6	10	6	34
Salts	22	5	10	7	30
Brighouse	22	6	6	10	30
Queensbury	22	5	9	8	29
Eccleshill	22	4	8	10	24

Division 2
	P	W	D	L	Pts
Windhill	22	11	6	5	50
Spen Victoria	22	9	12	1	48
Undercliffe	22	9	9	4	45
Bowling Old Lane	22	7	9	6	37
Baildon	22	6	9	7	33
Great Horton	22	5	12	5	32
East Bierley	22	5	9	8	29
Keighley	22	5	8	9	28
Saltaire	22	3	13	6	25
Bankfoot	22	3	11	8	23
Yeadon	22	2	10	10	18

Batting Averages
1. M.S. Woodcock (Bankfoot)   46.69
2. J.C. Rigg (Bingley)   46.06
3. H. Waterhouse (East Bierley)   42.40

Bowling Averages
1. W.H. Copson (Lidget Green)   42 wkts @ 9.89
2. E. Leadbeater (Pudsey St. Lawrence)   70 wkts @ 10.51
3. A. Goodwin (Keighley)   34 wkts @ 10.97

Note: Winner of Batting averages came from a side which won only 3 of its 22 league games. A surprising feature of the season.

1957

Division 1
	P	W	2 pts	1 pt	L	Pts
Lidget Green	22	15	0	6	1	66
Bradford	22	10	1	7	4	49
Idle	22	10	1	6	5	47
Salts	22	8	1	7	6	41
Pudsey St. Lawrence	22	8	1	5	5	39
Bingley	22	5	2*	10	5	34
Lightcliffe	22	5	2	8	7	32
Farsley	22	5	1	8	8	30
Brighouse	22	5	0	9	8	29
Spen Victoria	22	5	0	6	11	26
Windhill	22	3	1*	7	11	21

Division 2
	P	W	2 pts	1 pt	L	Pts
Baildon	22	14	0	4	4	60
East Bierley	22	11	3	4	4	54
Saltaire	22	9	1	8	4	46
Keighley	22	8	2*	7	5	43
Undercliffe	22	9	0	5	8	41
Queensbury	22	6	0	9	7	33
Yeadon	22	7	0	5	10	33
Bowling Old Lane	22	4	2*	8	8	28
Great Horton	22	5	0	7	10	27
Bankfoot	22	3	0	7	12	19
Eccleshill	22	3	0	7	12	19

Batting Averages
1. E.S. Barraclough (Bradford)   45.12
2. A.G. Padgett (Brighouse)   44.61
3. B. Jenkinson (Lidget Green)   39.90

Bowling Averages
1. B. Wood (Lidget Green)   67 wkts @ 8.67
2. C.H. Wood (Saltaire)   52 wkts @ 9.48
3. H. Aspinall (Great Horton)   40 wkts @ 10.62

* In league table signifies tied game.

1958

Division 1

	P	W	2 pts	1 pt	L	Pts
Bradford	22	10	3	9	0	55
Salts	22	8	2	8	4	44
Bingley	22	7	3	8	4	42
Lightcliffe	22	7	1	9	5	39
Idle	22	6	0	11	5	35
East Bierley	22	6	0	10	6	34
Farsley	22	5	1	11	5	33
Baildon	22	4	1	12	5	30
Lidget Green	22	4	0	12	6	28
Brighouse	22	4	2	7	9	27
Pudsey St. Lawrence	22	3	3	7	9	25

Division 2

	P	W	2 pts	1 pt	L	Pts
Yeadon	22	9	0	11	2	47
Great Horton	22	9	1	9	3	47
Undercliffe	22	9	2	6	5	46
Saltaire	22	8	1	9	4	43
Bowling Old Lane	22	7	2	8	5	40
Spen Victoria	22	7	1	8	6	38
Eccleshill	22	6	1	7	8	33
Keighley	22	5	0	10	7	30
Windhill	22	6	0	5	11	29
Queensbury	22	3	0	6	13	18
Bankfoot	22	1	2	7	12	15

Batting Averages
1 C. Helliwell (Bradford) 50.00
2 E.S. Barraclough (Bradford) 41.84
3 A. Hodgson (Salts) 40.85

Bowling Averages
1 M. Cowan (Bingley) 47 wkts @ 6.19
2 R.K. Platt (Bradford) 46 wkts @ 7.52
3 K. Speight (Yeadon) 32 wkts @ 8.78
4 C.H. Wood (Saltaire) 64 wkts @ 9.59
5 P. Roantree (Eccleshill) 49 wkts @ 9.91
6 T.G. Webster (Pudsey St. Lawrence) 49 wkts @ 9.93

1959

Division 1

	P	W	2 pts	1 pt	L	Pts
Bingley	22	12	1	5	4	55
Salts	22	12	1	2	7	52
Lidget Green	22	10	1	6	5	48
Bradford	22	9	3	4	6	46
East Bierley	22	9	2	6	5	46
Farsley	22	9	3	2	8	44
Yeadon	22	8	0	8	6	40
Baildon	22	8	1	5	8	39
Idle	22	6	0	5	11	29
Lightcliffe	22	6	0	4	12	28
Great Horton	22	2	1	5	14	15

Division 2

	P	W	2 pts	1 pt	L	Pts
Brighouse	22	11	2	4	5	52
Pudsey St. Lawrence	22	11	1	6	4	52
Spen Victoria	22	10	0	6	6	46
Bowling Old Lane	22	10	1	4	7	46
Undercliffe	22	10	0	6	6	46
Saltaire	22	8	1	5	8	39
Keighley	22	6	1	7	8	33
Eccleshill	22	6	3	2	11	32
Windhill	22	6	0	5	11	29
Queensbury	22	4	1	9	8	27
Bankfoot	22	2	1	4	15	14

Batting Averages
1 E.S. Barraclough (Bradford) 60.07
2 J.A. Phillips (Bradford) 55.07
3 A.G. Padgett (Brighouse) 48.00
4 M. Hellawell (Keighley) 46.40
5 F.A. Lowson (Brighouse) 44.72

Bowling Averages
1 P.E. Watson (Spen Victoria) 81 wkts @ 11.71
2 M.J. Cowan (Bingley) 72 wkts @ 11.83
3 B. Jenkinson (Lidget Green) 30 wkts @ 12.43
4 J. Cliffe (Lidget Green) 30 wkts @ 12.56
5 B. Stead (Farsley) 52 wkts @ 12.61

For the first time there was a tie for the fastest fifty trophy. D. Dent (Queensbury) and H.J. McIlvenny (Bradford) having scored 50 runs in 26 mins.

89

Chapter Ten
Nothing Idle at Cavendish Road (1960 – 1977)

The 1959 season had been the first to be played under the fifty, six ball overs system. At the end of that season, Clubs met to vote on their impressions. Brighouse and Farsley wanted to abolish the overs system. Each side of the argument was stated forcefully and when the voting came to eleven in favour and eleven against it was an indication that the League had problems, with half the teams playing under a system they did not want. The summer of 1960 gave the clubs a second chance to judge the situation after which many clubs realised they had been a bit hasty and once they became used to the fifty, six ball overs the vast majority got to like it, so much so the system still remains.

The opening day of a season has rarely passed quietly and in 1960 East Bierley left Baildon to get 172 runs for victory. Baildon reached 115 for 4 putting the final outcome very much in the balance. A few minutes later they were all out for 116. Their last six wickets had fallen for just one run. Barrie Jenkinson, after three years as an amateur with Lidget Green, started his professional career with Bowling Old Lane against Farsley and made a great start with 43 and a match winning 6 for 25. Newly promoted Brighouse played Salts who totalled 202 for 9. A Frank Lowson century however helped Brighouse reach 203 for 5, so they were off to a good start in the higher grade. On the second Saturday of the 1960 campaign came one of the biggest shocks of all time. The previous year Queensbury had applied for re-election and this particular fixture was Inter-Divisional against Bradford. Batting first, Bradford piled up runs as expected, Blackburn 65, Barraclough 52, Phillips 38 not out, King 35 and Thompson 20 not out, as they reached 220 for 4 wickets. In reply Queensbury had a partnership of 116 for the second wicket. Jack Moule (surely the best value for money professional of the time) made 82 not out, while newcomer Dent hit 64. Assisted by 32 from Woodford and 31 not out from Keeton, Queensbury won by eight wickets, their finest victory for many a day. Perhaps I should add that in the return game Bradford did gain revenge. Queensbury all out 135 were beaten by seven wickets and strangely both Blackburn and Barraclough, who made fifties in the first meeting did so again.

Despite the early clouds over the system the season had not been in progress for long before the Yorkshire Evening Post (Green Edition) carried a story of how bright play was in the Bradford League, with all Clubs being positive. It stated that there had been only two draws in the first twenty two fixtures and since then the total had hardly risen with almost all teams going out for victory. Farsley made 234 for 8 with Brian Claughton making an unbeaten 121 and in Bradford's reply Joe Phillips also made a 'ton' but the spirited reply failed. At Queensbury, Eccleshill were the visitors and Dobson for Eccleshill and Dent for Queensbury both reached 80. Though runs were usually plentiful there were always the exceptions and two low scoring matches on the fourth Saturday of the season ended in Bingley dismissing Yeadon for 52 with David Hay taking 6 for 10 and Bingley going on to win by six wickets. Over at Cleckheaton John Walker and Barrie Jenkinson whipped out Spen for just 91 only to find Eric Fisk (5 for 21) and Percy Watson (4 for 29) in match winning form. Old Lane despite 21 from both Keith Dimbleby and Geoff Thompson were all out for 76.

A fine partnership came on 21st May 1960 when Jim Chatburn (102 not out) and George Bottomley (77 not out), playing for Lightcliffe, put on 176 for the 5th wicket. Alas it was just one run short of the 41 year old record set up by George Gunn and W.H. Hickton in 1919 for Undercliffe, but 176 in 112 minutes mean't good entertainment for the Lightcliffe spectators even though Spen in the end held out for a draw. In the first five weeks of the 1960 season there were seven centuries compared to only ten in the whole of the previous season. Batsmen were having a really good time on the hard fast wickets, none more so than Frank Lowson. On the 5th June 1960 the top two sides in Division One, Brighouse and Pudsey St Lawrence, met at Brighouse. Often a top of the bill battle does not live up to expectations. This one did. Batting first Brighouse had a hard time against Eddie Leadbeater (5 for 16) and Chris Wood (3 for 34) and were all out for 93. All over bar the shouting one would think. Not a bit of it as Pudsey lost two wickets for ten runs in reply. Then Pudsey reached 54 for 2 and again the result seemed a foregone conclusion. Terry Webster broke through and he and John Hill spent an hour taking the last eight Pudsey wickets for 27 runs as Pudsey lost by two runs. One week later while Brighouse were failing to beat Bingley, Pudsey were back on the winning trail with success in the local derby, at Farsley, by three wickets. Here the Fearnley brothers were very much in evidence with Duncan top scoring for Farsley with 60 runs and Mike making 23 not out, in a total of 158. When Pudsey finally won by the three wickets Mike had taken all seven to fall at a cost of 55.

Two matches which should be mentioned come from the programme for the 11th June 1960. Firstly the Inter-Divisional fixture when Second Division Great Horton were hosts to First Division Lidget Green. The Division One side looked well set for victory as Great Horton tottered to 73 for 8, but a sparkling stand of 110, only five short of the League record, between Keith Robinson (28 not out) and Gordon Ormondroyd (78) took the score to an all out 187. Ormondroyd was in sparkling form with four sixes and eight fours. Then again Lidget were in control at 66 without loss until Ormondroyd was introduced into the attack. He took 4 for 22 and Lidget eventually ended at 130 for 7 wickets, hanging on desperately for the last few overs.

Meanwhile over at Pearson Road, Bankfoot were batting first against Spen Victoria. Percy Watson opened the bowling for Spen and after six overs he had taken six wickets without conceding a run. He eventually finished with 9 for 54, and Spen went on to win by seven wickets. On the 18th June Jack Douglas became the sixth bowler in League history to take four wickets in four balls. This he did against Idle who slumped from 104 for 4 to 104 for 8 as a result. Douglas was 54 years old at the time. Idle hung on for a draw at 147 for 9 chasing 203, with opener Sid Smith not out on 85. A word here about Sid who at times had infuriated many with his slow scoring. Here however was a match saving effort and no one could fault his dedication and loyalty to Bradford League cricket, in particular his worth to Idle with whom he spent 13 years. Sadly the death of Sid Smith was recorded earlier this year.

Before June was out Alec Hodgson had scored his fourth century of the season when making 116 not out for Salts at home to Bingley. It was needed too as Bingley had made 225 for 6 but Salts thanks to Hodgson and 20 not out from Sunderland went on to win. At Lightcliffe there was an unusual happening in the fixture v Brighouse. A ball from Brighouse fast bowler David Pickles shattered the stumps, moving one away at an angle, sending both bails up in the air. One bail actually came down firmly resting on the top of the middle stump. A real freak balancing act that one.

The 1960 review must contain a mention of the games between Bingley and Salts. When the sides met in the Priestley Cup, Salts scored 270 for 9 and Bingley replied with 166. In the first League game between the two that season there were 451 runs scored as Salts won by five wickets. In the return Salts totalled 190 for 9 dec. being passed by Bingley's 192 for 2 (Barry Whittingham 80 not out). By my reckoning that makes a total of 1269 runs in three games at five runs per over throughout. Not bad going. Now that is entertainment.

With three games to go in the 1960 programme Brighouse were firm favourites for the Title. When they made 99 for 3 at Lidget Green the game was rained off and so were all the others in the League which left Brighouse needing just one point, from the two games left, to clinch it. This they did in style at Yeadon dismissing the home side for just 84 runs and with 51 not out from Frank Lowson won by eight wickets to start celebrations with a week of the season still remaining. Yeadon probably didn't join in because that Brighouse win sent them down to Division Two. Coming up from the lower division would be Undercliffe who beat Saltaire, after Fred Binks (3 for 13) and Norman Fell (3 for 14) had dismissed the Roberts Park side for just 74 runs. Spen on the other hand had to sweat a little longer. All out 128 they needed every point to make sure of going up. Opponents Windhill were going to have to apply for re-admission and yet they very nearly spoilt Spen's party. Gradually getting nearer to the Spen total they kept losing wickets and at the end were only five runs short with their last pair at the wicket. Eric Fisk, who had earlier top scored with thirty-five was the man Spen had to thank most with some economical bowling, leading to figures of 5 for 25. It was the end of a tremendous tussle, for during August only four points had separated the top six clubs. It was 'topsy turvy' stuff and if you were top, as Lightcliffe were, on the 6th August you could drop four places as Lightcliffe duly did when losing to Great Horton on that date. Another great Bradford League season was over.

At the start of the 1961 season Undercliffe raced away to the top of the table before their home game with Farsley in late May. What a game it turned out to be. Farsley took first knock and were all out for 160. No one reached fifty and Norman Fell took 5 for 44. In reply the leaders Undercliffe were comfortably placed at 150 for 5 but then John White broke through and took four wickets in his last two overs and Undercliffe were all out for 160. A tie. What a way to save your unbeaten record. By the time Undercliffe and Farsley met again the Intake Road side were still top but failure to beat Farsley for the second time coupled with Salts win over Idle meant loss of the leadership. Against Farsley the Undercliffe side came up against another Fearnley brothers act. Duncan making 61 and Mike following with four wickets. Chasing 178 for 8 Undercliffe were 139 for 9 at the close. That Salts win was by a comfortable six wickets over relegation threatened Idle against whom Alec Broadbent took 6 for 38.

The Inter-Divisional fixture was still part of the League format in 1961. Usually of course the Division One side won and very often with comparative ease. In 1961 Second Division Bankfoot met Spen from the top flight. In the first meeting at Bankfoot, Spen were all out for 80 with Brian James taking 5 for 22. The Division Two side won by six wickets. In the return at Spen, Sylvan Farquarson (5 for 16) and Brian James, what a good bowler he was, (3-19) did the damage. Spen all out 54, Bankfoot winning by four wickets though Percy Watson did his darndest to stop them with 5 for 15. For a Division Two side to do the double was quite something, to dismiss Spen for 80 and 54 was really something else.

The 1961 Champions were Salts, a surprise, for they had won only five games in 1960. Phillips (36.38), Hodgson (29.25) and Clarke (27.07) were not exactly prolific scorers but were steady and got the runs when it mattered most. Often there were not very many to get after Stead (40 wkts at 12.62), Gott (37 wkts at 13.72) and Broadbent (34 wkts at 14.29) had done the early damage. King and Kendall added valuable runs and although their greatest day was the one that clinched the title, they would be proud of the performance which dismissed Brighouse for 47 with Barry Stead, who would later open the bowling for Notts with Gary Sobers, taking 9 for 15. The Division Two Champs were Bowling Old Lane and they also reached the Priestley Cup Final. There was no finer opening pair of pace bowlers than Malcolm Shackleton and Harry Rider who had taken 58 and 47 wickets respectively. No one reached 500 runs, nor averaged 30 but Clough, Dimbleby, Thompson, Hill and Woodford made up a very useful first five in that order. Only once did a player top 80 runs for Old Lane that season and that was Keith Dimbleby's 82 against East Bierley. Very unusual that, no one topping 82 in a Championship winning side. Shackleton had 8 for 35 v Great Horton and 8 for 23 v Baildon while Rider took 7 for 19 v Yeadon and 6 for 16 v Eccleshill helping to dismiss Bierley for only 33. The 55 not out made by Jackie Hill (Jnr) against Bankfoot was his last Bradford League fifty. His first two had come 21 years earlier when in 1940 he scored 63 against Windhill and 50 v Brighouse.

Jackie Hill like his father before him created a large chunk of Bradford League History. Hill (Snr) started at Bankfoot in 1922, moved to Low Moor for 1927, on to Brighouse in 1930 and followed with Bingley, Baildon Green and Bowling Old Lane. His finest days were with Brighouse with whom he twice topped the League Averages and had that record breaking partnership in 1932 with Crossley, of 248 for the third wicket. Maybe because he was at Bowling Old Lane in 1939 his son joined the same club. Jackie Hill (Jnr) has been a one club man at Old Lane and was an outstanding captain. He was a steady rather than spectacular batter, making in 1956 the League's highest individual score of the season with 148 not out against Windhill. This was a terrific triumph for the family for in 1930 his father made 136 not out for Brighouse against East Bierley and that too was the highest individual score of the season. Bowling Old Lane have much to thank Jack Hill for.

Outstanding bowling performance for 1961 belonged to Dennis Bateson, a superb all-rounder, who had figures against Yeadon of 11 overs, 10 maidens, 1 run, 6 wickets. He became the only player to perform the double of 10,000 runs and 1,000 wickets in the League.

As previously stated there are usually shocks on the opening day of a new season and in 1962 the shock came in the gate receipts at Queensbury. Only 12 shillings and 3 pence which represented 12 adults and 1 child. Out of that Queensbury had to pay two professionals, Dent and Moule, the scorer, tinboys, gateman, umpires and buy a new ball. Members are not included of course in that total of 13, and those who did turn up on that fine day saw Queensbury give real value for money. Batting first they scored 227 for 9 with 79 from Moule, 78 from Dent and 37 not out from Jackson. When Yeadon went in they found Queensbury too good in the bowling and fielding departments too and were all out for 45 (A. Watt 6 for 11). On the second Saturday most games ended in draws due to early evening rain. No one would be more disappointed than Spen who were 110 for 7 replying to Bankfoots 112 all out.

The 1962 title was won by Farsley, but if their supporters will forgive me, I feel second placed Bowling Old Lane were the more attractive of the sides to watch. They played positive cricket which gave them one more victory than the Champs and while Old Lane had just five one point fixtures, Farsley had twice as many losing draws. Somewhere along the line they decided not to adopt the 'Do or Die' policy of the Old Lane, and one of those ten one pointers made all the difference at the end when Farsley topped Old Lane's 45 points by one. Old Lane had the ability to bowl sides out. Twice I saw them batting first, reaching 164 and 122 but one each occasion it was enough. Neither Farsley nor Old Lane had a player in the top five of either the batting or bowling averages. John Woodford (33.91) from 12 innings was Old Lane's top batsman and what a fine one day player he was to be for Yorkshire. Brian Claughton led the way for Farsley ending with 499 runs at 31.19. Malcolm Shackleton a fine all-rounder for Bowling averaging over twenty with the bat and taking 52 league wickets at 13.62. John White was Farsley's leading bowler, a player who later became a long serving and much respected player at Undercliffe.

Despite being only an average Division Two side Keighley took some individual honours. J.A. Greenwood was top amateur batsman in the League, Derek Stow, top bowler. G.S. Greenwood, top wicketkeeper and J.S. Wilson leading fieldsman. Perhaps it was rather surprising to see them only in mid table.

At the head of Division Two in 1962 were Idle who became the team of the sixties. They only had a two point margin over Saltaire losing just three of twenty-two league fixtures. One of these defeats came five games from the end of the season and almost cost them the title, when they had no answer to Brian James who took 7 for 35 at Cavendish Road. Idle were all out for 115 and were beaten by six wickets but they were a good all round team and they deserved their success. Brian James put more than the Idle batsmen to rest for he was a fine bowler, one of the best left arm pacemen it has been my privilege to see. He had played first class cricket for Yorkshire in 1954. In his Bradford League days he was of course a professional. One Saturday we were both in a tearoom at a Bradford League ground when in came a newspaper seller with that days *Yorkshire Sports*. Inside were the half way stage averages for all Bradford League professionals. Now it was the custom of the paper to list both batting and bowling and Brian was, to be polite, never a man to score many runs. Seeing his batting average was 3.50 his face lit up and in celebration of such a large average bought drinks all round. His stay in the League was too short for my liking but not I expect for his victims that numbered nearly three hundred in six years spent equally at Brighouse and Bankfoot.

The 1962 season was one in which I witnessed a good deal of top class wicketkeeping. Peter Bretherick (Bowling Old Lane), Stan Longbottom (Bankfoot), Albert Firth (Windhill), Duggie Bates (Eccleshill, one of the top Table Tennis players in the City at the time), and Derek Wainwright of Brighouse. Ray Green at Baildon was a perfect keeper to Roger Bradley and Wilf Birkenshaw, two men who could turn it a bit. Green gained sixteen stumpings in league games.

The 1962 'fastest fifty' trophy went to Geoff Thompson, a powerfully built man who took just 17 minutes, the fastest time for almost twenty years. There were two ten wicket feats in that 1962 season, Bob Horrox taking 10 for 34 for Division Two champs Idle v Windhill but the second was the most amazing bowling feat in the history of the League. Percy Watson, by now at Spen Victoria, took ten wickets for eleven runs against Yeadon. It beat the 10 for 14 taken in 1915 by Sydney Barnes as the Leagues No. 1 performance. In 1962 there was some really positive cricket played in Division Two. Throughout the season on only eleven occasions was there a winning/losing draw. That's one every two weeks, a great tribute to all captains.

1963 taught me a great lesson about this great game of cricket. Reporting for the *Yorkshire Sports* I rang through some copy which ended, 'at 41 for 3 the home side are due for a small total, for the outfield is slow and Horne who has taken all three wickets is bowling brilliantly'. Never again should I make a prediction about the outcome of an innings. Imagine how I felt later when all spectators were able to read my report and Ken Hill 123 not out and Geoff Thompson 65 not had put on 191 for the 4th wicket, only a dozen runs short of the League record. A reporters life can be dangerous for one or two sought me out to 'have a go', good naturedly on this occasion. On another though I referred to a batsmans slow scoring being detrimental to his side, later that day he was looking for me I was told, he never found me, so I'm here to tell the tale.

Undercliffe were champions in 1963 and Jack Wainwright had a big hand in taking the title to Intake Road. Jack had 57 league wickets at 9.16 and his style of bowling which was strangley both penetrative and yet economical, brought discomfort to all who faced it. In 1960 Jack took five wickets in each game against Idle (5 for 22 and 5 for 32) having joined Undercliffe one year earlier. His first seven wicket haul came in 1962 with 7 for 27 against Eccleshill while in 1963 there were two more, 7 for 25 v Idle and 7 for 58 against Lightcliffe. There was no doubt that 1963 was his finest season. In 1970, by now at Bowling Old Lane, he took 8 for 40 against Hartshead Moor in the Priestley Cup and signed off in 1973 when he took 6 for 46 for new club Idle against his old mates from Bowling. Jack Wainwright was a bowler who never seemd to get collared and in recent years has pleased me talking a lot of common sense on cricket with local radio.

Back to that 1963 season and some more wicketkeepers to take the eye. David Pullan at Farsley, Ray Hirst at Spen Victoria, Donald Garside at Lightcliffe and Bill Jamieson at Lidget Green. Bingley ran Undercliffe very close and they too had men to catch the eye. Brian Lymbery, about whom much more later and Ken Standring. Ken was a class batsman right out of the textbook and while he was adding to his list of admirers weekly, Frank Lowson with the same type of elegant batting for Brighouse became the fourth player to score 1,000 league runs in a season.

There were two newcomers to the League in 1963, Hartshead Moor and Laisterdyke. The latter had been members before from 1903 to 1927. Both won only five of their 22 league games and while Laisterdyke lost ten games, Hartshead, being the more difficult to beat, lost six. Hartshead had some good players, Brian Collier, never short of confidence in his own ability topped 500 runs and there was fine support from the two Hirsts, Donald and Raymond, with Terry Evans adding 345 welcome runs. Donald Hirst is a man I came to admire but alas on one occasion he had been the brunt of some, in my opinion, unkind comment. Hirst recalled a batsman he knew to be not out, a decision which cost his side the game. I applaud Hirst for his action, just as I did in Test Cricket when Gundappa Viswanath recalled England's Bob Taylor. Taylor saved the game and Vishy was crucified by the Press. I cannot understand those who say Hirst was wrong. Cheating should never be a part of any game and if you lose by doing the 'right thing', be it recalling a batsman or losing wickets by entertaining then so be it. Now I did say that this book would not be controversial and so it won't. I would like to express one opinion of mine which first came to light in 1964. I was asked to cover, for a weekly paper, the match between Bankfoot and Salts on the seasons opening day. Bankfoot batting first made only 85 runs due to a fine piece of bowling by Tony Rowe who took 9 for 39. In reply Salts scored 86 for 2 to win by eight wickets. They deserved their win being far superior on the day but both Bankfoot and Salts were awarded a point due to the fact that no other game in the division had started due to the weather conditions. In Division One Undercliffe had commenced against Pudsey a match which was abandoned, with Pudsey 98 for 4 replying to 184 for 8 Dec. Had either side won in that game each would have only received a point. My personal opinion is that this Rule should simply not apply and that Salts should have received winning points. I know of many cases where one match has been rained off after starting and two clubs had to settle for one point while all other clubs, so widely spread gained points. There is sure to be days when one side, say Hanging Heaton or Keighley, or Brighouse or Yorkshire Bank will either be the only one rained off or the only area fit to play. To compensate for when they may be the only far flung area rained off I believe that if they are the only area able to play they should be able to compete for full points.

In those two openers of 1964 the receipts at Undercliffe were £2-3-9d while at Bankfoot the receipts were nil. I'll testify that only members were present but the players wanted to play and all credit to them on a raw cold wet afternoon for doing so. On the second Saturday of that season there was an unusual sequel, for while Salts, all out 90, were beating Baildon (Rowe 6 for 38), Bankfoot's match was rained off meaning they took as many points when being beaten by Salts as they did when not playing.

On the 9th May 1964 Pudsey St Lawrence were at Idle. The home team were all out for 45 with John White taking 6 for 32 and Chris Wood 3 for 10. Idle were nothing if not battlers and Ken Woodward 4 for 18 and Dick Sherred 6 for 15 brought Idle a six run victory against the odds.

Yeadon won only two games in 1962 and again only two games in 1963. Then quite remarkably in 1964 the won three games in four days. Starting on Whit Saturday, Yeadon dismissed Eccleshill for 122 and won by four wickets. On Whit Monday they chased 181 to beat Hartshead Moor with 86 from Goolam Abed, the winning run coming from the fourth ball of the last over. One day later Abed scored 75 as Yeadon made 166 for 8 and then with Garland 4 for 42, Smith 3 for 6 and Williams 3 for 24 taking the wickets, dismissed Great Horton for 79 to record their third successive win. They were the only Bradford League side to do so over that holiday weekend. Before the holiday they would have been the last team anyone expected to win all three matches. Such are the fluctuations of this great game.

One match I would like to mention from that Whitsuntide programme is Undercliffe against Bradford. Undercliffe reached 204 for 4 after 47 overs and declared. After their allotted fifty overs Bradford were a few runs short. They won thanks to the bonus of three overs given by Undercliffe and with their last pair at the wicket. The Undercliffe skipper had gambled and lost but I warmly applaud his action in giving himself more overs in which to bowl out the opposition. Bradford responded and went for the runs throughout and although Undercliffe lost I never question a team who loses whilst trying to win. Far too much emphasis is placed on avoiding defeat these days. You can lose with honour. I am reminded of a piece my father often quoted and by which Test cricketer Fred Root ran his life.

> When the One Great Scorer comes,
> To write against your name,
> It isn't if you won or lost,
> But how you played the game.

Many Bradford League supporters, with justification, say there is a great gulf between Division One and Division Two, so the fact that promoted Lidget Green in 1963, took the 1964 Division One title must have been the exception to the rule. They had two fine bowlers in Ray Peel and David Batty, both using an experienced head on young shoulders. Bob Fisher, Peter Atkinson and Mick Huddlestone were batsmen difficult to remove. When Jamieson, the wicketkeeper who had seven stumpings and fifteen catches, was unable to play in six games his deputy Mick Reynolds had a remarkable time with seven stumpings and nine catches.

The deputy of the year though must have been Peter Wear of Bingley. Ken Standring was unable to open the bowling against Bradford due to an injury and up stepped Peter in his place. Wear then took 9 for 10 as Bradford were dismissed for 28 runs. The wicket Wear didn't get was the first, previously he had only taken eleven. Ah, that unexpected 'defying the odds' had cropped up again. Behind Lidget Green were Idle who were about to embark on a hat-trick of titles in 1965 and keep Pudsey St Lawrence in second spot on all three occasions.

The 1965 season opened with Barrie Jenkinson performing the hat-trick at Bingley for Bradford, a stand of 136 by Harold Gill and A.H. Clarke for Laisterdyke and 8 for 40 by John White for Pudsey at home to Lidget. None of these feats helped their side to a victory though Laisterdyke came nearest when Idle replied to their 182 for 5 dec., with 131 for 8. In fact Idle won only one of their first three but from then on their talents became obvious, though Pudsey St Lawrence and Lightcliffe made it a very exciting Championship race. When each side had played ten games Lightcliffe had 29 points, Idle 28 and Pudsey 27.

One week later Pudsey failed to beat Undercliffe for whom that magnificent bowler Les Jackson, in his first Bradford League season took five of the eight Pudsey wickets to fall. After eleven games and with six successive wins behind them Lightcliffe were top but a century from East Bierley's Eddie Slingsby and six wickets from Brian Redfearn brought that run to an end. Meanwhile Idle won at Undercliffe. Having dismissed the team from Intake Road for 103 (Sherred 5 for 34 and Woodward 4 for 41) they now had to face Jackson. Les as always bowled his heart out despite only a small total on the board. He took 4 for 31 but Sid Smith held firm and his 38 not out was largely responsible for a three wicket Idle win. Five matches later and Lightcliffe had gone back to the top, very unexpectedly too. At tea Lightcliffe were all out 94 at Bingley while Idle scored 157 for 5 against Pudsey. At the end of the day however Idle lost and despite making only 94 runs Lightcliffe had won, by 14 runs, to regain top spot in the League. Then the top two, Idle and Lightcliffe, met in game eighteen at Idle. The home side were 85 for 9 of which John France had scored 42. Sherred (25) and Reynolds (35 not out) then had a last wicket stand of 61. Lightcliffe progressed to 37 without loss when the rain ended all hopes of a win for either side. One week later as Laisterdyke held Lightcliffe to a draw Idle, thanks to 8 for 33 from Dick Sherred, at Saltaire, won by eight wickets and took over by one point.

The Lightcliffe challenge faded when they lost to Bowling Old Lane only three games from the end of the season. Now it was a two team race with Idle having two points more than Pudsey and one game to play. This has been brought about by Pudsey scoring at nine runs per over to beat the rain and Saltaire while Idle were on 129 for 6 when their particular match was rained off. The last day saw both Idle and Pudsey unable to play and so Idle's two point margin was just about right in the final analysis. Ian Leng with his left arm slows had been a star among 'stars' for Idle. Sid Smith scored 603 runs at 33.50 while Ken Hill had 472 at 29.50. Sherred, Leng and Woodward were as good as any other combination in the League. Lewis Pickles, the ex-Somerset County all-rounder gave great service to Pudsey with his 752 runs and 36 wickets at 15.72. Donald Garside of Lightcliffe was a popular winner of the League's wicketkeeping trophy.

Winning a title is one thing, retaining it, when the likes of a very good Pudsey side was again in the way, made Idle's 1966 title a really worthy achievement under the captaincy of Ken Woodward. The 1966 season was another nailbiter, though this time third placed Lightcliffe soon fell by the wayside. However the season nearly didn't get started at all. Due to really dreadful weather the first two weeks fixtures were moved, en bloc, to the 27th and 28th June and the season saw the first ball bowled as late as the 7th May. Champs Idle were at Keighley and got a shock. Keighley had them all out for 102, top scorer Ken Woodward with just 19. Although Idle fought hard taking eight Keighley wickets they nevertheless started the new season with a loss. On the second playable Saturday in 1966 there were a few batsmen top scoring with under twenty. Now its common knowledge that each week a side will make a low score and probably have their top scorer with under twenty. On this day in 1966 there were a few such happenings more than is usual.

Kay of Farsley scored thirteen and was top scorer as they made only 63 losing to Idle. Meanwhile Morton and Sutton with 12 runs each were joint top scorers for Salts who made only 66. Laisterdyke were all out 66 too with John Hainsworth's nineteen their highest. Saltaire made only 61, their top man being Derek Webster with fifteen. Yeadon's top score was thirteen by M. Melrose, in their all out total of 59. Great Horton were the third side dismissed for 66 and again their top scorer was under twenty, this time seventeen by Arthur Aspinall. While all this mayhem was afoot East Bierley and Eccleshill were tieing on 109 runs each and even in those low scores two men Slingsby (69) for Bierley and Moore (66) for Eccleshill managed to make a large proportion of their sides total.

In June 1966 I witnessed a match which had a truly astounding turn around. Bankfoot were all out for 139 at home to Great Horton. With 23 overs left Horton were 74 for 1. Before they reached 80 they were playing for a draw. They had slumped from that winning position to a score of 80 for 8. With one over left they were 88 for 9 having just added fourteen runs whilst losing eight wickets in the previous 22 overs. Such a fightback deserved victory and justice was done with Bankfoot winning in the last over. So Horton, 74 for 1, had eventually been dismissed twenty three overs later for 88 runs. Allan Clarke (5 for 23) and Roger Pawson (3 for 18) had been the men responsible.

When Idle met Lightcliffe they struggled to an all out score of 94. Then Dick Sherred took nine wickets and caught the other off Ian Leng's bowling as Idle were successful by 25 runs. Another slump/fightback on the same day came at Queensbury who went from 67 for 3 to 84 all out, when the Spen captain, John Woodford, had a four wickets for no run spell and finished with five wickets for five runs. When Idle, second in the table, went to Pudsey the leaders, the home side rattled up 228 for 4 dec. Idle repled with 93 for 9 to gain just the odd point. In retrospect they will have been very pleased that they did gain that point because that was the margin by which they took the title over Pudsey at the seasons end.

Martin and Dick Sherred skittled Lidget Green, all out 87, and the resulting Idle win brought them a one point lead over Pudsey at the seasons half way point. At that time Bingley were in fourth place in Division Two after making 154 against Great Horton, taking six early Horton wickets and the finding Alan Douglas (59 not out) and Henry Webster (40 not out) immovable as Horton won by four wickets. That was Bingley's second defeat but it was also their last that season. In the eleven second half games Bingley won seven and drew four. Idle made sure of the title when they beat East Bierley, by seven wickets, on the penultimate Saturday, but the week before they had dismissed Pudsey for 74 with Dick and Martin Sherred taking five wickets each. Sid Smith steadied Idle, after four wickets had gone, with 47 not out. On the last day Idle of course wanted to end the season in style but batting first against Undercliffe they were bowled out for 100. They made a real game of it though before losing by one wicket. Pudsey meanwhile were beating Bradford but it was all too late because Idle had that extra point.

With 1966 being Football World Cup year there were many spectators missing during the League programme watching the progress of the England team on television or in person. It was a year when the sun shone and most Bradford League games had a definite result. Derbyshire's D.H.K. Smith and Les Jackson were proof that top class players were still in the Bradford League. 1966 opened well for Farsley. They won by four wickets on the opening day against East Bierley but this turned out to be their only win of the season. Another unusual feature of 1966 was that Idle had won the title without once reaching a score of two hundred in an innings. They dismissed their opponents for under a hundred on seven occasions and the Sherred brothers took 140 of the 170 wickets gained by the club that season.

With Ken Woodward again leading the side and with their full quota of professionals (Sid Smith, Malcolm Smith, and the Sherred brothers) Idle set out in an effort to win a third consecutive championship with an opening 1967 fixture v East Bierley. They found Brian Lymbery (27) and Denis Bateson (23) most stubborn but managed to dismiss the side for 102 and scrape home by three wickets for a winning start. Another fine opening day performance came from Pat McKelvey in the Saltaire visit to Bankfoot. The visitors were all out for 98 of which McKelvey had made twenty two. Then in Bankfoot's reply he took 7 for 39 to help his side to a ten run victory. McKelvey had first played Bradford League cricket in 1965 after County experience with Surrey.

Twenty two years later, Pat McKelvey was still playing in the League, again with Saltaire after a short spell with Hartshead Moor. In his First Class days Pat once took the only wicket to fall in a game. This was for Surrey against the Combined Services which was a First Class fixture in Pat's County days. It happened in 1960 at The Oval and the game was rain affected. Eventually play got underway, under the one day rule at that time and Surrey batted first making 138 without loss before declaring. The Combined Services had used four bowlers including Barry Stead. More than 54 overs had already been bowled by the Services side but no wicket. Then Surrey took the field and Gibson, Sydenham and Bedser bowled 23 overs between them also without a wicket. Along came McKelvey getting the wicket of Richard Langridge for 34 and he finished with figures of 5-3-7-1, the best figures of the match and the only wicket to fall. His left arm slows and knowledge of cricket, not to mention the helpfulness of his character, makes him a valuable servant to Saltaire Cricket Club where he spent the majority of his Bradford League seasons.

The first hat-trick of 1967 came from Tony Rowe of Salts in the Home game with Bankfoot, small reward for the day his nine wicket haul failed to bring full points. This time his 4 for 58 was for a losing side. A comfortable win over Lightcliffe at the end of May took Idle to the top of the League, a position to which they had become accustomed. Ken Woodward was the unsung hero. Unsung because maybe his performances were steady rather than spectacular but no less value to the team for all that.

At Idle's next match, the umpire was so annoyed by Idle's slow scoring he promptly resigned. The match was at Lidget Green where the home side declared at 166 for 5 wickets. In reply Idle lost seven wickets for 75 runs, at which point they put up the shutters. Malcolm Reynolds and Ken Woodward put on fifty-one facing six bowlers and ending at 126 for 7 to earn a point. Philip Cooper, a twenty-seven year old umpire from Heckmondwike, had been an umpire for seven years but objected to Idle putting up the shutters with 30 overs still to go in the innings. Now I am all in favour of entertainment but if all clubs put up the shutters early what a disaster the cricket would be, perhaps with seven or more wickets down the more acceptable it can be. It is clubs who lose three of four wickets for about fifty runs chasing a score in the region of two hundred, and then play for a draw which upsets me. Those who leave it as late as Idle did in this case, I don't feel deserve criticism. It also depends how vital the game is too. Two mid-table sides have nothing to lose by all out attack, an approach which is also pleasing for the spectator.

Undercliffe crept to the top of the table after twelve games and held a two point advantage over Idle. The next fixture was a meeting of the top two. Idle totalled 183 with Hill, France and Hogg all getting into the thirties. Les Jackson was his usual self and finished with 4 for 41. Undercliffe were a good side with Jim Brailsford a fine skipper and Ashley Harvey-Walker, another Derbyshire County player, a prolific scorer. Yet it was Idle who proved superior that day. Only Daley, Nicholson and Brailsford topped twenty as the Sherred brothers had three wickets each. After Undercliffe and Idle had led it was the turn of Pudsey to go to the top just one week later. They beat Undercliffe by one wicket while Idle had difficulty dismissing Great Horton. Replying to Idle's 148 for 4, of which Stuart Herrington made 92, Horton ended on 76 for 6.

In July of the 1967 season Ray Peel of Lidget Green was expelled by his club following a dressing room incident. Peel, upset at the lack of bowling since the first day of the season, when he bowled twenty overs had used some bad language and the club expelled him. It was a courageous step to take for he had already taken 95 runs off Pudsey and 130 from Great Horton while taking 12 wickets at a coast of 14.60. To dismiss a player who was an obvious asset to the cricket side of things was a great credit to Lidget Green. Peel himself was honest enough to admit his use of bad language and has played much Bradford League cricket since. He said at the time he believed it right in the confines of the dressing room and his offence was far less than some I have seen where players have used rank bad language on the field of play. The League's President for the last 9 years, Mr Bruce Moss, has made calls for an end to bad language and I feel his wishes have not fallen on stoney ground. He believes in good christian principles and his example makes him worthy of his post as League President. The management committee have never been slow to suspend players for foul language on the field, particularly in the eighties. It's action to applaud.

Unfortunately not long after the Peel incident there emerged another similar kind of problem to do with discipline. Stan Longbottom quit the East Bierley Club following a disagreement. Stan took 343 League victims behind the stumps, a record, in his Bradford League career. He was a cheerful chap, a schoolteacher from Horsforth. When Bradford beat East Bierley, Stan was blamed for the fact that the win was gained by an overthrow for three runs from the last scheduled ball of the game. What several players had said in the heat of the moment had upset Stan and he promptly left the League signing for Gomersal, in the now Central Yorkshire League.

With three games left in the 1967 programme the title was between Idle, Pudsey St Lawrence and Bradford. Pudsey cut the arrears to one point when they thrashed Bowling Old Lane while Idle were thwarted by Bradford. Idle made 140 for 3 and Bradford replied with 63 for 8 in a rain affected match. While this was going on Yeadon were all out for 50 runs against Bankfoot and won by ten runs. Only two games to go now and Idle were to play Pudsey. The top two. What a match in prospect and in fact it lived up to its 'Match of the Day' billing. Batting first Pudsey reached 170 for 9 dec. with 55 from A.D. Webster while Martin Sherred took 7 for 67. In reply Idle lost wickets but Stuart Herrington stood firm and in this intriguing encounter they ended at 161 for 9, with Herrington 108 not out. So Idle needed a last match win to complete a hat-trick of Championships. They soon had Eccleshill all out for 99 despite a knock of 53 from Billy Rhodes, father of County wicketkeeper Steve, who himself played for Nottinghamshire. In reply Idle reached 100 for 3 with Smith 53 not out and it was celebration time once again. Idle were undoubtedly worthy Champions because there was such fine opposition in the First Division, they had a lot of very good teams to beat and beat them they did. In Division Two that season there was an unexpected end to the programme of matches. With two games to go Hartshead Moor had a seven point lead over Saltaire yet failed to take the title. While Saltaire were beating both Baildon and Yeadon, Hartshead gained only one point out of ten and had to settle for second place.

There was another truly great battle for the Championship in 1968. Main participants were Idle, Bradford and Undercliffe. Neither won their first two matches and after five games it was Bingley and Bowling Old Lane at the top. After five too, Idle the Champs, had not even tasted victory and there were thoughts that the bubble had burst when in game five Idle needed 23 runs with six wickets left but only managed 17 of them. At the same time Pudsey were bottom and when they met Bradford at Park Avenue, Pudsey collapsed from FIFTY WITHOUT LOSS TO SIXTY FOUR ALL OUT. Idle put together two wins before meeting Bradford where again their batting failed. Bradford dismissed them for ninety-four. But we must not forget the Sherred lads, Martin had six wickets and Dick the other four and Bradford were all out for 78. Idle were buzzing again. It was four wins in a row when the Old Lane were beaten, five in a row when Pudsey were all out 99. However with thirteen matches gone Undercliffe had a ten point lead over Idle. Yet in their last nine matches Undercliffe picked up only fourteen points. On the last day of the season Bradford started the day with 57 points, Undercliffe had 57 also and Idle 54. Idle's title was likely to be removed. Firstly Undercliffe's game was rained off, leaving them with 58 points. Enough to take the title if the other two lost. But despite Idle beating Lightcliffe the Championship finished up at Bradford who early in the afternoon polished off Saltaire for 47 and raced home by ten wickets. Mike Fearnley had taken 6 for 11 to take number one spot in the League's bowling averages. Bob Fisher (22 not out) and Barrie Leadbeater (22 not out) saw Bradford to that ten wicket success, giving Fisher an average over fifty and Leadbeater 67.30 and top spot in the batting. Division Two Champs were Spen Victoria, by far the best team in that Division. They only had two defeats, one coming on the last day of the season when with the Championship secure they declared at 75 for 1 (the lowest declared total in the League's history) in a rain affected match and were beaten by five wickets. The other defeat was not so freakish and came at Keighley by thirty-three runs.

Never in the League's history has there been such a start than that in 1969. After five games Lidget Green, Brighouse, Hartshead Moor, East Bierley and Bradford had all played five, drawn five. In fact they had not 'played' five, they had simply not bowled a ball as all the games had been washed out by the weather. Many other clubs lost four out of their first five completely, also. The League tables looked decidedly odd particularly the First Division, when each side was down as having played eight matches only one club, Bingley, had won twice. Five others had just one win in eight whilst the remainder had no wins at all, and all this after eight fixtures of the '69 League programme. It was going to be a strange season with rain the real winner. With half the season gone Bankfoot had won only one match out of eleven and were third from the top of the League.

Farsley had a young sixteen year old playing for them, Phil Carrick, a man who would later lead the County side to a memorable win at Lords. Phil played for Farsley against Yeadon and was run out for 99. This must have been heartbreaking for the sixteen year old lad. He then took 3 for 40 to help his side to a 38 run win. After thirteen games Idle were second but came up against strong opposition in Saltaire. After Idle had made over two hundred for five wickets declared, Saltaire ended at 113 for 9, their last pair denying Idle for 17 overs. Bingley hadn't lost for fifteen games but tasted defeat in game sixteen, when Hartshead Moor scored 171 for 7 to win by three wickets. It was however to be Bingley's season.

With one game left, Bingley had 55 points and Spen Victoria 55 points also. Bingley made 187 for 7 and restricted Lightcliffe to 86 for 8, gaining three points. Spen in the meantime had dismissed Idle for 117 but lost by two runs. It gave Bingley the title by three points. Then it became a double as their 2nd XI won their teams championship also. After beating Spen in the Priestley Cup Final, it became a treble for the club. Then to crown it all the 2nd XI won the Priestley Shield to make it a double double. This is a unique performance in Bradford League cricket. Ken Standring had much to do with this success. He topped the League batting average and took 37 wickets at 11.27 and was quite brilliant at times. Captain John Harrison was as consistent as any I have ever known, at least statistically. In League games Harrison had only one score below twenty (against Spen Victoria) but only one score above thirty-three (against Saltaire). All but two scores therefore were between 20 and 33. Quite consistent I would say. He also skippered the League representative side well.

After many years of tight finishes and tense title battles 1970 was a one horse race due to an outstanding side. Undercliffe. In Les Jackson and John White they had two bowlers as good as any in the League, quite possibly in league cricket throughout the country. Just one League defeat came and that was only by three wickets, after topping the 200 mark against East Bierley. Wherever you looked Undercliffe had some fine players. County Class they were too. Ashley Harvey-Walker started with 90 v Idle, made 100 against Bankfoot and scored 149 not out v Lightcliffe. The latter being the highest score of the season. Skipper Jim Brailsford (from Derbyshire also) took a liking to Hartshead Moor's attack, making 62 and 52 against them and his bowling could be very useful too. His captaincy was outstanding. Then there was a young David Bairstow full of energy and positive thinking. He thrashed 100 not out against Idle in the League and 52 against them in the Cup, and scored 54 off the Pudsey attack and always gave good 'value for money' when available. Some steady batting from Claude Helliwell, fine wicketkeeping from Bill Jamieson and in addition to White and Jackson there were good all round performances from Ray Peel, including 124 runs and 3 for 57 in the match with Bingley. This was indeed a very good Undercliffe side, good enough to compare with any in the past I would think.

It was not surprising that Undercliffe retained their title in 1971 though Bradford cut down to eight points their margin of victory. Harvey-Walker, Peel and Helliwell were again largely responsible for the runs, while John White had another 'Les' from Derbyshire this time in Les Bradbury to open the attack. Bradbury took 35 league wickets at 14.46. In second team cricket that season only one player topped the 500 run mark, A. Harrison of Undercliffe being the honoured player. There were six 2nd team centuries throughout the League though not one of them was more than 107.

Salts had an excellent season in 1971 winning the Division Two title with 80 points, a large total but Lidget Green chased them all the way and finished only three adrift. Poor Windhill were without a win that year and only once, out of twenty-two games, did they take more points from a game than their opponents. There was a record 2nd XI total in 1971 when Bankfoot scored 314 for 8 in 44 overs against Spen Victoria. Four players, Roger Verity (52), John Tiffany (64), Ian Cooper (68) and wicketkeeper Dennis Walker (68) all topped the fifty mark. Little did we know at this juncture that the Bankfoot 1st XI would become the outstanding team of 1972.

At the start of the 1972 season I doubt if many would have backed Bankfoot to win their first ever title after a history going back 109 years. Yet win it they did and in some style too. In Allan Clarke they had a fine skipper who led by example, a player in his twentieth season with the club, so he hardly lacked experience. His seam up bowling, from the smoothest of actions, was a joy and as a batsman he was often accused of batting too low down the order. He was a fine team man who always put his side first with any personal glory very much in second spot. It was fitting that on the day they clinched the title, at Bingley, it should be Allan, with 4 for 5, who made it certain.

He was backed up by two players known nationally. John Woodford had played thirty-eight First Class matches for Yorkshire before Bankfoot clinched their Championship success and he'd been a more than useful 'one day' cricketer for his County. John was a real sportsman, not averse to saying 'well bowled' after a fine delivery had beaten or dismissed him. He gave credit where credit was due, even if that meant to the opposition.

Howard Cooper was a bowler who did not receive his just desserts with Yorkshire, an opinion shared by many Bradford League followers. Like Woodford, Cooper was an above average 'one day' player. At the time of Bankfoot's greatest season he was just starting a County career which eventually brought him ninety-eight First Class games up to 1980, his last season at the top level.

In 1972 Howard took 8 for 30 on the seasons opening day and followed with 8 for 40 in the second fixture played, the home game against Lidget Green having been rained off completely. At the seasons end that Lidget Green game was one of only five draws the club had that season. Most clubs had ten or more which indicates the positive cricket played under Allan Clarke. Ken Hill, all 6'4" of him, was a man who could, and often did, turn a game with his own special brand of batting. Ken has hit the ball harder and further than any batsman I have seen in the Bradford League and if a little ungainly at times, when the bat often got tangled between his legs, his clean hitting made many bowlers despair. Ken's first Bradford League fifty came in 1959, a not out fifty against Queensbury. He came up through the club's junior ranks where he was taught much of what he knew by Stanley Cowman, who emigrated to New Zealand in 1964, and became a much respected Umpire at Test level. In 1964 Ken moved to Idle but was back at Bankfoot for the 1969 campaign. 1972 saw an average of 44.46 from his fifteen League innings and none was more attractive than his 94 not out against Lightcliffe. Raymond Hirst was the club's wicketkeeper having first played Bradford League cricket when Hartshead Moor joined the League in 1963. In fact he was the first centurion for Hartshead in the League. Although he did not make another 'ton' his accumulation of runs, through nudges and pushes, kept the scoreboard ticking over and brought him into the wicketkeeper/batsman class. Brian Hudson will forgive me if I say that at times his mind could wander from the job in hand. More than once skipper Clarke had to 'gee him up' in the field but there were few finer openers in the League in Brians time. For all the periodic wanderings in the field he once snapped up five catches at short-leg in the same innings. To date no Bankfoot batsman has scored a thousand runs in a season, Brian Hudson 809 (1981) and Ken Hill's 740 (1963) being the highest. A margin of seventeen points, in the days of five points for a win, was a truly remarkable achievement for this likeable club. It was a popular win throughout the League and in addition to those mentioned, Ian Leng, John Tiffany, Phil Carter, Stuart Verity, Ted Senescall and Chris Metcalfe all played their part.

If Bankfoot's win of 1972 was unexpected, though thoroughly deserved, that of Bingley in 1973 was a little more predictable. Bingley are a club used to winning trophies, four times previously they had carried off the Division One title and twice been Division Two champions. They had a disappointing 1972 but signed Tony Lush (brother of Peter) a hard hitting batsman, Mike Fearnley and John Waring were acquisitions others would have liked. Strangely Lush (129 v Saltaire) and Waring (7 for 20 v Eccleshill and 6 for 24 v Hartshead Moor) saved their best performances for the Priestley Cup. John Harrison however averaged over fifty for each of his nineteen innings and though I have it on good authority that he was extremely nervous on the night before a game, his apparent nervousness never showed when he batted. Then there was

David Batty, 'George' as he is affectionately known throughout the League who took 62 League wickets at 10.67 and Mike Fearnley had 48 at 11.14 runs each. It was unusual to discover Bingley only exceeded 200 on three occasions, with a top score of 225 against Saltaire, but their bowling often meant only small totals to chase and Salts (41) and Lightcliffe (49) meant early finishes. One feature of Bingley's 1973 season was the fielding, at times brilliant. A leading light in that area was S.J.D. Core. Although he did score only one fifty (against Pudsey St Lawrence) he saved many runs in the field and was such an outstanding fieldsman that in 1976 he won the League's Fielding Award while still with Bingley and followed this success with the Federation Fielding Trophy when with Saltaire in 1979. Bingley were second in 1974, Harrison's runs dried up when from the same number of innings he had 297 runs less. Batty (55 wickets at 11.21) and Fearnley (41 wickets at 15.90) did their stuff with the ball, but a new light began to shine. Neil Hartley, stylish, straight from the textbook showed quality with some fine batting. His 75 not out v Saltaire and 68 against Lidget Green may have been his only League fifties that season but his potential was obvious as was shown to a wider audience in the Priestley Cup Final when he made fifty-four against Undercliffe and was named 'Man of the Match'.

It was Idle who slipped into top spot in the League, not quite the side of the mid-sixties but a very hard side to dismiss. Barrie Jenkinson topped the League batting and with Brian Lymbery second and Brian Hodgson fifth, it was obvious there was no lack of run-getters. Jimmy Spence and Stuart Speak added their weight too. They also had five top class bowlers. Steve Oldham took 5 for 47 against Bankfoot but took some stick from Allan Clarke in a late stand. Tony Burnett had 44 League wickets. Mike Clegg, who had probably the most unusual action ever seen in the League, scuppered Pudsey with 5 for 45. Perhaps I ought to add that I loved watching Clegg 'mix em up a bit'. Life was never dull when he was bowling. For those who haven't seen him, let me say he generated the same sort of expectation as Abdul Qadir, who of course performed for Hanging Heaton a few years later. Chris Fordham took 5 for 24 v Lidget Green adding weight to the attack but it was Idle's Mike Bailey who was the most 'feared' player they had. Mike was in his second season with Idle having taken 7 for 35 v Saltaire in the Priestley Cup, 7 for 53 v Bingley, backed up by five wicket feats against Bradford and Pudsey St Lawrence in his first season. His tidy, dare I say stingy, mean and miserly left arm medium pace guided Idle to the Championship, including 8 for 43 v Bingley. Mike followed this success by becoming a prolific wicket taker after moving to Pudsey St Lawrence in 1981.

It was Pudsey who took the Division One Championship trophy in both 1975 and 1976, but they were two contrasting seasons. A ten point margin in 1975 illustrates that Pudsey were not hard pressed, with Undercliffe and Idle putting up token resistance, but Bowling Old Lane in fourth place in the League were twenty-eight poinys behind.

The 1975 Pudsey side was noted for being positive and only one game was lost, with fourteen victories. Keith Smith gave the ball a fair old 'tonk' to the tune of a 39.25 average while Test batsman Salim Uddin, Stuart Speak (having moved from Idle) and Richard Coates also topped an average of 32 per innings. V.J. Modgill bowled only 220 overs yet had 56 wickets and Steve Southwart gained 39 wickets but at 19.23. It could not be said that 1975 had many potential champions, 1976 did. It was a hard fought season with many sides likely contenders. Undercliffe and Baildon fell away, but Bowling Old Lane who won as many matches as Pudsey ran them close and Idle, despite winning only eight games, even closer, to just one point in fact. The Pudsey side could be said to be stronger in 1976, Harry Atkinson had joined to open the attack. Phil Carrick who had taken 8 for 15 and scored 64 against Baildon was no longer available having moved more permanently to 'higher' things with the County. Modgill had 50 wickets, Uddin, Reekie, Speak, Miller, Page and Coates all helped in this second consecutive win, a win of more merit than the previous one. The 1976 battle had been hard fought which made victory so much sweeter.

During 1975 and 1976 there were, as always, some top class individuals delighting spectators week in and week out. One of my favourites was John Harvey of Undercliffe. John won the League batting averages in 1975 and was a man of graceful, unhurried strokes. How many times do you read of a player having 'plenty of time' to play his shots and with John Harvey it always seemed so. Hopefully that description is one with which readers can identify should you not have had the pleasure of watching him. He was of course County Class having played over 200 First Class matches for Derbyshire. After seeing Harvey make a quite superb century at Bankfoot, in 1975, I dubbed him 'The Beethoven of the Bradford League', because it was put together with such craft and artistry. Wilson Rose who played as goalkeeper for Bradford Park Avenue and Gainsborough Trinity was pleasing supporters at Brighouse. His 1976 average of 42.22 is the sort of average you like to see attractive players finish up with.

When Salts met Manningham Mills in 1976 they tied in both meetings, home and away. Unique. Pudsey from Idle by a point became Idle from Pudsey by two points in 1977. The same two sides were joined in the race by Bingley who had disappointed and nearly went down in 1976. Keighley who had won the Division Two Championship proved a stubborn outfit also taking part in the seasons only tie when meeting Bowling Old Lane.

Many people said that Idle only had five players in 1977, a statement which would be hard to dispute on figures alone. Malcolm Mawson and Tony Moore scored most runs whilst Mike Bailey and Paul Willis took the vast majority of wickets to fall while all-rounder Peter Kippax averaged 37.41 with the bat and was a match winner with the ball, witness his 5 for 8 as Laisterdyke were sent packing for just 43. Yet it takes more than five men to win a Bradford League Championship. Its often the 'bits and pieces' players who make all the difference.

When Pudsey won Division One in 1976, their 2nd XI won their respective title. Meanwhile Keighley were Division Two Champions and their 2nd XI were also Champions. In 1977 Farsley won Division Two and the 2nd XI also completed a double, but when Idle won Division One in 1977 their 2nd XI was unable to bring about a club double. They tried hard however finishing second to a Spen Victoria side which boasted fine performers such as Pete Hodgson and Dave Tee with the bat, Ralph Emsley and Stuart Brooke and Hodgson again with the ball. Poor old Queensbury, despite pleasing performances from batsman Naylor and bowler Sunter they went through the season without a win, but their fortunes were to turn for the better in the not too distant future. The club which made most headlines in 1977 was Manningham Mills. It was not a surprise the club did well, in fact maybe it was a surprise they failed to win the Division Two title but they were second, and duly gained promotion. With the likes of Phil Sharpe and Don Wilson the Second Division had players of the highest class. There was Jackie Heron too, a hard hitter, a man of great entertainment, one of those who causes a buzz of excitement in a crowd as he walks to the wicket.

The period covered by this Chapter saw four more 'all ten' performances. Roger Pawson playing for Baildon against Yorkshire Bank took 10 for 32 in 1974 and it couldn't have happened to a nicer chap. Roger was one of crickets 'grunters', that is to say he gives his bowling everything and maybe the resultant noise, from his efforts has frightened the odd batsman or at least made him look lively from time to time. V.J. Modgill took 10 for 45 for Lightcliffe v Eccleshill in 1977 and he too is associated with noise. In V.J.'s case the noise once startled the crowd, for while he was fielding an alarm went off, which appeared to be coming from his person. The crowd were even more shocked when Modgill then raced from the field sounding as if he were about to explode. In fact Dr Modgill was on call at a nearby Hospital and the alarm was an indication that he was needed immediately. Peter Hill had 10 for 52 for Bingley v East Bierley in 1968 and the fourth 'all-ten' feat came in 2nd XI cricket when Ben Serotsky took 10 for 31 for Farsley in 1976, becoming only the fifth 2nd XI bowler to do so. Serotsky was very fast and gave the Farsley 2nd XI, where he and his son played, excellent service.

In 1970, K. Sutcliffe and B. Aziz put on 150 for the last wicket, for Lidget Green v Salts, to create a new League record. While on the subject of records, in 1969, G. Blackburn and R. Bickley playing second team cricket for Salts each had a hat-trick in the same innings. Bankfoot 2nd XI had created a new record with their 314 for 8 in 1971, but the 1976 score of 330 for 5, by Hartshead Moor's second eleven, caused yet another alteration to the League's records. Prior to 1977 there had been just four players making 1,000 runs in a season and never had it been done in 2nd XI cricket. In that year Phil Sharpe, of Manningham Mills, became the fifth player with 1048 runs, in 22 innings, while R. Jackson of Lightcliffe, scored a record 1036 League runs in second eleven affairs, ending with a staggering average of 94.18, over 45 per innings ahead of his nearest rival.

My strongest memory of the 1977 season concerns four men sat on a seat near a sightscreen. To avoid a hard hit straight drive all four gentlemen leaned back and over went the seat along with four slightly shaken bodies, much to the amusement of all present. After the next ball was sent sailing over their heads for six, they moved. The story doesn't end there for that six went straight through a bedroom window of a semi and when the home club secretary went sheepishly to ask for the ball back he found no one in the house, but a neighbour told him that the couple, whose house it was, had set off that morning for a two week holiday, so it would be a fortnight before they could retrieve the ball. The batter responsible, who better remain anonymous was, so rumour had it, almost responsible for the club going bankrupt, so many balls did he lose. This same batsman had a love of potato crisps and one day a committee member offered him a tin of crisps (48 packets) if he made a fifty that day. He did too and he was presented with his four dozen packets. Later in the season it was noticeable that he had put on considerable weight.

FINAL LEAGUE POSITIONS

1960
Division 1

	P	W	2 pts	1 pt	L	Pts
Brighouse	22	10	2	10	0	54
Bradford	22	11	2	4	5	52
Bingley	22	8	4	4	5	47
Idle	22	8	2	6	6	42
Pudsey St Lawrence	22	8	0	8*	6	41
East Bierley	22	8	2	3	9	39
Farsley	22	8	2	3	9	39
Salts	22	5	3	5	9	31
Lidget Green	22	4	2	7*	9	28
Baildon	22	5	0	7	10	27
Yeadon	22	4	0	7	11	23

* Denotes 1 pt added for a tie

Division 2

	P	W	2 pts	1 pt	L	Pts
Undercliffe	20	11	1	3	5	49
Queensbury	20	10	2	4	4	48
Spen Victoria	20	11	0	3	6	47
Bowling Old Lane	20	8	3	5	4	43
Lightcliffe	20	8	2	7	3	43
Great Horton	20	9	0	6	5	42
Keighley	20	8	0	4	8	36
Saltaire	20	7	1	4	8	34
Eccleshill	20	4	0	6	10	22
Bankfoot	20	3	1	3	13	17
Windhill	20	1	2	4	13	12

Batting Averages
1. J.A. Greenwood (Keighley) — 60.50
2. A. Hodgson (Salts) — 56.13
3. E.S. Barraclough (Bradford) — 51.80
4. J.H. Chatburn (Lightcliffe) — 49.73

Bowling Averages
1. M.C. Fearnley (Bradford) — 74 wkts @ 11.13
2. A. Fielding (Keighley) — 42 wkts @ 11.26
3. J. Wainwright (Undercliffe) — 40 wkts @ 11.32
4. B. Jenkinson (Bowling Old Lane) — 39 wkts @ 11.64

1961
Division 1

	P	W	2 pts	1 pt	L	Pts
Salts	22	13	1	5	3	59
Undercliffe	22	10	2	8	2	52
Farsley	22	9	4	5	4	49
Bingley	22	7	2	8	5	40
Pudsey St Lawrence	22	7	2	8	5	40
East Bierley	22	7	0	6	9	34
Lidget Green	22	5	2	9	6	33
Bradford	22	5	1	9	7	31
Brighouse	22	4	2	7	9	27
Spen Victoria	22	5	0	6	11	26
Idle	22	2	1	10	9	20

Division 2

	P	W	2 pts	1 pt	L	Pts
Bowling Old Lane	22	12	1	7	2	57
Lightcliffe	22	11	0	8	3	52
Windhill	22	10	0	6	6	46
Bankfoot	22	9	1	5	7	43
Keighley	22	7	5	4	6	42
Saltaire	22	7	3	7	5	41
Queensbury	22	6	0	9	7	33
Eccleshill	22	5	0	8	9	28
Baildon	22	5	1	5	11	27
Yeadon	22	4	0	7	11	23
Great Horton	22	1	2	5	14	13

Batting Averages
1. J.D.H. Blackburn (Bradford) — 47.42
2. J. Moule (Queensbury) — 44.36
3. C.D. Fearnley (Farsley) — 43.08
4. C. Helliwell (Keighley) — 39.71

Bowling Averages
1. D. Bateson (Saltaire) — 61 wkts @ 7.52
2. B. Askham (Eccleshill) — 37 wkts @ 8.05
3. M. Shackleton (Bowling Old Lane) — 58 wkts @ 8.48
4. B.J. Whitham (Lightcliffe) — 62 wkts @ 10.35

1962
Division 1
	P	W	2 pts	D 1 pt	L	Pts
Farsley	22	8	2	10	2	46
Bowling Old Lane	22	9	2	5	6	45
Salts	22	6	6	5	5	41
Bingley	22	6	2	10	4	38
Pudsey St Lawrence	22	6	3	8	5	38
Bradford	22	7	1	8	6	38
Undercliffe	22	6	1	9	6	35
East Bierley	22	6	2	7	7	35
Lightcliffe	22	6	1	8	7	34
Brighouse	22	6	2	3	11	31
Lidget Green	22	3	0	11	8	23

Division 2
	P	W	2 pts	D 1 pt	L	Pts
Idle	22	13	0	6	3	58
Saltaire	22	11	4	4	3	56
Windhill	22	8	3	5	6	43
Bankfoot	22	9	0	7	6	43
Keighley	22	8	0	7	7	39
Eccleshill	22	7	2	6	7	38
Great Horton	22	6	1	9	6	35
Queensbury	22	7	0	7	8	35
Baildon	22	6	1	4	11	30
Spen Victoria	22	5	0	5	12	25
Yeadon	22	2	0	5	15	13

Batting Averages
1. N.B. Whittingham (Bingley) — 56.14
2. F.A. Lowson (Brighouse) — 54.82
3. J.A. Greenwood (Keighley) — 45.00
4. S. Smith (Idle) — 43.20
5. E.S. Barraclough (Undercliffe) — 41.47

Bowling Averages
1. D. Stow (Keighley) — 39 wkts @ 11.49
2. D. Bateson (Saltaire) — 55 wkts @ 11.96
3. M.C. Fearnley (Bradford) — 74 wkts @ 12.35
4. A. Walfi (Eccleshill) — 57 wkts @ 12.51
5. B. James (Bankfoot) — 58 wkts @ 12.52

Wicketkeeper R. Green (Baildon) had the unusual distinction of stumping more victims than he caught – 16 stumpings and 10 catches in league games.

1963
Division 1
	P	W	2 pts	D 1 pt	L	Pts
Undercliffe	22	10	2	7	3	51
Bingley	22	10	0	8	4	48
Pudsey St. Lawrence	22	9	1	7	5	45
Bradford	22	7	5	6	4	44
Lightcliffe	22	7	1	8	6	38
Saltaire	22	7	1	6	8	36
Idle	22	7	0	8	7	36
East Bierley	22	6	0	7	9	31
Windhill	22	5	1	8	8	30
Farsley	22	3	3	10	6	28
Salts	22	5	0	8	9	28
Bowling Old Lane	22	4	2	5	11	25

Division 2
	P	W	2 pts	D 1 pt	L	Pts
Brighouse	22	13	2	6	1	62
Lidget Green	22	10	2	10	0	54
Great Horton	22	10	3	5	4	51
Spen Victoria	22	8	1	8	5	42
Bankfoot	22	4	6	7	5	35
Eccleshill	22	5	2	9	6	33
Hartshead Moor	22	5	1	10	6	32
Keighley	22	4	2	10	6	30
Laisterdyke	22	5	1	6	10	28
Queensburry	22	3	2	9	8	25
Baildon	22	3	0	9	10	21
Yeadon	22	2	0	9	11	17

Batting Averages
1. A. Hamer (Spen Victoria) — 69.92
2. F.A. Lowson (Brighouse) — 60.29
3. K. Hill (Bankfoot) — 52.86
4. K.B. Standring (Bingley) — 51.00
5. B. Collier (Hartshead Moor) — 45.91

Bowling Averages
1. J. Wainwright (Undercliffe) — 57 wkts @ 9.16
2. M.C. Fearnley (Bradford) — 63 wkts @ 9.90
3. A. Clarke (Bankfoot) — 38 wkts @ 12.76
4. D. Sullivan (Eccleshill) — 36 wkts @ 13.00
5. K.B. Standring (Bingley) — 38 wkts @ 13.05

In 1963 there was a great battle to be leading wicketkeeper. Stan Longbottom of Bankfoot and Eric Sutton of Salts each had 30 victims and shared the honour. David Pullan of Farsley was just one victim behind.

1964
Division 1
	P	W	2 pts	D 1 pt	L	Pts
Lidget Green	22	10	2	7	3	51
Idle	22	10	2	4	6	48
Bingley	22	8	3	8	3	46
Saltaire	22	8	3	7	4	45
Pudsey St. Lawrence	22	8	1	7	6	41
East Bierley	22	6	2	7	7	35
Lightcliffe	22	4	4	10	4	34
Bradford	22	5	1	9	7	31
Farsley	22	5	1	9	7	31
Undercliffe	22	4	3	8	7	30
Brighouse	22	3	3	6	10	24
Windhill	22	3	0	9	10	21

Division 2
	P	W	2 pts	D 1 pt	L	Pts
Bowling Old Lane	22	11	1	6	4	52
Laisterdyke	22	9	3	6	4	48
Keighley	22	9	3	5	5	47
Eccleshill	22	8	1	8	5	42
Baildon	22	8	2	6	6	42
Spen Victoria	22	9	0	6	7	42
Yeadon	22	7	0	7	8	35
Bankfoot	22	7	0	7	8	35
Queensbury	22	5	1	8	8	30
Salts	22	4	1	8	9	26
Hartshead Moor	22	4	0	8	10	24
Great Horton	22	3	2	7	10	23

Batting Averages
1. K.B. Standring (Bingley) — 43.82
2. D. Field (Pudsey St. Lawrence) — 39.61
3. B. Collier (Queensbury) — 38.54
4. D.H.K. Smith (Undercliffe) — 37.86

Bowling Averages
1. M. Sherred (Baildon) — 42 wkts @ 10.00
2. A.A. Johnson (Laisterdyke) — 41 wkts @ 10.97
3. R. Peel (Lidget Green) — 47 wkts @ 11.32
4. E.G. Smith (Bingley) — 46 wkts @ 11.50

In 2nd XI cricket Saltaire did not win a match and gained just 4 pts from 4 losing draws. Meanwhile Undercliffe 2nd XI had 19 wins and 3 draws in 22 league games and gained 8 pts more than had been totalled in a season before.

1965
Division 1
	P	W	2 pts	D 1 pt	L	Pts
Idle	22	12	2	7	2	55
Pudsey St. Lawrence	22	11	2	5	4	53
Lightcliffe	22	11	0	6	5	50
Bowling Old Lane	22	9	2	5	6	45
Lidget Green	22	6	3	8	5	38
Bradford	22	7	1	7	7	37
East Bierley	22	8	1	3	10	37
Undercliffe	22	6	1	7	7	35
Laisterdyke	22	6	2	7	7	35
Farsley	22	6	0	6	10	30
Bingley	22	4	2	7	9	27
Saltaire	22	1	1	6	14	12

Division 2
	P	W	2 pts	D 1 pt	L	Pts
Eccleshill	22	15	1	4	2	66
Keighley	22	9	2	6	5	46
Bankfoot	22	8	1	9	4	43
Baildon	22	8	2	7	5	41
Brighouse	22	7	1	8	6	38
Spen Victoria	22	7	2	4	9	36
Great Horton	22	5	3	7	7	33
Queensbury	22	6	0	8	8	32
Hartshead Moor	22	5	2	6	9	30
Windhill	22	3	5	7	7	29
Salts	22	4	3	6	9	28
Yeadon	22	4	1	9	8	27

Batting Averages
1. A. Warren (Lightcliffe) — 54.78
2. L. Pickles (Pudsey St. Lawrence) — 41.78
3. F.A. Lowson (Bradford) — 41.14
4. E. Slingsby (East Bierley) — 40.32

Bowling Averages
1. D. Sullivan (Eccleshill) — 42 wkts @ 6.74
2. B. Askham (Eccleshill) — 67 wkts @ 7.97
3. K.B. Standring (Bingley) — 60 wkts @ 10.31
4. I. Leng (Idle) — 32 wkts @ 11.53

Top all-rounder in the 1965 season was Lewis Pickles (Pudsey St. Lawrence). He scored 752 league runs and took 36 league wickets at 15.72 runs each.

1966

Division 1

	P	W	3 pts	1 pt	L	Pts
Idle	22	14	0	5	3	75
Pudsey St. Lawrence	22	12	4	2	4	74
Lightcliffe	22	10	1	6	5	59
Undercliffe	22	9	2	7	4	58
Eccleshill	22	9	3	3*	7	58
Bradford	22	9	1	5	7	53
Lidget Green	22	7	2	6	7	47
Keighley	22	6	2	9	5	45
Bowling Old Lane	22	5	0	6	11	31
East Bierley	22	3	2	6*	11	28
Laisterdyke	22	4	0	8	10	28
Farsley	22	1	0	6	15	11

Division 2

	P	W	3 pts	1 pt	L	Pts
Bingley	22	12	2	6	2	72
Great Horton	22	12	0	5	5	65
Spen Victoria	22	11	1	7	3	65
Baildon	22	9	1	4	8	52
Hartshead Moor	22	8	1	6	7	49
Windhill	22	7	1	7	7	45
Bankfoot	22	7	1	7	7	45
Salts	22	6	2	8	6	44
Queensbury	22	8	0	4	10	44
Brighouse	22	7	0	5	10	40
Yeadon	22	4	0	6	12	26
Saltaire	22	2	1	3	16	16

* Denotes 1 pt extra for tied match.

Batting Averages
1 D.H.K. Smith (Undercliffe)   47.66
2 F.A. Lowson (Bradford)   42.43
3 B. Sutherland (Pudsey St. Lawrence)   40.60

Bowling Averages
1 L. Jackson (Undercliffe)   63 wkts @ 9.05
2 B.J. Whitham (Lightcliffe)   57 wkts @ 9.91
3 E.G. Smith (Bingley)   52 wkts @ 10.40

Five points for a win commenced in the 1966 season replacing the four points for victory which had started in the 1950 season.

1967

Division 1

	P	W	3 pts	1 pt	L	Pts
Idle	22	8	4	9	1	61
Pudsey St. Lawrence	22	8	3	8	3	57
Bingley	22	9	1	9	3	57
Bradford	22	9	0	10	3	55
Undercliffe	22	7	2	7	6	48
Lightcliffe	22	6	1	9	6	42
Bowling Old Lane	22	4	3	8	7	37
Eccleshill	22	5	0	11	6	36
Lidget Green	22	4	1	11	6	34
East Bierley	22	3	3	9	7	33
Keighley	22	4	0	7	11	27
Great Horton	22	0	0	14	8	14

Division 2

	P	W	3 pts	1 pt	L	Pts
Saltaire	22	11	1	7	3	65
Hartshead Moor	22	10	2	7	3	63
Spen Victoria	22	10	0	9	3	59
Salts	22	10	0	7	5	55
Laisterdyke	22	6	4	8	4	50
Bankfoot	22	6	2	7	7	43
Brighouse	22	6	0	9	7	39
Yeadon	22	5	2	8	7	39
Queensbury	22	5	1	9	7	37
Baildon	22	3	2	9	8	30
Farsley	22	1	0	12	9	17
Windhill	22	1	0	12	9	17

Batting Averages
1 J.D. Woodford (Spen Victoria)   61.20
2 J.S. Herrington (Idle)   38.46
3 R.J. Parker (Pudsey St. Lawrence)   39.19

Bowling Averages
1 K. Illingworth (Salts)   46 wkts @ 8.15
2 A. Stilgoe (Saltaire)   60 wkts @ 8.40
3 J. Smith (Yeadon)   42 wkts @ 9.31

In 2nd XI cricket an unusual feature was the fact that only three bowlers took more than 40 wickets. Brook (Farsley) 48, Barens (Saltaire) 44, Smith (Hartshead Moor) 42. The averages were shattered by Harry Hoyle (Spen Victoria) who bowled only 87 overs, but it brought 33 wickets @ 6.30.

1968

Division 1

	P	W	3 pts	1 pt	L	Pts
Bradford	22	10	2	6	4	62
Idle	22	10	1	6	5	59
Undercliffe	22	9	2	7	4	58
Bingley	22	7	3	6	6	50
Bowling Old Lane	22	7	1	11	3	49
Saltaire	22	7	1	5	9	43
Eccleshill	22	6	2	7	7	43
Hartshead Moor	22	5	3	8	5	42
East Bierley	22	6	1	8	7	41
Lightcliffe	22	5	2	7	8	38
Lidget Green	22	4	1	9	8	32
Pudsey St. Lawrence	22	2	1	8	11	21

Division 2

	P	W	3 pts	1 pt	L	Pts
Spen Victoria	22	11	4	5	2	72
Bankfoot	22	10	3	4	5	63
Queensbury	22	9	4	3	6	60
Keighley	22	8	2	7	5	53
Salts	22	8	0	9	5	49
Great Horton	22	7	1	10	4	48
Windhill	22	7	1	9	5	47
Baildon	22	7	1	9	5	47
Laisterdyke	22	7	0	8	7	43
Brighouse	22	5	2	5	10	36
Farsley	22	2	0	8	12	18
Yeadon	22	1	0	5	16	10

Batting Averages
1 B. Leadbeater (Bradford)   67.30
2 J.D. Woodford (Spen Victoria)   53.54
3 R.A. Fisher (Bradford)   51.73
4 N.B. Whittingham (Saltaire)   42.16

Bowling Averages
1 M.C. Fearnley (Bradford)   69 wkts @ 9.71
2 H.P. Cooper (Bankfoot)   46 wkts @ 9.83
3 P.M. Stringer (Bradford)   35 wkts @ 10.63
4 A.J. Burnet (Bradford)   31 wkts @ 11.22

In 2nd XI cricket A. Bloore (Bowling Old Lane not only topped the League Bowling Averages but also hit the season's top score — 119*

1969

Division 1

	P	W	3 pts	1 pt	L	Pts
Bingley	22	9	1	10	2	58
Spen Victoria	22	9	0	10	3	55
Undercliffe	22	6	2	11	3	47
Idle	22	5	3	10	4	44
Bankfoot	22	5	3	10	4	44
Lightcliffe	22	6	0	11	5	41
Bradford	22	5	0	14	3	39
East Bierley	22	5	0	11	6	36
Hartshead Moor	22	5	0	11	6	36
Bowling Old Lane	22	4	0	11	7	31
Saltaire	22	1	1	12	8	20
Eccleshill	22	1	1	10	10	18

Division 2

	P	W	3 pts	1 pt	L	Pts
Farsley	22	12	0	7	3	67
Pudsey St. Lawrence	22	8	2	8	4	54
Laisterdyke	22	8	1	8	5	51
Yeadon	22	8	0	11	3	51
Windhill	22	7	0	9	6	44
Salts	22	6	0	9	6	40
Keighley	22	5	1	11	5	39
Lidget Green	22	5	1	10	6	38
Queensbury	22	3	3	10	6	34
Baildon	22	4	0	11	7	31
Brighouse	22	2	0	13	7	23
Great Horton	22	1	0	11	10	16

Batting Averages
1 K.B. Standring (Bingley)   49.27
2 B. Lymbery (East Bierley)   46.50
3 S. Smith (Idle)   39.33
4 J. Hainsworth (Laisterdyke)   39.09

Bowling Averages
1 W.A.J. Bowes (Lidget Green)   44 wkts @ 9.04
2 M.C. Fearnley (Farsley)   66 wkts @ 9.42
3 R.A. Rowe (Queensbury)   36 wkts @ 9.64
4 P. McKelvey (Saltaire)   39 wkts @ 10.51

Note that the winner of the Bowling Averages was Tony Bowes the son of the great Bill Bowes, alas no longer with us. Unlike his son Bill did not play in the Bradford League.

1970
Division 1

	P	W	3 pts	1 pt	L	Pts
Undercliffe	22	12	4	5	1	77
Farsley	22	11	0	4	7	59
Bradford	22	10	2	3	7	59
Bingley	22	8	4	4	6	56
Bankfoot	22	9	1	5	7	53
Idle	22	7	2	8	5	49
Pudsey St. Lawrence	22	8	1	5	8	48
Lightcliffe	22	7	1	6	8	44
East Bierley	22	6	2	6	8	42
Spen Victoria	22	6	1	5	10	38
Bowling Old Lane	22	6	1	4	11	37
Hartshead Moor	22	3	1	3	15	21

Division 2

	P	W	3 pts	1 pt	L	Pts
Saltaire	22	14	2	4*	2	81
Great Horton	22	12	1	4	5	67
Laisterdyke	22	12	1	3	6	66
Eccleshill	22	12	0	3	7	63
Lidget Green	22	11	1	5	5	63
Yeadon	22	9	2	3	8	54
Salts	22	8	2	5	7	51
Keighley	22	7	2	3	10	44
Brighouse	22	7	0	4*	11	40
Windhill	22	6	1	4	11	37
Baildon	22	3	0	7	12	22
Queensbury	22	1	0	3	18	8

* Denotes 1 pt extra for tied match.

Batting Averages
1. B. Lymbery (East Bierley) — 48.21
2. N.B. Whittingham (Saltaire) — 47.80
3. R.A. Fisher (Saltaire) — 46.22
4. R. Taylor (Laisterdyke) — 44.40

Bowling Averages
1. C.P. Fordham (Yeadon) — 90 wkts @ 9.24
2. L. Jackson (Undercliffe) — 34 wkts @ 10.12
3. J. White (Undercliffe) — 62 wkts @ 10.84
4. A. Pickersgill (Great Horton) — 66 wkts @ 10.98

At the seasons end Queensbury 2nd XI had an identical record to the 1st XI — unusual.

1971
Division 1

	P	W	3 pts	1 pt	L	Pts
Undercliffe	22	10	5	4	3	69
Bradford	22	9	3	7	3	61
Bingley	22	10	1	7	4	60
Farsley	22	8	1	5	8	48
Saltaire	22	6	3	8	5	47
Idle	22	6	3	7	6	46
Bankfoot	22	5	3	8*	6	43
Spen Victoria	22	4	4	7	7	39
Great Horton	22	5	1	11	5	39
Lightcliffe	22	5	1	8*	8	37
Pudsey St. Lawrence	22	5	0	8	9	23
East Bierley	22	3	1	6	12	24

* Denotes 1 pt extra for tied match.

Division 2

	P	W	3 pts	1 pt	L	Pts
Salts	22	14	2	4	2	80
Lidget Green	22	12	5	2	3	77
Hartshead Moor	22	9	4	3	6	60
Laisterdyke	22	6	6	4	6	52
Brighouse	22	8	1	7	6	50
Keighley	22	8	0	8	6	48
Queensbury	22	8	1	5	8	48
Eccleshill	22	7	2	4	9	45
Baildon	22	6	0	7	9	37
Bowling Old Lane	22	4	3	5	10	34
Yeadon	22	5	0	8	9	33
Windhill	22	0	1	8	13	11

Batting Averages
1. M. Mawson (Salts) — 47.81
2. B. Lymbery (East Bierley) — 40.63
3. R.A. Fisher (Saltaire) — 38.06
4. R. Taylor (Laisterdyke) — 37.72

Bowling Averages
1. R.K. Platt (Bradford) — 40 wkts @ 8.95
2. D.M. Ross (Lidget Green) — 61 wkts @ 9.14
3. W.A.J. Bowes (Lidget Green) — 68 wkts @ 10.26
4. D.A. Batty (Bingley) — 56 wkts @ 10.86

It is not often that a club has a 1st & 2nd XI tie in the same season, but Lightcliffe did, tieing with Bankfoot 1st XI and Undercliffe 2nd XI. These were the season's only ties.

1972
Division 1

	P	W	3 pts	1 pt	L	Pts
Bankfoot	22	14	0	5	3	75
Bradford	22	8	3	9	2	58
Undercliffe	22	8	3	6	5	55
Idle	22	4	4	10	4	42
Spen Victoria	22	5	3	6	8	40
Salts	22	5	1	10	6	38
Lidget Green	22	4	1	11	6	34
Lightcliffe	22	4	1	11	6	34
Saltaire	22	2	3	13	4	32
Bingley	22	4	1	9	8	32
Great Horton	22	3	2	11	6	32
Farsley	22	3	1	12	6	30

Division 2

	P	W	3 pts	1 pt	L	Pts
Hartshead Moor	22	12	2	6	2	72
Pudsey St. Lawrence	22	11	0	7*	4	65
Baildon	22	9	2	9	2	60
Bowling Old Lane	22	10	1	6	5	59
Eccleshill	22	10	1	5	6	58
Yeadon	22	5	3	11*	3	46
Laisterdyke	22	6	2	9	5	45
Brighouse	22	6	1	9	6	42
Queensbury	22	4	2	4	12	30
Keighley	22	4	0	7	11	27
Windhill	22	2	2	8	10	24
East Bierley	22	2	0	5	15	15

* Denotes 1 pt extra for tied match

Batting Averages
1. B. Lymbery (Idle) — 87.12
2. D.E.V. Padgett (Bowling Old Lane) — 67.62
3. I.H. Moore (Pudsey St. Lawrence) — 44.82

Bowling Averages
1. R.K. Platt (Bradford) — 42 wkts @ 8.69
2. H.P. Cooper (Bankfoot) — 50 wkts @ 8.92
3. R.W. Elviss (Pudsey St. Lawrence) — 38 wkts @ 9.55

It was Bankfoot's first Division One Championship and to make it a double the 2nd XI were also top of their League. The club also had the top wicketkeeper (Ray Hirst) with 28 caught and 2 stumped — top 2nd XI bowler (Walt Sheppard) with 46 wkts @ 9.17 runs.

An unusual feature of their success was that two of their three defeats came from the bottom club, Farsley, who only won three games all season.

1973
Division 1

	P	W	3 pts	1 pt	L	Pts
Bingley	22	9	5	5*	3	66
Undercliffe	22	8	3	9	2	58
Saltaire	22	9	0	9	4	54
Lightcliffe	22	8	2	7*	5	54
Pudsey St. Lawrence	22	7	3	8	4	52
Spen Victoria	22	6	4	6	6	40
Idle	22	6	1	9*	6	43
Bankfoot	22	4	3	11*	4	41
Bradford	22	6	0	8*	8	39
Lidget Green	22	4	2	9	7	35
Hartshead Moor	22	3	0	8*	11	24
Salts	22	2	1	7	12	20

* Denotes 1 pt extra for tied match

Division 2

	P	W	3 pts	1 pt	L	Pts
Windhill	22	13	1	6	2	74
Bowling Old Lane	22	12	0	3	7	63
Laisterdyke	22	10	1	8	3	61
Baildon	22	11	0	5	6	60
Eccleshill	22	10	1	3	8	56
Farsley	22	9	1	7	5	55
Great Horton	22	7	1	7	7	45
Keighley	22	6	1	6	9	39
East Bierley	22	4	4	3	11	35
Queensbury	22	4	0	4	12	30
Yeadon	22	5	0	5	12	30
Brighouse	22	3	1	6	12	24

Batting Averages
1. C.J.C. Reekie (Farsley) — 53.62
2. J.K. Harrison (Bingley) — 51.68
3. A.P. Moore (Saltaire) — 46.12

Bowling Averages
1. H.J. Rhodes (Bowling Old Lane) — 50 wkts @ 9.20
2. B. Redfearn (Yeadon) — 52 wkts @ 9.68
3. A. Stilgoe (Windhill) — 96 wkts @ 9.81

In 2nd XI cricket Alan Jennings (Bradford) became the first batsman to win the batting averages in two consecutive seasons.

1974
Division 1

	P	W	3 pts	1 pt	L	Pts
Idle	22	12	3	4	3	73
Bingley	22	12	1	5	4	68
Undercliffe	22	9	5	3	5	63
Saltaire	22	9	2	8	3	59
Lidget Green	22	8	3	4	7	53
Bankfoot	22	8	2	7	5	53
Pudsey St. Lawrence	22	8	0	5	9	45
Bowling Old Lane	22	6	2	6	8	42
Lightcliffe	22	5	3	5	9	39
Spen Victoria	22	4	5	4	9	39
Windhill	22	3	1	7	11	25
Laisterdyke	22	2	0	7	13	17

Division 2

	P	W	3 pts	1 pt	L	Pts
Hartshead Moor	24	12	3	7	2	76
Baildon	24	12	1	8**	3	73
Farsley	24	12	1	7*	4	71
East Bierley	24	7	6	6	5	59
Keighley	24	9	2	7*	6	59
Great Horton	24	9	2	8	5	59
Yorkshire Bank	24	8	1	9	6	52
Eccleshill	24	8	2	5	9	51
Brighouse	24	7	1	9	7	45
Queensbury	24	6	1	5	12	38
Manningham Mills	24	5	0	10	9	35
Salts	24	6	0	5	13	35
Yeadon	24	1	0	4	19	9

* Denotes 1 pt extra for tied match.

Batting Averages
1 B. Jenkinson (Idle) 71.14
2 B. Lymbery (Idle) 56.00
3 A.P. Moore (Saltaire) 48.23
4 D.S. Dobson (Undercliffe) 44.86

Bowling Averages
1 W.H. Brown (Hartshead Moor) 46 wkts @ 8.93
2 P. Carrick (Pudsey St. Lawrence) 39 wkts @ 9.77
3 P. Taylor (East Bierley) 67 wkts @ 10.55
4 B. Serotsky (Farsley) 32 wkts @ 10.87

The two ties of the season both concerned Baildon and they along with Farsley and Keighley were awarded 2 points for each tie.

1975
Division 1

	P	W	3 pts	1 pt	L	Pts
Pudsey St. Lawrence	22	14	2	5	1	81
Undercliffe	22	12	3	2	5	71
Idle	22	11	4	3	4	70
Bowling Old Lane	22	8	3	4	7	53
Lightcliffe	22	8	3	4	7	53
Bingley	22	8	3	3	8	52
Lidget Green	22	8	2	4	8	50
Spen Victoria	22	7	2	7	6	48
Bankfoot	22	8	1	5	8	48
Baildon	22	4	1	7	10	30
Saltaire	22	2	1	8	11	21
Hartshead Moor	22	1	0	3	17	13

Division 2

	P	W	3 pts	1 pt	L	Pts
Laisterdyke	24	18	2	3	1	99
Yorkshire Bank	24	18	1	2	3	95
Farsley	24	13	2	4	5	75
Great Horton	24	14	0	3	7	73
East Bierley	24	11	2	4	7	65
Keighley	24	10	3	3	8	62
Eccleshill	24	11	0	3	10	58
Manningham Mills	24	8	0	6	10	46
Salts	24	7	2	3	12	44
Windhill	24	6	2	4	12	40
Yeadon	24	6	0	4	14	34
Brighouse	24	2	0	4	18	14
Queensbury	24	2	0	3	19	13

Batting Averages
1 J. Harvey (Undercliffe) 54.41
2 A.P. Moore (Idle) 49.23
3 J.K. Harrison (Bingley) 48.81
4 G. Boothroyd (Yorkshire Bank) 48.64

Bowling Averages
1 J. Hebron (Great Horton) 91 wkts @ 7.37
2 H.J. Rhodes (Bowling Old Lane) 52 wkts @ 9.61
3 A.P. Moore (Idle) 34 wkts @ 10.41
4 M. Naylor (Laisterdyke) 74 wkts @ 10.44

1976
Division 1

	P	W	3 pts	1 pt	L	Pts
Pudsey St. Lawrence	22	10	3	5	4	64
Idle	22	8	6	5	3	63
Bowling Old Lane	22	10	1	6	5	59
Undercliffe	22	6	5	4	7	49
Baildon	22	5	4	8	5	45
Yorkshire Bank	22	4	5	9	4	44
Laisterdyke	22	6	1	9	6	42
Bankfoot	22	6	1	9	6	42
Spen Victoria	22	6	2	5	9	41
Bingley	22	6	2	4	10	40
Lightcliffe	22	5	2	8	7	39
Lidget Green	22	4	1	7	10	30

Division 2

	P	W	3 pts	1 pt	L	Pts
Keighley	26	15	0	8	3	83
East Bierley	26	11	5	6	4	76
Farsley	26	11	3	7	5	71
Brighouse	26	11	2	7	6	68
Eccleshill	26	7	6	6	7	59
Saltaire	26	9	0	8	9	53
Manningham Mills	26	8	0	9**	9	51
Windhill	26	8	1	8	9	51
Yeadon	26	8	1	7	10	50
Hartshead Moor	26	7	1	9	9	47
Salts	26	6	2	9**	9	47
Great Horton	26	5	4	9	8	46
Cleckheaton	26	6	1	6	13	39
Queensbury	26	3	0	7	15	27

* Denotes 1 pt extra for tied match

Batting Averages
1 B. Lymbery (Idle) 51.00
2 D.S. Dobson (Undercliffe) 50.60
3 A.E. Douglas (Great Horton) 43.76

Bowling Averages
1 P.J. Kippax (Idle) 57 wkts @ 9.70
2 D.S. Dobson (Undercliffe) 45 wkts @ 11.13
3 D. Brown (Farsley) 59 wkts @ 11.23

A remarkable oddity concerned the seasons only two tied games. They were Manningham Mills v Salts and Salts v Manningham Mills. Unique in Bradford League History.

1977
Division 1

	P	W	3 pts	1 pt	L	Pts
Idle	22	10	3	8	1	67
Pudsey St. Lawrence	22	9	5	5	3	65
Bingley	22	10	1	8	3	61
Undercliffe	22	8	4	5	5	57
Baildon	22	6	2	5	9	41
Keighley	22	5	2	9*	6	41
Bowling Old Lane	22	5	2	7*	8	35
Bankfoot	22	5	1	10	6	38
Laisterdyke	22	5	2	6	9	38
East Bierley	22	5	1	8	8	36
Spen Victoria	22	3	5	6	8	36
Yorkshire Bank	22	5	0	7	10	32

* Denotes 1 point extra for tied match

Division 2

	P	W	3 pts	1 pt	L	Pts
Farsley	26	18	1	6	1	99
Manningham Mills	26	15	6	4	1	97
Lightcliffe	26	10	3	8	5	67
Eccleshill	25	10	3	7	6	66
Lidget Green	26	11	0	10	5	65
Brighouse	26	8	6	7	5	65
Great Horton	26	9	3	7	7	61
Saltaire	26	9	2	6	9	57
Cleckheaton	26	9	1	8	8	56
Salts	26	6	1	6	13	39
Hartshead Moor	26	5	1	8	12	36
Yeadon	26	5	0	8	13	33
Windhill	26	4	1	6	15	29
Queensbury	26	0	2	5	19	11

Batting Averages
1 P.J. Sharpe (Manningham Mills) 65.50
2 J.G. Heron (Manningham Mills) 53.26
3 A. Gilliver (Brighouse) 52.00

Bowling Averages
1 K.S. Barrett (Lidget Green) 31 wkts @ 10.12
2 D. Wilson (Manningham Mills) 64 wkts @ 10.51
3 A.J. Burnett (Saltaire) 54 wkts @ 11.18

In 2nd XI cricket R. Jackson (Lightcliffe) had the amazing average of 94.18, topping 1000 runs with a total of 1036.

BANKFOOT CRICKET CLUB v BRADFORD C. CLUB

PLAYED AT BANKFOOT ON 12TH MAY 19 73

INNINGS OF BRADFORD

	BATSMEN	HOW OUT	BOWLER	TOTAL
1	TOWNSLEY R.A.J.	c TART	CLARKE	38
2	LEATHLEY J.M.	LBW	CLARKE	15
3	SANT D.P.	b.	CLARKE	0
4	SMITH N.	LBW	COOPER	0
5	SYKES A.J.	c LENG	COOPER	13
6	THOMAS B.	c CARTER	COOPER	5
7	MURPHY R. (wk)	c SENESCAL	COOPER	18
8	WAINWRIGHT D.	b.	COOPER	7
9	BORE M.K.	LBW	COOPER	0
10	ALLISON B.	NOT	OUT	21
11	McGLENNON G.	NOT	OUT	18

EXTRAS 9
TOTAL 144 FOR 9 WKTS.

FALL OF EACH WICKET

1	2	3	4	5	6	7	8	9	10
36	36	38	62	70	84	91	97	102	

BOWLERS

		OVERS	MDNS	RUNS	WKTS	AVGE
1	COOPER H	23	5	59	6	9·8
2	SENESCAL E.	3	1	15	1	—
3	CLARKE A.	14	2	42	3	14
4	LENG I.	10	1	19	1	—

THIS WAS THE FINEST BRADFORD LGE MATCH I HAVE SEEN AND EVER EXPECT TO SEE.
PP.

INNINGS OF BANKFOOT

	BATSMEN	HOW OUT	BOWLER	TOTAL
1	HUDSON B.	c & b	McGLENNON	39
2	VERITY S.	c WAINWRIGHT	McGLENNON	4
3	HIRST R. (wk)	b	McGLENNON	0
4	CARTER C.P.	LBW	McGLENNON	11
5	LENG I.	b	THOMAS	23
6	COOPER H.	c SMITH	TOWNSLEY	9
7	TART S.	NOT	OUT	21
8	METCALFE C.	st WAINWRIGHT	BORE	5
9	HALL A.	st WAINWRIGHT	BORE	2
10	CLARKE A.	c TOWNSLEY	BORE	0
11	SENESCAL E.	b	BORE	6

EXTRAS 24
TOTAL 144 FOR 10 WKTS.

FALL OF EACH WICKET

1	2	3	4	5	6	7	8	9	10
11	11	37	69	90	111	128	132	132	144

BOWLERS

		OVERS	MDNS	RUNS	WKTS	AVGE
1	BORE M.K.	22	7	42	4	10·5
2	McGLENNON G.	18	3	56	4	14
3	TOWNSLEY R.A.J.	7	3	14	1	14
4	THOMAS B.	3	8	1	8	

PLEASE LOOK CAREFULLY AT SCORCARD, FALL OF WICKETS ETC TO THE GAMES MANY FLUCTUATIONS.

Chapter Eleven
Marquis of Queensbury Rules (1978 – 1988)

The first basic principle of cricket is to score runs and the decade commencing 1978 certainly had many batsmen capable of doing just that.

Leading the way in 1978 was Rahul Mankad, son of the great Vinoo. Rahul totalled 1251 in League games for Cleckheaton which was a new record. His average of 65.84 enabled him to top the League batting averages. Close behind came Graham Boothroyd of Yorkshire Bank averaging 65.50, while at Brighouse three players exceeded forty-five. Ross Chapman (45.05), Brian Bolus (52.81) and Alan Gilliver (53.73). Gilliver, like Mankad, passed the one thousand mark but up at Lightcliffe there was a double celebration. Martin Radcliffe scored 1003 runs in league matches while Mike Bore became only the third player in league history to take over 100 league wickets in a season. The great S.F. Barnes had done this three times and John Burton (1948) once. No fewer than twenty one batsmen made a century in League games and I don't think it would be wasted space if I list them.

Kevin Sharp (150*), Martin Radcliffe (123), James Dracup (121), Alan Gilliver (121*), John Oxley (119), Arthur Tickle (114), Mike Bailey (Yes, Mike Bailey 113), Ross Chapman (112*), Tony Lush (112*), Philip Sharpe (111*), Andrew Whiteley (109*), Rahul Mankad (108), Mike Page (107*), Marsden Claughton (104*), Rodney Ford (104*), Alan Douglas (102), Lewis Pickles (102), Steve Lawrence (101*), John Hall (101*), Neil Hartley (100) and Dave Hallett (100*).

There was much positive cricket played, none more so than by Yorkshire Bank, who won eighteen games in a season, where only they and Lightcliffe, with fourteen victories, won more than a dozen. Although Keighley 2nd XI had reached 101 league points in 1976, no side had reached three figures in 1st XI cricket until Yorkshire Bank totalled 105 points as Division Two Champions in that 1978 season.

Despite Mankad's runs, Cleckheaton were unable to gain a promotion spot, but as Mankad's league record still stands, a look at it in more detail would be appropriate. Taking his total runs (from both the home and away games in most cases) Mankad's record was as follows. Against Saltaire (25), Queensbury (61), Salts (196), Eccleshill (160), Yeadon (206), Spen Victoria (148), Lightcliffe (127), Windhill (54), Great Horton (40), Lidget Green (79), Hartshead Moor (84), Brighouse (54), Yorkshire Bank (17).

As can clearly be seen only Saltaire and Yorkshire Bank kept his scoring to manageable proportions over the two games. His lowest scores being six at home to Yorkshire Bank and eight at home to Great Horton. There were two centuries and eight half centuries and manner, sportsmanship, as well as ability were well respected by colleague and opponent alike. Mankad is the only person I know of who has 'walked' for LBW in the League. He was a great credit in all he did.

During the season the tragic news of his fathers death came, but after returning home for the funeral, he returned to play the last three games of the season, such was his loyalty. In 1980 the Cleckheaton Club had a benefit match against an International XI on his behalf.

Another batsman who whilst not scoring as many runs as Mankad was a vital cog in a well-oiled side was John Crowhurst. John scored 742 league runs and averaged over thirty without having a 'not out' to aid his average. This is not often performed, though in 1983 Terry O'Connor did likewise for Bowling Old Lane. This same O'Connor led Bowling to the 1978 Divison One Title and how well they deserved it. A real team effort from Old Lane with much to commend it. They opened the season against Manningham Mills and won by twenty-three runs, largely through a knock of 56 from Bill Athey. When Athey made his next appearance three games later he scored 75 but Undercliffe kept Old Lane to a point. Athey batted only three more times for the club that season and it was maybe a surprise in some quarters that the title was won without many contributions from him.

Starting on 13th May, wicketkeeper/batsman Derek Wainwright hit a bad run with the bat and seven of his next eleven innings in the League were 'ducks'. I have the greatest respect for Derek's wicketkeeping, after all he is the only player ever to take two catches off my bowling in the same innings, which he did in his Woodlands days. He was at his best in 1978 behind the stumps, not always reflected in victims.

Captain O'Connor did a splendid job when after four wins in a row, commencing 30th May the team were easily beaten at East Bierley (by 7 wkts) and Manningham Mills (by 6 wkts) in their next two matches. This was followed by a spell of seven games, six of which were won — the other a winning draw. The club had pulled itself together after a small hiccup and went on to win a much deserved title. Steve Sylvester (52 wkts) and Russell Heritage (53 wkts) led the bowling with John Wood and David Pepper lending fine support.

The fielding of Lidget Green in 1978 was quite special. They took eighteen and a half league fielding points in the season, a record breaking eleven to David Dunne. Ian Phillips, who was captain, led by example and added 748 league runs to his most capable leadership. Lidget also had two players who raised an odd eyebrow with their names. S.Core was a batsman and fine fielder who started the season by failing to 'Score' in three of his first four matches, after which he settled down and justified selection. Then they had Duck, who lived up to his name in the first two matches and three times more in the season, but Peter Duck kept wicket well and had twenty-four victims at the seasons end.

1978 was also the season that Pudsey St Lawrence signed John Snow. Former England Test Cricketer John had never impressed me in County and Test matches and in my opinion only Raymond Illingworth seemed to be able to motivate him. However he had a sparkling debut of seven wickets for ten runs as Idle were dismissed for just 27. In his fourth game Snow came up against bottom club Bankfoot. Having made 210-9 Pudsey probably felt safe until Bankfoot openers Stuart Verity and Brian Hudson scored 60 off the first ten overs in reply. Verity went for thirty-two but Hudson, never a respecter of reputations went on to make 83 and Bankfoot ran out winners by five wickets and Snow had the unenviable figures of 16 overs, 2 maidens, 74 runs, 0 wickets. He was 'not available for Pudsey again'.

As Snow melted away Queensbury's new signing Haroon Rashid, Pakistan Test Player of some note, made his entrance. His very first shot in the League was quite remarkable. He cracked a ball from Geoff Cowgill (Saltaire) with style and assurance and the ball sped off to the boundary. Neither he nor opener Naylor ran, but the ball went right into the corner of the field where a chasing Phil Baren hurled it in with both batsmen admiring a shot which brought no runs at all. However in his seven innings Rashid made 24, 26, 59, 68, 35, 24 and 114. His presence assisted the Club to three of their four wins that season and gave great hopes for the '79 season.

During the 1978 season it was discovered that Geoff Fryers of Keighley had not made a 'duck' since the 28th May 1973, at home to Yeadon to be exact. That was a total of 125 innings without failing to score. Geoff then played five more league games that season also without the dreaded 'blob' to bring his total to 130 innings. In 1979 his first six innings went by well enough but on the supposed 'lucky 7th' at Undercliffe he failed 'at long last' to get off the mark. Still 136 games, without a 'duck' is something to be very proud of.

Following the discovery of a Hundred Year Old Minute Book, Windhill decided to revive a hundred year old custom. In 1878 the club presented a cigar and photograph to the batsman making most runs in the match v Saltaire. Came the great day in 1978 and Neil Robson scored 42 runs earning him a 'large root' and choice of photograph. 'Raquel Welch' he eagerly cried when the *Telegraph and Argus* sportingly entered into the spirit of things and sure enough they gave him an eight inch cigar and framed photo of the lady in question. What photographic choice was made in 1878 is not recorded, though suggestions are that it could have been W.G. Grace, Queen

Victoria or indeed the player himself. The winner came from a cricketing family, for his grandfather Hugh played for Windhill in the 1925 Priestley Cup Final. Father was N.O. 'Pat' Robson who started cricket in the mid-thirties and finished in 1964 after a career mainly as opener, sometime stumper, but always an obdurate batsman not afraid to praise an opponent and a man of delightful company who fascinates with stories of days with Constantine, or receiving advice from the likes of Emmott Robinson and George Hirst. The 'Pat' Robsons of this world are the 'salt of the earth'. Always a pleasant word. I admire people who praise rather than criticise or condemn.

The two most unfortunate sides in 1978 were Hartshead Moor, who needed to win against Lidget Green to avoid having to apply for re-election. They had five Lidget wickets down for 89 runs when the match was abandoned while Laisterdyke had no luck at all winning only just two of their games and being subjected to a real thrashing from Farsley. Tony Lush (112*) and Kevin Sharp (150*) had an unfinished second wicket stand of 243 in Farsley's 294-1 dec.

A fifteen year old Andy Wilsdon made his Eccleshill debut at home to Salts and pleasingly is still playing ten years on at Idle.

Before the 1979 season started followers must have been heartened by the signings of players of the calibre of Jim Love, Ray Illingworth and Vanburn Holder to League ranks. Holder alas was only available for one match while Love did manage seven matches for Eccleshill and Illingworth five for Farsley.

Freddie Upfold, a very sprightly sixty-nine year old, celebrated fifty years as an umpire. Much of his life was spent in India, in fact Freddie was a top referee in boxing, hockey and soccer. He refereed the first Asian Cup Final between India and Persia in 1951. He could tell you with a smile on his face that his school, Queen Mary's G.S. Basingstoke, Hampshire, boasted three famous people, Lord Wigg, John Arlott and Freddie himself. Many are his tales of happenings on the field. Bill Voce once started bowling spinners to give more time for his collection to be taken, rather than polish off the innings.

In one match, Freddie was at square leg counting the deliveries and after six balls moved to the wicket where he found the wicketkeeper still in position. 'What do you want', enquired the keeper. 'It's over', said Freddie. 'Oh no it isn't', boomed a voice from the other end, a large black bearded man who reminded Freddie in no uncertain terms to get back to square leg and that he, not Freddie, was doing the counting. He umpired in M.C.C. games abroad and was therefore well suited to using his talents to keep up the high standard of Bradford League umpiring, whose motto is 'Without Fear or Favour'.

On his debut for Eccleshill, at Hartshead Moor, Jim Love became the first batsman in the League to wear a protective helmet. The match was a nailbiter too. Hartshead needing five to win off the last over. The scores were level with one ball remaining at which point the fielders were brought in to save the single and Martin Evans promptly hit the ball for six to bring victory in the grand manner.

After three matches in 1979 Lightcliffe were top of Division One but then failed to win another in the first half of the season. There was a very dark shadow however over the 1979 season. The death of Mike Fearnley while playing for Farsley at East Bierley. Mike was a tremendous worker for cricket, his 1324 League and 222 Priestley Cup total of wickets is likely to stand for many years. In a career with Farsley, Bradford and Bingley he made the most of his ability. Bespectacled and not a natural athlete Mike Fearnley worked hard to make something of himself in the world of cricket. There is no doubt that he succeeded. The brother of Worcestershire Chairman Duncan he also became one of the coaches to the Yorkshire County Cricket Club.

When Cleckheaton met Laisterdyke there were three visits, with injuries, to hospital and one player went twice. Russell Hutchinson the Cleckheaton captain was struck on the forehead as he tried a hook shot, was helped off the field and taken to hospital where he had five stitches inserted. While he was away his opening partner Dave Hallett, (who in 1980 was to make 5 stumpings in an innings) suffered a broken finger and he too went to hospital. Hutchinson returned, swathed in bandages, and after changing his blood stained flannels went back to the crease. After two overs there was an action replay of the earlier incident. Once more he was hit in the face and returned to have five more stitches inserted. Not surprisingly he did not bat again on his next return to the ground.

Glen Rhodes, the Yeadon bowler, saved the life of the Hartshead batsman Graham Clarke after he was struck in the mouth by a rising ball. Rhodes had taken a first aid course only four months earlier and had the necessary knowledge to cope as Clarke became unconscious.

On a lighter note The Lord Mayor of Bradford, Councillor John Senior took the opportunity of honouring the League when he entertained nearly two hundred players, members and officials of all twenty six clubs, plus the Executive Committee to a Civic Reception at the City Hall.

When the last day of the 1979 season arrived, five clubs were hopeful of taking the Division Two title. Pudsey led from Idle but only on runs per wicket, while Manningham Mills, who were to meet joint leaders Idle, Bingley and fifth placed Yorkshire Bank had high hopes if results elsewhere went in their favour and they themselves won of course. The season concluded however with much sourness and dis-satisfaction around. At Bankfoot, needing only 131 to take the title, Pudsey lost Rodney Ford for three, James Dracup for four and Rodney Cass for five, whereupon a championship winning partnership took place between Baboo Meman (45*) and Phil Carrick (72*). The question here was should Carrick 'morally' have played having made only two previous appearances that season. Similar questions were being asked at Keighley where David Bairstow played for Undercliffe, he scored 109 and sent Keighley down to Division Two.

Over at Farsley, Yorkshire Bank needed thirty-one runs to win with five overs left when at 7.25 pm the umpires brought both teams off even though both teams wanted to continue. Ray Illingworth was not amused and it has always been a surprise to me that if both teams wish to play, they should not be allowed to do so. Over at Laisterdyke around the same time two other umpires were thwarting Laisterdyke's promotion hopes. Needing only thirty-five off thirteen overs with six wickets left to guarantee promotion, Laisterdyke were brought off by the umpires without either side appealing.

Barrie Jenkinson and Brian Redfearn, two long standing players and both all-rounders of more than average ability announced their retirement from Bradford League Cricket. Ironically in their last innings Jenkinson, for Idle at home to Manningham Mills and Redfearn, for Yeadon at home to Saltaire, both made just a single.

The 1979 season saw a woman 'stand' for the first time in a League match when Catherine Haley stood in the Farsley v Pudsey match after umpire Geoff Mallinson had injured his ribs in a fall. It was also the season which members of the East Bierley club will never forget, for they reached the Final of the Whitbread National Village Competition and went for a marvellous day out to play the Final at Lords, the headquarters of Cricket. They conquered the pride of the Welsh Valleys—Ynysygerwn— by ninety-two runs, with Phil Taylor and his lads putting the Bradford Cricket League even more firmly on the National Cricket Map.

When I knew Hanging Heaton were to be admitted to the League for the 1980 season I set out trying to find out something about them. I found it was the ground on which Bill Bowes made his league cricket debut for Kirkstall Ed. I, like he, had to ask, 'Where is it?' They had been a quite outstanding side in the Yorkshire Council for many years. In addition I discovered what I believe to be a record for League cricket in Yorkshire and probably beyond. In May 1958 Liversedge made 28 all out against Hanging Heaton in reply to 151-2 dec and there was no boundary in the Liversedge innings. Not a record as many teams have been dismissed for a low total and had no boundary but when the two sides met again Liversedge batted first, were again all out 28 and once more had no boundary in their knock. This time neither did Hanging Heaton for in their 29-1 reply there were 14 singles, 4 two's, 2 three's and a leg bye. Thus no boundary in the whole match. The Liversedge innings had more overs than runs, 33.2 overs for 28 runs. As a footnote to this, in 1970 Liversedge were dismissed for 52 runs by Hanging Heaton although they had no four in their innings there was one six.

Hanging Heaton had only been in the League for three weeks when a Bradford League side went crashing, as Liversedge had done, for 28. It was the first round of the Priestley Cup against Yeadon, whom they had met the previous day in a league match, bowling them out for 83 to win

113

by nine wickets. Against Queensbury Ruel Hudson scored a century, the club's first in the Bradford League, his first fifty coming in 31 minutes and his second fifty in 28 minutes giving him a 59 minute 'ton'. Later in the season brother Ronnie reached fifty in 31 minutes against Salts and with his second fifty coming in 27 minutes pipped his brother's feat by one minute. It was Ronnie who hit the highest ever score in a League match when against Keighley on 3rd August 1980 he scored 201 as Hanging Heaton reached 305-5 in 47 overs and declared. Keighley's 53 over reply of 72-6 amused no one. At the seasons end Hanging Heaton were unbeaten in League games and had earned a place with the elite. They were not Champions however for Eccleshill managed to gain four points more.

At the foot of the table were Yeadon but rather surprisingly had the League's top batsman. Barrie Leadbeater although playing for a club which drew six and lost twenty of its twenty-six fixtures, averaged 78.11. Yorkshire Bank wanted one point from their final fixture to take the 1980 Championship. With Peter Graham taking 6-66 they dismissed Idle for 119 and then Marsden Claughton scored an unbeaten 70 as the Bank won in style by eight wickets. Captain Graham Boothroyd had been a shrewd skipper and Bank's first title was thoroughly merited.

Spectators at Baildon on the seasons last day did not feel that Keighley's point was merited. In a match reduced to forty overs a side Keighley needed just one point to accompany Eccleshill and Hanging Heaton into Division One. Restricting Baildon to 123-5 in forty overs Keighley found themselves in trouble in reply. John Harrison batted over an hour, faced eighty-three deliveries and scored one run. At the end Keighley were 39-7 in 40 overs but the point gained brought promotion. Not exactly sparkling cricket I agree, but to any reader who says they should have not put the shutters up when the first wicket fell as Keighley did, I ask 'What would you have done in their place?', promotion was the prize.

Before leaving the 1980 season, there are three other items which deserve a mention. Paul Topp playing for East Bierley against Spen Victoria took four wickets in four balls. Spen were 43-2 when with the last three balls of an over Paul did the hat-trick. Then with the first ball of his next over he made it four in four, becoming only the ninth player in 77 years to perform the feat. Then we must not forget the Pudsey v Spen Victoria match when Roy Pienaar (now with Kent) faced the games last over from Spen's John Burton with his side needing 23 runs to win. By striking 6-2-2-6-4 from the first five deliveries it still needed a boundary or a three from the final ball. Pienaar hammered home a four to complete twenty-four runs in the over and bring a most remarkable and unexpected victory with Spen, and bowler Burton in particular, devastated. Yet the last word on the 1980 season belongs to Ronnie Hudson who was outstanding during his first Bradford League season with 1210 league runs. Playing at Laisterdyke, Ronnie hit a ball into the clubhouse and onto the snooker table, prompting the man at the table to complain, 'Hey there's one red too many on this table'.

In December 1980 Harry Elam retired as Vice President of the League. Harry played his first Bradford League match in an emergency in 1922 for Bowling Old Lane and played regularly from 1924 to 1951. He had just one season away, at Undercliffe in 1933 when he won a Priestley Cup winners medal. His other five Finals, all with Old Lane, only brought losing ones. Harry was often confused with brother Eddie and although he always said he never made a century and that 93, against Lidget Green in the Cup in 1936, was his highest score, he is credited with 116 not out against Bankfoot in 1934. His final first team fifty was against the same opposition in 1951.

More exciting signings were made for 1981. South Australian Steve Wundke was signed by Farsley and Ali Zia, who had played in Under 19 Test Matches for Pakistan, joined Queensbury. In addition Yeadon brought the ex-Yorkshire and England off-spinner Geoff Cope into the League so another exciting season was in prospect.

The 1981 season belonged entirely to East Bierley. Though Brian Lymbery ended the season with a duck and Bob Sanderson started with one, they invariably gave East Bierley a good start. Lymbery had seven half centuries to add to his knock of 111 scored against Bowling Old Lane. Sanderson made only two League half centuries but nineteen times in League and Cup reached at least twenty and while not unique, his half centuries in the quarter final, semi-final and Final of the Priestley Cup was an indication of his talent in a pressure situation.

Phil Taylor as skipper led his side extremely well, his field placings for his own bowling and that of Paul Topp, Grant Forster and Tony Pickersgill came from long experience in the League and although he did not take five wickets in any League innings his 49 wickets backed up by 54 from Topp, 42 from Pickersgill and 20 from Forster completed a Bierley attack that was defensive or offensive as the occasion demanded. Paul Topp ripped the heart out of Pudsey St. Lawrence with 6-39. Tony Pickersgill had 5-15 in 17 overs against Bingley, while Taylor himself was always economical (apart from four overs for thirty runs against Cleckheaton).

First sensations of the year came in the Bankfoot v Lightcliffe matches. Playing for Bankfoot 2nd XI Geoff Scott took six wickets for one run. Having joined the club at thirteen it was his nineteenth season, a loyalty that deserves its reward. Martin Radcliffe scored the seasons first century, 134* in the 1st XI fixture between the same two sides. What a century it was too, five sixes included, he was merciless on anything slightly short of a length. Bowling Old Lane were fortunate enough to have Martyn Moxon for twelve games in the League in which his contribution amounted to six half centuries and an average of 39.5. His even tempered batting was literally reflected in his scores, with his first nine innings all being even numbers.

A 41 year old started a Bradford League career in 1981, Mel Holmes. On the strength of 85 wickets in the Bradford Central League in 1980 and the departure of Idle's 1980 opening attack he was given his chance despite having given up cricket from the age of sixteen up to being thirty.

Happenings of the infrequent variety in the 1981 season included a rabbit scampering across the field at Spen Victoria in a Priestley Cup game. Deep third man made a dive to catch it but the rabbit evaded his clutches and sped up the bank disappearing among parked cars. Later in the year Leonard Squire came back to help his club, Hartshead Moor, at the age of fifty-seven. Len played with his son, vice-captain Peter and although he did not score, swinging the bat in a run chase, his appearance did help Hartshead spring a surprise over promotion contenders Windhill. Richard Peel who began at Bankfoot as scorer at the age of nine had now graduated to the 1st XI by 1981 and scored 90 against Laisterdyke. But what a ninety. Seventy-eight of the runs came in boundaries and his nine sixes is the highest number by a player not making a century in League history. Despite his ninety his side lost as Laisterdyke's first three batsmen, Tony Clarkson (105*), Malcolm Mawson (54) and Brian Smart (69*) knocked off the runs. Later in the season Laisterdyke had a similar victory when once more the first three, this time, Mawson (100), Smart (59) and Roy Myers (50) again totalled over two hundred between them.

It was a good summer for weather once the first three fixtures had been cleared. Snow had caused the postponement of the seasons opening fixtures. Bingley took part in two news making matches in succession. Their game with Yorkshire Bank ended in a tie and the Bingley skipper ended up in hospital. Phil Padgett dived to make a brilliant stop from a shot by Graham Boothroyd and in doing so dislocated a shoulder and lay motionless. Yorkshire Bank's scorer who had some St. John Ambulance experience assisted until an ambulance arrived and this was driven onto the field to take top scorer Padgett to hospital. In the following match Bingley had second teamer Paul Ellis in the side at Spen where he hit 50 runs in eighteen minutes.

Richard Illingworth playing for Salts scored 195 runs and took 14 wickets in three consecutive matches, since when he has graduated into a fine County Cricketer much respected on the circuit and a loss to the Bradford League where his batting and bowling was always worthy of attention by spectator and opponent alike.

All credit to Cleckheaton who spent £2,000 on three covers, wicket covers I hasten to add, not three fielders. Playing for Farsley in mid-June Yorkshire's Kevin Sharp scored 157, the highest league total so far that year but he bettered this with 164 on 5th September in the penultimate match. It was in this game that Farsley and Keighley set a record aggregate for the Bradford League under the fifty overs rule.

Batting first Farsley scored 334-6, as well as Sharp's 164 there were fifties for Billy Holmes and Steve Wundke. Holmes and Sharp put on 215 runs for the first wicket. Keighley's reply was spirited to say the least. Peter O'Sullivan (72) and John Harrison (82) led the charge which ended at 288-6 and that through bad light. There was also 48 for an eighteen year old Phil Robinson who in 1988 really established himself as a County player for Yorkshire.

The son of a former Test 'Great' played in the League from game nine, for Idle. Pronab Roy, son of the great Pankaj Roy who made 2442 runs in 43 Test Matches for India. Pronab found the wickets not exactly as firm as he would have wished but he made 45 against Farsley and 53* in the return, then contributed ten other useful scores. Talking of useful scores the Idle captain Tony Moore ended the 1981 season with a century and seven half centuries in his last ten innings. His other two scores were 1 and 19 and on four occasions when he scored a half century during the season Phil Woodliffe did likewise in the same match. Very surprising therefore that Idle did not do better than three league wins and relegation. Pudsey St. Lawrence with captain Rod Ford having a fine spell with the bat commencing 27th June when his next innings' produced scores of 59, 79, 83*, 13, 2, 115*, 56, 59*, 24, 79 and 36, almost took the title but by failing to win any of their last five games the championship slipped away.

When the Bradford League met the Pontefract League in the Joe Lumb Trophy, Phil Robinson scored a superb 178 unbeaten as Bradford won by 156 runs.

Undercliffe were only able to have David Bairstow for one game in 1981 but David in one game can give more enjoyment than many do in ten. Playing in the home game against Yorkshire Bank he scored 68, took two wickets for twenty-six runs and then won the fielding point. Oh I nearly forgot, Undercliffe lost. Brian Lymbery swallowed his tongue after being hit in the throat against Spen Victoria. He was saved when a first-aid expert ran onto the pitch, to save Brian's live. Playing on after the event Brian remarked, 'I was close to deaths door but I couldn't go yet, I had to carry on, it was a vital match'. They make 'em tough in the Bradford League. A special word of praise should be given for the former Kathryn Bell. Who? you might ask. Well Kathryn was to marry John Anderson the Idle opening bowler and knowing of his love for the game of cricket and the fact that he did not want to miss the game at Hanging Heaton she agreed to go there and watch him play the day after the ceremony. Not many have spent part of a honeymoon at Bennett Lane. Anderson's 0-36 and a 'duck' leaves no further words necessary, readers will no doubt draw their own conclusions.

In 1978 the Spen Victoria 2nd XI scored 335-3 to record the highest second team score under the '50 overs' rule. On the last day of the 1981 season it was beaten twice. Firstly Bankfoot amassed 344-3 against Lidget Green which included a fifty-six minute century by Gareth Terry. This lasted only a short time as Salts made 347-6 in 48 overs against Queensbury with the Salts skipper, Alan Dorymeade, breaking the record with a six.

At the seasons end Eric Sharpe retired after twenty-one years as the League Secretary. Eric was a kindly man, meticulous and nothing was too much trouble. His tireless work for the Bradford League will not be forgotten.

Leaving the best till last as they say, 1981 was the season of the Marquis of Queensbury. Ali Zia had played first class cricket in Pakistan for four years before signing for Queensbury, shortly before his 23rd birthday. His ability with bat and ball was unquestionable and despite playing attractive cricket under Terry McGuire, Queensbury had not had much tangible success. Ali Zia was just the man to change all that. In his home country he had scored 102 in a Test Trial and made a record double century for Punjab.

His debut brought a single run and 2-65 in a defeat by Windhill, but at the seasons end Ali Zia had really made his mark. 1,110 runs at 61.66 (only Kevin Sharp had a better average). He had 50 league wickets at 21.70 and won the 'Federation' Fielding Trophy. What a man. He would bat and bowl all day every day if he could. He lived for cricket and recorded an amazing fact, when it was noted at the seasons end that eleven overs was the LOWEST NUMBER HE DELIVERED IN ANY MATCH. To my mind that proves he never had an off day which shows remarkable consistency. Three times he did fail to take a wicket but even in these games (12-3-25-0, 16-8-26-0, and 15-6-21-0) you could hardly say he hadn't done his stuff, for that is excellent economy in limited overs cricket. In two Priestley Cup-ties Ali scored 71* and 79 also taking 10 wickets for 104 runs). His enthusiasm was unbelievable. He would run round the ground an hour before net practice and then run round after it. Such enthusiasm and devotion deserves reward and although his success was individual, the team caught some of this infectious enthusiasm, named him 'The Marquis' and playing to his entertaining rules Queensbury became Division Two champions in 1982 with 99 points.

For 1982 Ali Zia had assistance at Queensbury from fellow countryman Asad Rauf. Playing for National Bank in Pakistan, Rauf had scored over 2,500 runs at an average of thirty-two, his highest score being 130. In Queensbury's opening game of 1982 Rauf made 106, a great start, Ali Zia scored 68 and although the last Laisterdyke pair hung on for a draw, the die was cast. Five wins in their next six games took Queensbury to the top. With three games still to play they were still there and playing at home to Brighouse. Rauf needed just 68 runs to reach 1,000 league runs for the season. Brighouse totalled 158-8 in their fifty overs with three wickets for Rhodes and three for Zia. In reply after 87 minutes Queensbury were 119-4 with Rauf 100*. His first fifty took an hour, his second just 27 minutes. After reaching his thousand for the season at 68 he threw the bat at everything, hitting three consecutive sixes and a five wicket win left Queensbury having to beat second placed Idle on the penultimate Saturday for the title.

Again Queensbury were in the field first, once more Rhodes and Zia had three wickets each and Idle's 145 all out was not expected to cause too many problems. At one point it looked as if Zia and Rauf may be there at the end but after Ali (28) and Asad (46) had been dismissed Stan Caines took up the example set and thrashed 54* in 29 minutes which brought the Title.

The Division One championship in 1982 went to Bingley. Their twelve point margin over Keighley was substantial and most people believed that the title had gone to the best club. One or two detractors complained that when clinching the title against Eccleshill by eight wickets they had the service of Yorkshire's Neil Hartley. True but Neil played for Bingley whenever he could and earlier in the season he had made seven other appearances. It was sour grapes, for in Billy Holmes, Gordon Ibbotson, Phil Padgett, Andrew Arundell and David Howes they had men capable of big scores. Dave Holden, David Batty and David Howes were the main bowlers with Steve Sylvester having a disappointing season. Padgett, Brown and Duffy also took vital wickets. It was ironic that skipper Phil Padgett was missing from the game which clinched the title, through suspension. He was suspended for the manner in which he made comments to the umpires about what he considered to be excessive use of the roller in a match with title rivals Keighley.

The League have in my opinion not been slow to suspend players and their action has I am sure, saved many such further outbursts. Padgett came back for the last match of the season and scored 79.

1982 saw the League's first, and hopefully its last, streaker. At Baildon a man stripped off his clothes and ran the length of the pitch and dashed over a wall disappearing into some bushes. The game was drifting slowly along and one of the batsmen gave him a pat with his bat on his backside as he ran past. His appearance enlivened proceedings against Cleckheaton but both clubs denied all knowledge of the man and it was thought it may have been done as a dare, egged on by friends who later returned him his clothes.

At the age of forty-four Don Wilson was a real threat to batsmen that year and against Bowling Old Lane he took a career best of 9-24. Test 'Stars' were still playing in the League. In the persons of Haroon Rashid at Undercliffe, Abdul Qadir at Hanging Heaton and Geoff Cope at Yeadon spectators could watch players who had reached the top.

In Mike Valetta who played for Manningham Mills and Lalchand Rajput who assisted Spen Victoria there were two stars of the future, while Shahid Mahboob took 89 wickets in league games for Hartshead Moor and had 'all ten' for thirty-nine runs against Idle. While his Saturday matches were in the Bradford League, Mahboob played his mid-week cricket for Notts Seconds and oddly enough one such appearance brought him to Bradford Park Avenue to play against Yorkshire's 2nd XI. The Pakistan bowler was just one of many Asians who had joined the League in the 1980's. Almost without exception they have been a great credit to the League, superb cricketers and fine sportsmen.

In 1983 Lightcliffe brought in a second teamer John Foster to bowl against Bankfoot. He bowled through taking 4-45 in his 25 overs, less than two runs per over which is a feat not often performed. In 1978 Brian Redfearn and Glenn Rhodes, both playing for Yeadon, had 25 overs each v Windhill and returned 4-34 and 5-43 respectively. Then there was Mike Bore's 25 overs for a 6-25 return at Yorkshire Bank in 1978. John Burton of Spen Victoria had figures of 25-18-23-2 in a match against Saltaire but the peak of these performances belongs to Paul Topp. In successive matches in 1976 he recorded 4-42 in each match bowling through and then took 6-21 in 25 overs for Baildon at East Bierley in August 1978. Never slow to take action, East Bierley had him in their ranks for 1979. It was in that year that Paul became one of very few men to bowl 26 overs in an innings. This is possible of course if a side bats first and declares giving overs to the other side. What tends to happen is that the team batting second is bowled out or many bowlers are used in an attempt to dislodge the stubborn batsmen who are usually batting for the draw. Playing against Undercliffe it worked slightly differently. Bierley were all out 183 in less than their allotted overs and Paul was able to bowl 26 overs before Undercliffe in their 52nd over won by three wickets. Paul took 3-72, though it was a surprise to many that only three bowlers were used.

Back to 1983. The opening games of the season as usual made some wonderful headlines. Mick Cartwright of Undercliffe performed the hat-trick against Manningham Mills in his fourth over. Exactly ten years earlier David Dobson performed a first day hat-trick for Undercliffe on his first appearance for them. Mark Sample made his Bradford League debut in April 1983, scoring 22 against Hanging Heaton. His father was present at the match and revived memories of Gordon's great hitting for Yeadon, Bankfoot and Idle. His throwing in to the keeper was so swift and accurate that he was worth his place just for his fielding. So good was his long accurate throwing that while a 'pro' at Rastrick Cricket Club, after his Bradford League days, Gordon was given a challenge. To throw a cricket ball over Lockwood viaduct. This had been done in 1935 by Jack Crump and as the viaduct was 129 feet high players since then had found it impossible. Up stepped Gordon, not only to accept the challenge but in front of a crowd of two hundred people he threw the ball over the viaduct four times in succession for the record.

Son Mark has remained in the League and become a more than useful all rounder himself and I am sure that dad approves. The season had only just got underway when Eccleshill Cricket Club banned Malcolm Hartley from their ground following an article he wrote for the *Telegraph & Argus*. Malcolm was simply expressing his opinion as he had every right to do and I never found anyone outside the Eccleshill club agreeing with their decision. At that time Malcolm Hartley was the Bradford League correspondent for the *Telegraph & Argus*. a job he did with great competence.

Shahid Maboob left the Bradford League for a month to join his Country in the Cricket World Cup. He got his name into the record books too with a partnership of 144 with Imran Khan, the highest partnership for the sixth wicket in Prudential Cup history. When he returned to the Hartshead side he scored 67* in 41 minutes reaching fifty in 31 minutes and along with Shashir Hattangadi, who made 95 took his team to a six wicket win at Drighlington. Mahboob also took part in one of the strangest endings to a match in cricket history. Brian Hudson, captain of Bankfoot, declared his teams innings closed at 18-7 batting second. Hartshead Moor had batted first on their own wicket and totalled 121. Bankfoot paceman Duncan Leng took nine wickets mainly to catches close to the wicket from batsmen defending themselves. In Bankfoot's reply Hudson considered players were in real physical danger and when the seventh wicket fell he declared to save his last three batsmen from possible injury. Hudson thus conceded the match but paid tribute to Mahboob who, knowing the state of the wicket kept the ball well up. Shahid had taken 5-9 when the declaration came.

After two innings of 25 runs each Martin Crowe, like Mahboob, had gone to play for his country (New Zealand) in the Prudential World Cup. On his return he faced Undercliffe in a vital match for Pudsey St. Lawrence with whom he played. Playing for Undercliffe was David Bairstow. The match largely revolved around these two as Crowe scored 52 in a rain affected match, Pudsey totalled 170-6. In reply Bairstow thrashed 79 off eleven overs in 42 minutes as Undercliffe raced to 173-3 in only 25.5 overs. Thrilling stuff and Crowe after taking an early wicket went for 66 in six overs. Pudsey failed to take the title by just two points as there was a complete washout on the seasons final day.

Champions Yorkshire Bank led by experienced Graham Boothroyd had some fine batsmen, for in addition to himself, Marsden Claughton, Mike Smith, Tony Page and John Walters were always likely to make a high score. Walters was perhaps the 'star' turn making 599 league runs despite missing a few matches, and his eight half centuries in the League found company with two more in the Priestley Cup. In Abbott, Hespe, Petty and David Atkinson theirs was a fine balanced attack but in August they brought on Walters against Bowling Old Lane and he took 4-10 in twelve overs, only the second occasion he had bowled that season. In Division Two, Cleckheaton were Champions leading from first to last. This 1983 success was founded on the enterprising captaincy of Bob Clark, the batting of twins Martin and Chris Pickles, Robert Taylor, Steve Archer and wicketkeeper batsman Ian Gatenby. Ralph Emsley had a disappointing season with just 26 league wickets but in Andy Baxter, Alan Stansfield, David Lee and the evergreen Ian Leng there was more than enough ability to compensate.

1984 may be remembered as the year of Pudsey's revenge. They took the Championship by twenty-three points from Hanging Heaton and were far and away the best side in the League. Mark Greatbatch, from New Zealand, topped their batting with over 800 league runs but with James Dracup, Steve Rhodes, Keith Smith and Russell Gaunt, all averaging over thirty, the Pudsey batting was strong to say the least. So was their 2nd XI who won the Second teams Division One Championship with 115 points. Added to the 1st XI's 117 points, the two sides gained 232 points in total. It was not a record for while they were accumulating this Bankfoot were gaining promotion from Division Two in second place to Manningham Mills with 105 points while their 2nd XI went through twenty-six League games without defeat and totalled 135 points. Manningham Mills were 'dare I say it' too good for Division Two. Their Championship was not surprising and was caused largely by the club's previously unsung heroes all hitting batting form together. Paul Holdsworth topped the Second Division batting averages with 895 runs at 47.11 but Numan Shabbir wasn't far behind. These two backed up by Zeb, Woodley and Sugden who all averaged over thirty-four made sure Manningham were not short of runs. It is said that its bowlers who win matches and that certainly applies in the Bradford League when you need to bowl out the opposition to take maximum points if you batted first but you don't have to bowl out the opposition for maximum points if batting second. David Jay and Numan Shabbir took 159 league wickets between them and Mills won a very creditable nineteen fixtures. David Legood with thirty-nine victims (28 caught and 11 stumped) did great stuff behind the timbers for Division One runners-up Hanging Heaton, while Bingley's Billy Holmes became the first Bingley player to top 1,000 league runs in a season. Their was some fine wicketkeeping again at Bingley with David Smith, who was joint winner of the wicketkeeping award in 1982, winner in his own right in 1983, having thirty-five victims and going close to another award.

Pudsey St. Lawrence were again the League's outstanding team in 1985 winning the title, once more, by a large margin. The match which decided it was the game at Farsley. The home side made only 83 with bowlers Pete Graham 4-41, Mike Bailey 2-37 and David Robertshaw three wickets without conceding a run in thirty-one deliveries, sharing the spoils. All over bar the shouting it seemed but at 21-4 and with Russell Gaunt, retired hurt after being struck by a ball from Australian Lennie McKeown, a shock looked possible. Skipper Colin Johnson led them home with 49* backed up by David Robertshaw 12*. This was Pudsey's 22nd game and they had the most remarkable record. It was their fourteenth win, but all their eight draws had been winning draws, eg four point draws, which means they had taken more points than the opposition in 22 consecutive matches. It became 23 matches when they took four points from Yeadon. Then in match 24 Pudsey were beaten at last when Bingley, thanks to 99 from Jerry Mytton and 51 from Billy Holmes reached 169-3 to win by seven wickets.

Individual performance of the season was probably by Raj Venkatraman, Hartshead Moor's Indian batsman. Raj scored 1007 runs in 21 innings but despite his success the club were only one point in front of an application for re-election. His highest score of 138* made at Eccleshill was beaten only by Marsden Claughton's 147* for Yorkshire Bank against Manningham Mills.

It was a fine summer with many centuries but these were shared around, not rivalling the four in a row by Simon Lax in 1983 nor the five in a season by Asad Rauf one year earlier.

The first team to perform a hat-trick of Championships was Bradford commencing 1927. Brighouse had a similar triumph beginning in season 1930, while Windhill had that amazing five division one championships in a row, starting in 1937, Baildon had done 'three in three' too beginning in 1950 and Idle had joined in with three in succession commencing 1965. It was nothing new, but even so the question, 'would Pudsey complete a hat-trick in 1986?' was on everyone's lips at the start of the season. Many remembered that Pudsey won the Championships in 1975 and 1976 but were unable to make it a hat-trick.

In 1986 they were again unable to do so, finishing third behind Hanging Heaton and Champions Undercliffe. While Mark Greatbatch was thrashing his 1097 runs for Pudsey in 25 innings, Hanging Heaton were as always scoring lots of runs in an attractive manner through Chris Pickles, Peter Ingham, Chris Lethbridge, Chris Leathley and the amazing Ronnie Hudson. Yet Undercliffe were able to match them run for run, Simon Kellett, Jerry Mytton, Peter Booth, David Dobson, Howard Reeve all having more than satisfactory seasons with the bat. This season no League bowler took his wickets at less than ten runs apiece but Peter Booth, the ex-Leicestershire pace bowler, was the most economical with 38 wickets at 10.05 in Undercliffe's triumph.

Manningham Mills completed a new club points record when the 1st XI, as Division Two Champions, totalled 125 and their 2nd XI also became Champions and ammassed 120 points for a well earned double. John Roberts of Keighley had taken 10-43 against East Bierley in 1985 and the 1986 season nearly produced such a feat very early when Bankfoot's Derek Robinson took 9-45 against Saltaire and the tenth wicket escaped him due to a player going to hospital 'retired hurt'.

There was an 'all ten' eventually in 1986 and it went to Murphy Walwyn of East Bierley ironically against Keighley making up a little for what Roberts had done to them a year earlier. The highest score of '86 was a mammoth 173* by Shahid Tanvir for Lidget Green at Eccleshill. If you ignore Ronnie Hudson's 201 in 1980 you have to go back to Payton's 187 in 1919 before one larger. Strangely enough two other batsmen have totalled 173 in a league game. George Leach did so in 1916 for Great Horton v Bowling Old Lane and Edgar Robinson did so in 1940 for Great Horton v Lightcliffe. Tanvir's was only the second such score since limited overs were brought in. Lidget Green made 256-4 with Tanvir taking part in a stand of 172 with David Peers for the third wicket. In reply Eccleshill had an opening partnership of 162 between Gordon Ibbotson and Malcolm Pringle and went on to win by seven wickets. What a match, 514 runs for seven wickets in 96.1 overs. There were some very close matches in the Bradford League in 1986. Tied games for example. Division One had just one, when Bingley and Laisterdyke each scored 174-7. The first tie in Division Two came when Cleckheaton 137-6, and Lidget Green 137-8, shared the spoils in a low scoring affair. Next tie in the Second Division came when Spen Victoria met Brighouse. Spen made 186-6 and Brighouse bowler Wilson was run out going for the winning run off the games last ball. Eccleshill had two tied matches in the season. Making 231-9 they probably expected to beat Bowling Old Lane, but Old Lane got to within twenty with two overs left. They were left needing three from the last ball, Steve Lee (67*) managed just two leaving the scores level, each side with seven wickets down. Having given their supporters a real nailbiter Eccleshill then took part in another. Salts reached 157-6 in 50 overs thanks largely to opener Tatton who batted through for 60*. Eccleshill were then bowled out for 157, the fifth tie in league matches that season.

David Batty will remember 1986 for he took his 1,000 wicket for Bingley. In 1979 he had reached 1,000 wickets in league and cup. Then in 1982 he reached his 1,000th league wicket but nearly 200 had been taken for Lidget Green, so it was 1986 before he reached 1,000 for the same club, Bingley. His triumph met with widespread approval.

The last day of the 1986 season was a day I believe should never have been. On the first day of the season all matches were washed out and it was decided that those fixtures should be played at the end of the season. Now certain players had already arranged their holidays to start after the final Saturday so were not available for this re-arranged fixture. There were other thoughts too. Raymond Illingworth was not able to play on the opening day due to his daughters wedding but was able to play on the final Sunday. He did so against Baildon, unfair to Baildon? Various people I spoke to said they found it surprising that after fixing a date for the seasons opening matches, those games but no others should be re-scheduled, under similar circumstances.

What happened in 1986 was that Bankfoot who should have shared one point each with Bingley for a first day washout found themselves having to play them on a Sunday in September with their Division One status at stake. Its all history now but many people know that Bankfoot lost with eleven balls remaining and were relegated. This same arrangement meant that instead of being promoted (if they'd been given one point at the seasons start) Drighlington had to win this 'extra' fixture to gain promotion. Fortunately in their case justice was done when they beat Queensbury. I know there are many who felt as I did, that when the fixtures are made they should be adhered to, for on the strength of those arrangements many cricketers plan their diaries and then clubs are deprived of personnel when movement of fixtures takes place.

For 1987 the League extended allowing Pudsey Congs and Ben Rhydding to join. As is now commonplace the opening day had its sensations. Pudsey St. Lawrence's opening pair James Dracup and Russell Gaunt shared an opening partnership of 272 as they won by ten wickets at Drighlington. This broke the previous record by Denis Dobson and Jim Thompson, also for Pudsey in 1956 against Bradford Park Avenue.

Meanwhile newcomers Ben Rhydding came face to face with a whirlwind when meeting Salts. Bryn Robinson thrashed 155 from their attack and while his was the highest individual total for Salts, their 301-7 was the club's highest in a league game. They have passed the three hundred mark in cup-ties. Ben Rhydding's reply was a credit to them as they managed to draw at 236-9 and had their first century maker in John McGregor, from New Zealand who scored 113. Pudsey Cong's first match found their attack wanting as Brighouse reached 184-1 to win by nine wickets.

Another Test batsman graced the scene when Dilip Vengsarkar made 79 on his debut for Hanging Heaton. If the scoring by Pudsey, Salts and Ben Rhydding on the seasons opening day was large in total, nothing could compare with Saltaire's match against Bankfoot in week two. Bankfoot batting first ended their fiftieth over at 135-5. At no time did Bankfoot have enough runs to declare but with rain interruptions Saltaire were left only thirteen overs to attempt the 136 to win. With only thirteen overs to use I did not expect Saltaire to be bowled out, so I expected them to make some sort of effort. They did too. Not only did they make the effort to succeed but they triumphed by scoring 141-1, their winning hit was a six off the very last ball. England Schoolboy Anthony Gilgrass annihilated the home attack with 89*, which included twelve fours and a six. Keith Woodhead scored his 46 off 21 deliveries and along with Gilgrass had a partnership of 116 in 45 minutes. Saltaire deserved their six points which helped considerably towards promotion which they gained as runners-up. Fortune does favour the brave.

Scoring over three hundred in fifty overs was becoming the 'norm' and by game four Yorkshire Bank reached 311-5 with Mike Smith hitting 179. Soon it was the turn of Hanging Heaton, who against no lesser club than Undercliffe, totalled 301-7. Simon Lax made 169 and the League was awash with high scoring. With eleven games gone only East Bierley, in the First Division, Spen Victoria and Bowling Old Lane in the Second were unbeaten. No one expected that Spen would still be unbeaten in League games at the seasons end but unbeaten they were. Their Championship success was due to positive play which brought more wins than anyone else in the division.

After the tied games of '86 there was just one in '87, Manningham Mills v Yorkshire Bank. The Bank reached 147-7 and in reply the Mills had Richard Sladdin (21*) and Paul Topp (1*) their last pair together at the end. East Bierley and Hanging Heaton fought tooth and nail for the 1987 honours. There was very little to separate them in the League at any time during the season. On the last day Bierley began four points ahead and the favourites. Chasing Idle's 141-9 Hanging Heaton had a few scares before making 145-7. Now all they needed was an East Bierley defeat but Bierley were looking like possible champions chasing Manningham Mills's 178-7 dec. Paul Topp so often doing his stuff for East Bierley was now with Manningham and his 3-64 which backed up Parkinson's 7-82 left his old chums at Bierley twenty-four runs short and the title went to Hanging Heaton by two points. Its nailbiters like that which make for spectator interest.

Pudsey Congs won the Priestley Shield in their first season and needed to beat Bankfoot on the final day to make it a double. Bankfoot, thanks to 77 from John Tiffany got home with a six by Mark Greenwood from the game's penultimate ball and took the 2nd XI championship right from under Pudsey's noses.

The individual honours for 1987 had two outstanding recipients amongst them. Murphy Walwyn took 'all ten' for the second year in succession, this time 10-45 against Yeadon, thus becoming only the second player in league history after Sidney Barnes to take 'all ten' more than once. David Legood took the League's wicketkeeping laurels for the third time in four years. To say that he's playing in the top division of the strongest league in the country speaks volumes for his ability.

The closeness of the 1987 championship left many supporters saying they thought the 1988 season could be extremely exciting, with honours possible for most clubs. How right they were. The 1988 season was wet, windy and usually heavy clouded making batting second a hazardous occupation as the light faded early.

Opening day brought just one century, that by Geoff Fisher of Bankfoot who scored 102* in his teams nine wicket win over Hartshead Moor. East Bierley were dimissed for only 116 and lost to Pudsey St. Lawrence. With five matches gone Undercliffe led from Saltaire and Manningham in Division One, and thereafter followed one of the most topsy turvy races for the Championship there has ever been. Every side was capable of beating any other with the possible exception of Lightcliffe who had a terrible time and were not up to Division One standard. The Bradford and Bingley Club looked at one time as if they may be going to add another title, then Farsley reached top spot, followed by Pudsey after seventeen matches. With only two defeats in seventeen games Bowling Old Lane had crept into fourth place just seven points behind the leaders. It was a great surprise that Hanging Heaton had won only once in seventeen matches for they too had a fine side in this very competitive season. Hanging Heaton then started dishing out thrashings and soared up the table, alas too late for a championship challenge. Positive cricket was being played by 90 per cent of clubs as witnessed by Undercliffe chasing Spen's 271 and getting it. They were not alone in their bright approach.

The shock of the season came from Salts in Division Two. Having lost by a massive 180 runs on the Saturday at Keighley they met promotion contenders Drighlington who were having a fine run one day later. Six wickets from Buckroyd and three from Tordoff dismissed the strong Drighlington batting side for only ninety five. Salts reply reached a nailbiting 95-9, but every dog has its day, and Ian Derbyshire (a match winning 55*) struck the winning boundary to give the bottom team a shock but welcome win.

When the final double weekend came East Bierley were firm Division One title favourites after a good run which left them wanting one point from two matches. Opponents in the penultimate fixture were 'Crest of a Wave' team Hanging Heaton. Bierley whipped them out for seventy four and raced to a championship which they could really be proud of, for it was in the face of the strongest possible challenge from a considerable number of clubs. David Dobson of Undercliffe had his best Bradford League season and his never say die attitude typified not only his club, but the League as a whole in 1988. More captains believed in trying to win even at the expense of losing. The cricket was entertaining, more sides than ever winning against the odds, and the season could be described as highly satisfactory on all counts.

With one match left to play the positions in Division Two were:

Keighley	93 pts
Bankfoot	93 pts
Pudsey Congs	92 pts
Cleckheaton	90 pts
Yeadon	90 pts

With three teams to be promoted it meant not only the Championship, but all three promotion spots were dependent of the final days matches.

Keighley won at Lidget Green to take the title with 99 points, the same number as Bankfoot who beat Eccleshill but had one victory less. Pudsey Congs late run gave them the third promotion spot, in only their second season in the League, and with Azhar and Grayson they had two players who were match winners and inspirations. Cleckheaton were probably the best Division Two side to fail to get promotion. Needing two wins on that final weekend they were robbed by the rain on the Saturday and a big win on the Sunday left them tantalisingly short.

Would I be wrong if I admonish the East Bierley player who having made twenty eight at Lightcliffe in quick time failed to acknowledge the fine ovation given him as he left the field. Maybe so, for the power of the pen is mightier than the sword and we can't expect perfection in all things.

The main individual achievement of the year was Paul Topp reaching 1000 Bradford League wickets. He achieved this in the game v Idle, in May and joined a select band. His father who also played some Bradford League cricket, took 1000 Huddersfield League wickets so Paul made it a real family double.

What the 1988 season did provide was near perfection in nearly all things, the likes of Mansoor Akhtar and Mark Greatbatch show the League can still attract the best. In fact at the end of 1988 the League could be said to be alive and well and looking forward to its future.

FINAL LEAGUE POSITIONS

1978
Division 1

	P	W	3 pts	D 1 pt	L	Pts
Bowling Old Lane	22	12	2	4	4	70
Undercliffe	22	10	4	3	5	65
Bingley	22	9	3	5	5	59
Manningham Mills	22	9	2	5*	6	57
East Bierley	22	7	5	4	6	54
Keighley	22	9	0	8	5	53
Pudsey St Lawrence	22	5	6	3	8	46
Farsley	22	4	5	7	6	42
Idle	22	5	3	5*	9	40
Bankfoot	22	6	0	7*	9	38
Baildon	22	3	2	8*	9	30
Laisterdyke	22	2	1	10	9	23

* Denotes 1 pt extra for tied match

Division 2

	P	W	3 pts	D 1 pt	L	Pts
Yorkshire Bank	20	18	4	3	1	105
Lightcliffe	26	14	5	4	3	89
Spen Victoria	26	10	8	4	4	78
Great Horton	26	13	2	4	7	75
Brighouse	26	10	5	7	4	72
Cleckheaton	26	9	4	4	9	61
Lidget Green	26	8	3	6	9	55
Eccleshill	26	7	2	6	11	47
Saltaire	26	7	2	6	11	47
Windhill	26	7	0	7	12	42
Salts	26	6	2	6	12	42
Yeadon	26	3	4	9	10	36
Hartshead Moor	26	3	3	9	11	33
Queensbury	26	4	2	5	15	31

Batting Averages
1 R.V. Mankad (Cleckheaton) 65.84
2 G.A. Boothroyd (Yorkshire Bank) 65.50
3 A. Gilliver (Brighouse) 53.73

Bowling Averages
1 M.K. Bore (Lightcliffe) 103 wkts @ 9.36
2 J.A. Marshall (Yorkshire Bank) 85 wkts @ 9.68
3 D. Wilson (Manningham Mills) 40 wkts @ 10.72

Mike Bore (Lightcliffe) became only the third bowler in the League's history to take 100 league wickets in a season. Martin Radcliffe also of Lightcliffe topped the 1000 run target to establish a unique double for the club.
David Dunne (Lidget Green) collected the League fielding award with eleven awards — a League record.

1979
Division 1

	P	W	3 pts	D 2 pts	1 pt	L	Pts
Pudsey St Lawrence	22	8	5	0	6	3	61
Bingley	22	6	8	0	5	3	59
Manningham Mills	22	9	3	0	3	7	57
Idle	22	7	6	0	3	6	56
Yorkshire Bank	22	6	5	0	8	3	53
Farsley	22	7	1	0	11	3	49
East Bierley	22	6	2	0	7	7	43
Lightcliffe	22	5	3	0	7	7	41
Undercliffe	22	3	4	0	10	5	37
Bowling Old Lane	22	4	2	0	9	7	35
Keighley	22	4	2	0	8	8	34
Bankfoot	22	2	1	0	11	8	24

Division 2

	P	W	3 pts	D 2 pts	1 pt	L	Pts
Spen Victoria	26	12	3	0	7	4	79
Cleckheaton	26	12	2	1*	7	4	75
Great Horton	26	11	4	0	7	4	74
Brighouse	26	10	5	0	8	3	73
Laisterdyke	26	11	3	0	7	5	71
Windhill	26	11	2	0	7	6	68
Lidget Green	26	10	3	1*	5	8	68
Saltaire	26	9	1	0	9	7	57
Salts	26	7	0	0	9	10	44
Baildon	26	6	0	0	11	9	41
Queensbury	26	3	4	0	6	13	33
Eccleshill	26	3	3	0	8	12	32
Hartshead Moor	26	3	1	0	8	14	26
Yeadon	26	2	2	0	8	14	24

* Denotes tied match - 3 pts each

Batting Averages
First Teams
1 S.N. Hartley (Bingley) 61.70
2 J.B.H. Dracup (Pudsey St Lawrence) 50.54
3 B. Bolus (Brighouse) 45.78

Bowling Averages
First Teams
1 A. Rothwell (Great Horton) 60 wkts @ 10.62
2 D.A. Batty (Bingley) 43 wkts @ 11.95
3 G. McLennon (Saltaire) 62 wkts @ 12.42

123

1980

Division 1

	P	W	3 pts	D 2 pts	1 pt	L	Pts
Yorkshire Bank	24	12	2	1*	5	4	85
Farsley	24	10	4	0	5	5	77
Pudsey St Lawrence	24	8	7	0	8	1	77
Undercliffe	24	9	4	0	7	4	73
Manningham Mills	24	9	4	0	5	6	71
Spen Victoria	24	8	3	0	6	7	63
East Bierley	24	7	3	0	8	6	59
Cleckheaton	24	6	6	0	5	7	59
Idle	24	6	5	0	5	8	56
Bingley	24	5	2	1*	8	8	46
Bowling Old Lane	24	4	4	0	8	8	44
Lightcliffe	24	5	0	0	7	12	37
Great Horton	24	1	1	0	8	14	17

Division 2

	P	W	3 pts	D 2 pts	1 pt	L	Pts
Eccleshill	26	16	2	0	6	2	108
Hanging Heaton	26	12	9	0	5	0	104
Keighley	26	10	6	0	7	3	85
Baildon	26	10	4	0	10	2	82
Brighouse	26	7	7	0	8	4	71
Bankfoot	26	7	3	1*	9	6	62
Lidget Green	26	6	5	0	9	6	60
Laisterdyke	26	6	4	0	12	4	60
Saltaire	26	7	2	0	9	8	57
Hartshead Moor	26	6	2	1*	8	9	52
Salts	26	5	2	1*	9	9	47
Windhill	26	5	1	1*	5	14	40
Queensbury	26	4	2	0	6	14	36
Yeadon	26	0	0	2*	4	20	8

* Denotes tied match - 3 pts each

Batting Averages
1 B. Leadbeater (Yeadon) 78.11
2 E.R. Hudson (Hanging Heaton) 63.68
3 J. Heaton (Brighouse) 62.11

Bowling Averages
1 R.S. Pawson (Baildon) 33 wkts @ 10.51
2 R. Braithwaite (Hanging Heaton) 64 wkts @ 11.26
3 S.A. Myers (Keighley) 34 wkts @ 11.73

1981

Division 1

	P	W	4 pts	D 3 pts	1 pt	L	Pts
East Bierley	26	12	3	0	8	3	92
Pudsey St Lawrence	26	9	8	0	3	6	89
Hanging Heaton	26	9	4	0	9	4	79
Eccleshill	26	8	6	0	7	5	79
Yorkshire Bank	26	9	2	1	8	6	73
Manningham Mills	26	5	10	0	3	8	73
Keighley	26	8	4	0	6	8	70
Spen Victoria	26	6	7	0	6	7	70
Undercliffe	26	8	2	1	7	8	66
Farsley	26	6	4	1	9	6	64
Bingley	26	7	1	2	5	11	57
Bowling Old Lane	26	6	0	1	10	9	49
Cleckheaton	26	4	2	1	9	10	44
Idle	26	3	3	1	10	9	43

Division 2

	P	W	4 pts	D 3 pts	1 pt	L	Pts
Yeadon	24	12	3	0	6	3	90
Lidget Green	24	9	3	2	3	7	75
Brighouse	24	7	5	1	6	5	71
Laisterdyke	24	10	1	0	6	7	70
Salts	24	10	0	1	7	6	70
Windhill	24	9	2	0	4	9	66
Saltaire	24	8	1	3	3	9	64
Great Horton	24	9	0	0	6	9	60
Lightcliffe	24	7	2	0	6	9	56
Bankfoot	24	4	6	0	8	6	56
Queensbury	24	6	3	0	7	8	55
Baildon	24	5	2	1	8	8	49
Hartshead Moor	24	2	3	1	7	13	29

Batting Averages
1 K. Sharp (Farsley) 78.70
2 Ali Zia (Queensbury) 61.66
3 D.C. Wyrill (Eccleshill) 54.52

Bowling Averages
1 G.A. Cope (Yeadon) 65 wkts @ 8.81
2 C.P. Smith (Yeadon) 30 wkts @ 10.63
3 R.K. Illingworth (Salts) 58 wkts @ 10.81

1982

Division 1

	P	W	4 pts	D 3 pts	1 pt	L	Pts
Bingley	26	10	8	0	3	5	95
Keighley	26	9	5	0	9	3	83
Yeadon	26	10	3	0	9	4	81
Hanging Heaton	26	7	8	0	5	6	79
Pudsey St Lawrence	26	10	1	0	11	4	75
Manningham Mills	26	7	6	0	5	8	71
Yorkshire Bank	26	6	6	0	10	4	70
Farsley	26	8	2	0	8	8	64
East Bierley	26	4	8	0	7	7	63
Eccleshill	26	6	4	0	9	7	61
Undercliffe	26	4	7	0	8	7	60
Bowling Old Lane	26	7	1	0	8	10	54
Spen Victoria	26	5	3	0	11	7	53
Lidget Green	26	2	2	0	7	15	27

Division 2

	P	W	4 pts	D 3 pts	1 pt	L	Pts
Queensbury	26	14	3	0	3	6	99
Idle	26	13	4	0	4	5	98
Lightcliffe	26	11	2	1*	6	6	83
Baildon	26	10	2	1*	8	5	79
Hartshead Moor	26	10	4	0	3	9	79
Salts	26	7	7	0	5	7	75
Brighouse	26	7	6	0	4	9	70
Windhill	26	8	3	0	8	7	68
Cleckheaton	26	7	4	0	7	8	65
Drighlington	26	8	3	0	4	11	64
Bankfoot	26	4	3	0	9	10	45
Great Horton	26	2	5	0	13	6	45
Saltaire	26	5	2	0	6	13	44
Laisterdyke	26	3	2	0	14	7	40

* Denotes tied match - 3 pts each

Batting Averages
1 A.M. Valetta (Manningham Mills) 79.78
2 A. Clarkson (Windhill) 68.50
3 A. Rauf (Queensbury) 49.86

Bowling Averages
Division 1
1 G.A. Cope (Yeadon) 72 wkts @ 12.51
2 G. Binks (Lightcliffe) 77 wkts @ 12.57
3 S. Mahboob (Hartshead Moor) 89 wkts @ 12.85

1983

Division 1

	P	W	4 pts	D 3 pts	1 pt	L	Pts
Yorkshire Bank	26	12	2	0	8	4	88
Pudsey St Lawrence	26	10	4	0	10	2	86
Undercliffe	26	10	2	0	11	3	79
Hanging Heaton	26	8	4	0	13	1	77
Bingley	26	7	7	0	7	5	77
East Bierley	26	7	4	0	10	5	68
Keighley	26	7	3	0	12	4	66
Farsley	26	4	6	0	11	5	59
Idle	26	4	7	0	7	8	59
Yeadon	26	6	1	0	13	6	53
Queensbury	26	2	4	0	10	10	38
Eccleshill	26	4	0	0	12	10	36
Manningham Mills	26	2	2	0	15	7	35
Bowling Old Lane	26	1	0	0	11	14	17

Division 2

	P	W	4 pts	D 3 pts	1 pt	L	Pts
Cleckheaton	26	12	2	0	9	3	89
Spen Victoria	26	10	3	0	11	2	83
Baildon	26	11	1	0	2	12	82
Lightcliffe	26	7	4	0	11	4	69
Salts	26	8	2	0	12	4	68
Windhill	26	7	4	0	9	6	67
Saltaire	26	8	2	1*	6	9	65
Laisterdyke	26	9	0	0	8	9	62
Hartshead Moor	26	7	1	0	10	8	56
Drighlington	26	5	2	0	10	9	48
Brighouse	26	5	0	2*	11	8	47
Bankfoot	26	4	3	0	10	9	46
Great Horton	26	4	2	0	9	11	41
Lidget Green	26	2	0	1*	6	17	21

* Denotes tied match — 3 pts each

Batting Averages
1 S. Hattangadi (Hartshead Moor) 62.36
2 C. Johnson (Pudsey St Lawrence) 59.29
3 K. Smith (Pudsey St Lawrence) 57.33

Bowling Averages
1 M. Sherred (Baildon) 49 wkts @ 10.43
2 A. Baxter (Cleckheaton) 57 wkts @ 11.12
3 D.A. Batty (Bingley) 65 wkts @ 11.42

1984

Division 1

	P	W	4 pts	D 3 pts	1 pt	L	Pts
Pudsey St Lawrence	26	17	3	0	3	3	117
Hanging Heaton	26	9	9	0	4	4	94
Bingley	26	11	6	0	3	6	93
Yorkshire Bank	26	10	6	0	7	3	91
East Bierley	26	11	5	0	3	7	89
Keighley	26	10	6	0	4	6	88
Yeadon	26	7	4	0	8	7	66
Farsley	26	7	3	0	11	5	65
Idle	26	5	7	0	7	7	65
Undercliffe	26	5	4	0	8	9	54
Spen Victoria	26	6	1	0	6	13	46
Cleckheaton	26	6	0	0	8	12	44
Eccleshill	26	3	2	0	8	13	34
Queensbury	26	4	1	0	5	16	33

Division 2

	P	W	4 pts	D 3 pts	1 pt	L	Pts
Manningham Mills	26	19	2	0	1	4	123
Bankfoot	26	13	5	1*	4	3	105
Baildon	26	12	3	0	4	7	88
Laisterdyke	26	9	5	0	3	9	77
Brighouse	26	12	0	0	3	11	75
Drighlington	26	11	1	0	5	9	75
Lightcliffe	26	11	1	0	4	10	74
Salts	26	10	1	0	4	11	68
Saltaire	26	7	4	1*	5	9	66
Windhill	26	9	1	0	4	12	62
Great Horton	26	5	4	0	5	12	51
Lidget Green	26	6	1	0	8	11	48
Bowling Old Lane	26	4	4	0	8	10	48
Hartshead Moor	26	4	3	0	5	14	41

* Denotes tied match - 3 pts each

Batting Averages
1. J.M. Greatbatch (Pudsey St Lawrence)   51.38
2. M. Chadwick (Farsley)   50.25
3. P.E. Robinson (Keighley)   47.42

Bowling Averages
1. R. Braithwaite (Hanging Heaton)   51 wkts @ 12.63
2. D.A. Batty (Bingley)   68 wkts @ 13.22
3. P.H. Topp (East Bierley)   60 wkts @ 13.98

1985

Division 1

	P	W	4 pts	D 3 pts	1 pt	L	Pts
Pudsey St Lawrence	26	16	9	0	0	1	132
Farsley	26	15	4	0	3	4	109
Idle	26	13	2	0	2	9	88
Hanging Heaton	26	11	4	0	4	7	86
Bingley	26	11	3	0	7	5	85
East Bierley	26	6	11	0	1	8	81
Baildon	26	9	4	0	7	6	77
Yeadon	26	9	1	0	7	9	65
Keighley	26	7	4	0	6	9	64
Undercliffe	26	7	1	1*	5	12	54
Bankfoot	26	7	1	0	6	12	52
Manningham Mills	26	6	0	0	5	15	41
Spen Victoria	26	4	3	0	4	15	40
Yorkshire Bank	26	4	1	1*	8	13	35

Division 2

	P	W	4 pts	D 3 pts	1 pt	L	Pts
Lightcliffe	26	17	2	0	3	4	113
Laisterdyke	26	16	2	1*	1	6	108
Saltaire	26	11	8	0	4	3	102
Drighlington	26	13	3	0	2	8	92
Bowling Old Lane	26	14	1	0	2	9	90
Eccleshill	26	11	4	0	3	9	85
Great Horton	26	9	3	0	7	7	73
Cleckheaton	26	8	2	1*	7	8	66
Lidget Green	26	7	3	0	5	11	59
Windhill	26	6	2	0	6	12	50
Brighouse	26	6	2	0	4	14	48
Hartshead Moor	26	6	2	0	4	14	48
Salts	26	7	0	0	5	14	47
Queensbury	26	4	0	0	5	17	29

* Denotes tied match — 3 pts each

Batting Averages
1. J.M. Greatbatch (Pudsey St Lawrence)   60.76
2. B.A. Butt (Bowling Old Lane)   60.41
3. A. Metcalfe (Farsley)   53.57

Bowling Averages
1. P.C. Graham (Pudsey St Lawrence)   85 wkts @ 10.75
2. G.A. Cope (Yeadon)   63 wkts @ 11.78
3. J.M. Foster (Lightcliffe)   51 wkts @ 12.33

1986

Division 1

	P	W	4 pts	D 3 pts	1 pt	L	Pts
Undercliffe	26	15	6	0	3	2	117
Hanging Heaton	26	14	6	0	3	3	111
Pudsey St Lawrence	26	14	3	0	5	4	101
East Bierley	26	12	6	0	3	5	99
Idle	26	11	2	0	5	8	79
Baildon	26	9	4	0	8	5	78
Keighley	26	10	1	0	5	10	69
Yeadon	26	8	3	0	8	7	68
Farsley	26	7	2	0	8	9	58
Lightcliffe	26	7	1	0	4	14	50
Bingley	26	5	3	1*	5	12	50
Bankfoot	26	6	2	0	5	13	49
Saltaire	26	3	2	0	6	15	32
Laisterdyke	26	2	0	1*	7	16	22

Division 2

	P	W	4 pts	D 3 pts	1 pt	L	Pts
Manningham Mills	26	19	2	0	3	2	125
Yorkshire Bank	26	17	4	0	4	1	122
Drighlington	26	12	6	0	3	5	93
Eccleshill	26	12	3	2*	5	4	95
Bowling Old Lane	26	11	2	1*	4	8	81
Spen Victoria	26	8	5	1*	3	9	74
Cleckheaton	26	8	1	1*	9	7	64
Great Horton	26	7	3	0	5	11	59
Windhill	26	7	1	0	7	11	53
Lidget Green	26	6	2	1*	5	12	52
Queensbury	26	6	2	0	5	13	49
Brighouse	26	2	7	1*	5	11	48
Hartshead Moor	26	6	1	0	5	14	45
Salts	26	3	0	1*	6	16	27

* Denotes tied match - 3 pts each

Batting Averages
1. A. Jabbar (Spen Victoria)   61.53
2. J.M. Greatbatch (Pudsey St Lawrence)   60.94
3. G.A. Boothroyd (Drighlington)   59.47

Bowling Averages
1. P. Booth (Undercliffe)   38 wkts @ 10.50
2. J.P. Hespe (Yorkshire Bank)   50 wkts @ 10.94
3. A. Jabbar (Spen Victoria)   54 wkts @ 10.96

1987

Division 1

	P	W	4 pts	D 3 pts	1 pt	L	Pts
Hanging Heaton	26	11	6	0	7	2	97
East Bierley	26	13	2	0	9	2	95
Manningham Mills	26	7	7	1*	7	4	80
Farsley	26	10	2	0	8	6	76
Baildon	26	7	5	0	10	4	72
Pudsey St Lawrence	26	4	9	0	9	4	69
Idle	26	7	4	0	9	6	67
Bingley	26	9	0	0	9	8	63
Undercliffe	26	7	2	0	10	7	60
Yorkshire Bank	26	6	2	1*	9	8	56
Lightcliffe	26	5	1	0	8	12	42
Drighlington	26	4	2	0	10	10	42
Keighley	26	4	0	0	11	11	35
Yeadon	26	2	1	0	11	12	27

Division 2

	P	W	4 pts	D 3 pts	1 pt	L	Pts
Spen Victoria	28	13	4	0	11	0	105
Saltaire	28	12	3	0	9	4	93
Bowling Old Lane	28	12	3	0	8	5	92
Queensbury	28	9	4	0	11	4	81
Great Horton	28	11	1	0	7	9	77
Cleckheaton	28	9	3	0	10	6	76
Bankfoot	28	8	3	0	8	9	68
Pudsey Congs	28	9	0	0	12	7	66
Eccleshill	28	7	3	0	8	10	62
Brighouse	28	7	2	0	11	8	61
Hartshead Moor	28	5	4	0	10	9	56
Lidget Green	28	5	2	0	12	9	50
Windhill	28	6	1	0	8	13	48
Salts	28	4	2	0	7	15	39
Ben Rhydding	28	4	1	0	10	13	38

* Denotes tied match — 3 pts each

Batting Averages
1. R. Talwar (Brighouse)   55.60
2. J.B.H. Dracup (Pudsey St Lawrence)   50.05
3. J. Holah (Pudsey Congs)   47.00

Bowling Averages
1. J. Poutch (Bowling Old Lane)   48 wkts @ 11.33
2. R.S. Braithwaite (Hanging Heaton)   54 wkts @ 12.54
3. S. Gill (Saltaire)   30 wkts @ 12.90

1988

Division 1

	P	W	4 pts	D 3 pts	1 pt	L	Pts
East Bierley	26	14	2	0	8	2	100
Farsley	26	9	3	2*	11	1	83
Pudsey St Lawrence	26	9	5	0	9	3	83
Bradford & Bingley	26	7	7	0	8	4	78
Undercliffe	26	8	4	1*	7	6	74
Hanging Heaton	26	7	4	0	11	4	69
Manningham Mills	26	6	6	0	9	5	69
Saltaire	26	8	2	1*	8	7	67
Bowling Old Lane	26	8	2	0	9	7	65
Baildon	26	4	4	0	9	9	49
Yorkshire Bank	26	5	1	0	14	6	48
Spen Victoria	26	4	2	0	11	9	43
Idle	26	1	3	0	12	10	30
Lightcliffe	26	0	0	0	9	17	9

* Denotes a tied match – 3 points each

Division 2

	P	W	4 pts	D 3 pts	1 pt	L	Pts
Keighley	28	14	2	0	7	5	99
Bankfoot	28	13	3	0	9	3	99
Pudsey Congs	28	11	6	0	8	3	98
Cleckheaton	28	13	2	0	10	3	96
Yeadon	28	10	5	0	10	3	90
Brighouse	28	10	3	0	7	8	79
Bankfoot	28	8	3	0	8	9	68
Drighlington	28	8	4	0	10	6	74
Eccleshill	28	7	4	0	10	7	68
Queensbury	28	7	3	0	9	9	63
Ben Rhydding	28	5	2	0	12	9	50
Great Horton	28	6	1	0	9	12	49
Hartshead Moor	28	5	2	0	9	12	47
Windhill	28	4	0	0	15	9	39
Lidget Green	28	2	5	0	6	15	38
Salts	28	3	0	0	11	14	29

Batting Averages
1. D.S. Dobson (Undercliffe) — 54.38
2. J.B.H. Dracup (Pudsey St Lawrence) — 51.60
3. M. Akhtar (Spen Victoria) — 50.79

Bowling Averages
1. J.N. Robinson (Cleckheaton) — 69 wkts @ 8.93
2. J. Marshall (Baildon) — 56 wkts @ 10.59
3. D. Lee (Cleckheaton) — 41 wkts @ 11.46

More than a century of Test players – 102 in fact

Cricketers who have played at test match level either before or after playing in the Bradford League. All played for England except those listed with their country in brackets.

Sir Len Hutton
Sir Jack Hobbs
S.F. Barnes
H. Sutcliffe
E. Paynter
L.E.G. Ames
F.E. Woolley
P. Holmes
W. Barber
E.W. Clark
G. Gunn
E.P. Robinson
E. Robinson
C.H. Parkin
C.W.L. Parker
J.W. Hearne
M.W. Booth
L.F. Townsend
A. Waddington
T.B. Mitchell
G.G. McCauley
M.S. Nicholls
C.F. Root
M. Leyland
A. Wood
A. Mitchell
T.W. Goddard
F. Smailes
D. Smith
J.H. King
A.D.G. Matthews
R. Illingworth
D.B. Close
R. Appleyard

W. Voce
W.W. Keeton
P.A. Gibb
G. Duckworth
J.F. Crapp
R.T. Simpson
A.E. Fagg
C. Gladwin
G.H. Pope
W. Place
C. Washbrook
W.H. Copson
A. Coxon
E. Leadbeater
G.A. Smithson
F.A. Lowson
D.V. Brennan
J.C. Laker
J.H. Wardle
D.E.V. Padgett
K. Taylor
D. Wilson
H.J. Rhodes
J. Birkenshaw
J.B. Bolus
H.L. Jackson
A. Ward
S. Haigh
D. Brookes
J.W. Hitch
A. Dolphin
P.J. Sharpe
J.A. Snow
R.A. Hutton

J.C. Balderstone
G.A. Cope
D.L. Bairstow
N.G.B. Cook
L.B. Taylor
A. Sidebottom
C.W.J. Athey
M.D. Moxon
D. Leng (Ire)
M.R.J. Veletta (A)
M.J. Greatbatch (NZ)
M.D. Crowe (NZ)
G.B. Troup (NZ)
A. Qadir (P)
D. Vengsarkar (I)
P. Roy (I)
H. Rashid (P)
I. Qasim (P)
S. Uddin (P)
C.B. Llewellyn (SA)
E.A. Vogler (SA)
M.P. Donnelly (NZ)
C.S. Dempster (NZ)
G.M. Parker (SA)
E. St Hill (WI)
E. Achong (WI)
E.A. Martindale (WI)
Sir Learie Constantine (WI)
R. Gilchrist (WI)
L. Rajput (I)
S. Mahboob (P)
V. Holder (WI)
K. James (NZ)
M. Akhtar (P)

76 – England, 6 – West Indies, 6 – New Zealand, 6 – Pakistan,
3 – India, 3 – South Africa, 1 – Australia, 1 – Ireland

Chapter Twelve
The Future

The Bradford League name has been made largely through the 'Top Class' players who have played in it, but I firmly believe its future is in the hands of those unsung heroes, the long standing servants.

Sam Patchett, Eddie Hanlon, George Hudson, Ernest Jones have all been umpires of long standing. Often only heard about when controversy arrives. Their loyalties are deserving of praise for unlike a player they are not able to find the spotlight and their dedication is largely unrewarded.

So too is the sort of dedication shown by players like Vic Fletcher. Vic was first introduced to Bradford League Cricket in 1946 when his idol was Johnnie Wardle, at Eccleshill. It was in the days of time limit cricket when the umpires used to wave a white handkerchief to signify the last fifteen minutes. In 1957 Vic made his debut for Queensbury 1st XI at Lightcliffe. Like many illustrious players before, and after, started with a 'duck' and a golden one at that. A short spell at Bankfoot, during which he made a name for himself as a very capable and speedy outfielder, followed. If some reward were given for time spent at the crease Vic would surely have earned it, for in the last thirty years he has probably stayed longer at the wicket in Bradford League games than any other player. The fact that this is not hinted at in total runs is because, to put it mildly, Vic did not score quickly but my how difficult it was to shift him. In 1985, when many his age would have retired, he was still good enough to make 74 runs against Undercliffe in first team cricket for Queensbury, where he had returned from Bankfoot in 1966. While at Bankfoot Vic, all 5'4" of him and eight stones wet through used to open the innings with Ken Hill, a foot taller and four stones heavier, a sight I never managed to find captured on film.

There was no controversy ever surrounding Vic Fletcher, such was his dedication that in the 1960's he travelled from Liverpool each week by bus or train (having no car) to play in the League. His is the attitude that often is unnoticed by most, the sort of person on whom you can always rely but that dependability sometimes makes a person simply part of the furniture.

Yet it is dedicated people, the likes of Vic Fletcher, that are the backbone of any organisation. The scorers, the tea-ladies, the mothers and wives, such as Rosemary Batty, Sue Taylor, Betty Aspinall, Dorothy Fearnley, Rachael O'Connor, Margaret Greenwood, Audrey Spencer, Annie Burton, Vera Hodgson, Marjorie Demaine, Doris Carter, Joan Peel, Joan White, Doris Hopkinson and many others who unfortunately are too numerous to mention, who support relatives close or otherwise. It is to these 'backroom' people that the Bradford League owes thanks to and the fathers, such as Denis Dobson, Dennis Leng, Gordon Sample, Russell Peel, Ken Hill, David Batty, Leonard Squire, John Dickinson, Keith Illingworth, Billy Rhodes who having played in the League themselves have guided their sons to follow in their footsteps.

We must not forget the likes of Brian Lymbery who started in the late 50s and is still enjoying his cricket 30 years on. Brian has now made more scores over 50 than any other Bradford League player. Then there are the supporters. Many give a lifetime to one club, and most go unheralded. Its to these that the League owes its gratitude.

The vast number of players at present playing Bradford League Cricket would I am sure recommend it to any outsider. It is very competitive and contains many of the countries leading club cricketers (and often County and Test players). The standard is high and yet it is a 'friendly' league. By that I mean you can enjoy being within its confines.

During my Bradford League viewing which began as a teenager in the late 1950's, I have made many friends, lasting friendships and received much joy from the fellowship gained.

Over the years the Bradford League format has changed, with points alterations, Sunday play, loss of Inter-Divisional fixtures, league enlargement and much more. Change is inevitable in life, and while change is not always good, it is my belief that the League is in the hands of some first rate administrators who will look into things very carefully before making drastic alterations to the countries top cricket league.

With this in mind it is my considered view, shared I know with many others, that there is not much wrong with the Bradford Cricket League and it would be no surprise if we could peep into the future to find that in another 85 years time it would be still thriving with very little unrecognisable from the present. While like all other sports the League has lost a large number of spectators to a new age of TV watching, other choices of leisure activities, holidays abroad, etc., it has not lost its attraction for players wanting to play in it (and this includes Test and County players). This in itself must show that it has plenty to offer. It is still in demand. I believe it always will be.

Acknowledgements

Sincere thanks go to the following for helping in a variety of ways re the publication of this book.

My good friends Russell Peel (who typed the manuscript and made many helpful suggestions) and Malcolm Hartley who loaned his Bradford League records and cuttings books. To Phil Robinson, Pat Robson, David Batty, Rachael O'Connor, Dorothy Fearnley, Angela Walker of the *Spenborough Guardian*, Geoff Collinson, Len Squire, Pat McKelvey, A.H. Lawrence, Undercliffe CC, Hanging Heaton CC, Graham Red, David Pedley, Charles Hodgson, Geoff Fisher, Albert Smith, Ray Dawes, Alec Higson, Tony Rowe, Ken Woodward, H. Goulding, Brian Clough, Ken Taylor, *Keighley News*, Jeff Slater, Jack Emslie, *Halifax Courier*, Keighley CC, Bankfoot CC, Yorkshire Bank CC, Peter Walker.

Not forgetting the stars who contributed to Chapter 8.

To Bruce Moss, the League President, Donald Grant, Carters Sports, Allanwood Press, Ken Hill, Tom Mathers, Harry Hoyle, Kevin Hopkinson, Sandy Jacques, Duncan Fearnley, Bruce Deadman, Sportshoes Unlimited, *Telegraph and Argus, Yorkshire Post Newspapers*, D & R Sports Frizinghall and to the Libraries of Bradford, Cleckheaton and Kirklees.

To anyone whom I may have inadvertently forgotten, apologies and thanks.

Attempts have been made to trace all photos re copyright. However one or two were loaned without a copyright stamp on the back making an appropriate acknowledgement impossible.

My sincere thanks to all who have in anyway contributed, without your assistance there could be no book.

Peter Pickup, October 1988

Bradford Cricket League – Tour Results

1923	Draw	Cupar	123 for 8	v	Bradford League	228 for 7 dec.
	Won	Forfarshire	100 all out	v	Bradford League	190 all out
	Won	Perth County	79 all out	v	Bradford League	263 for 7 dec.
1929	Won	Cupar	170 all out	v	Bradford League	171 for 8
	Draw	Forfarshire	165 for 9 dec	v	Bradford League	114 for 9
	Draw	Perth County	117 for 8	v	Bradford League	225 for 9 dec
1946	Won	Cupar	62 all out	v	Bradford League	63 for 0
	Draw	Forfarshire	169 for 8 dec	v	Bradford League	d.n.b.
	Draw	Perth County	124 for 8 dec	v	Bradford League	128 for 9
1947	Won	Ayr	76 all out	v	Bradford League	80 for 2
	Draw	Greenock	138 for 7	v	Bradford League	175 for 5 dec.
	Won	West of Scotland	50 all out	v	Bradford League	51 for 3
1949	Draw	Stroud	148 for 9 dec	v	Bradford League	101 for 7
	Lost	Cheltenham	77 for 3	v	Bradford League	75 all out
	Draw	Gloucester Gypsies	157 for 8 dec	v	Bradford League	132 for 5